W9-CMJ-250

MONEY
FOR
FILM&VIDEO
ARTISTS

MONEY
FOR
FILM&VIDEO
ARTISTS

Edited by SUZANNE NIEMEYER

aca BOOKS
American Council for the Arts
New York, New York

Copublished with Allworth Press

93 92 91   5 4 3 2 1

Book and Cover Design by Celine Brandes, *Photo Plus Art*
Typesetting by *The Desktop Shop*, Baltimore, MD

Printing by *Capital City Press, Inc.*

Director of Publishing: Robert Porter
Assistant Director of Publishing: Doug Rose
Publishing Assistant: Tiffany Chez Robinson

Library of Congress Cataloging-in-Publication Data:

Money for film and video artists / edited by Suzanne Niemeyer.
       p.   cm.
   Includes indexes.
   ISBN 0-915400-93-6
    1. Motion pictures — Scholarships, fellowships, etc. — Directories.
  2. Video art — Scholarships, fellowships, etc. — Directories.
  I. Niemeyer, Suzanne. II. American Council for the Arts.
  PN1998.A1M56 1991
  791.43'079 — dc20   91-20784
                                                CIP

TABLE OF CONTENTS

ACKNOWLEDGMENTS

This publication would not have been possible without the hard work and support of many people. Special thanks goes to Doug Oxenhorn, a tireless and diligent researcher. Thanks also to David Bosca, Library Director at the Arts Resource Consortium Library, who provided space and support during the research for this volume, and to his assistant Eleanor Zimmer. Comments from videographers Les Crandell and Sally Sass were invaluable in clarifying technical questions. Others who gave special assistance and provided leads on little known sources of support included Alene Abouaf of the Long Beach Museum of Art's Video Annex; Kathryn Bowser of the Association of Independent Video and Filmmakers (AIVF); Mary Esbjornson of the Media Alliance; and Toni Treadway of the International Center for 8mm Film and Video. Finally, thanks to the many individuals who took time out of their busy schedules to respond to our surveys. Without their help this book would not exist.

—S.N.

HOW TO USE THE GUIDE

In this single volume, we have assembled a unique resource compendium of the myriad programs of support and assistance for professional, individual film and video artists in the U.S. and Canada.

What we have learned by collecting the 193 organization profiles that appear on the following pages is that support for filmmakers and videographers comes in a wide variety of forms and from diverse sources. We have uncovered programs that offer free or low-cost access to production and post-production equipment and facilities. Other programs offer several million dollars in fellowships or act as nonprofit fiscal sponsors for independent producers seeking funding from other sources. Some organizations operate on an international scale, while others provide service community wide. We've tried to collect information from the largest government agencies to regional media centers to smaller nonprofit groups. You may be surprised at the number of places that can provide assistance to you.

This book is intended to simplify your search for the various kinds of assistance that you need to advance your career. We have arranged the profiles alphabetically by organization name. Each entry includes detailed sections about the organization's specific programs for film and video artists. Following the name, address, phone number, and contact person for the organization, each entry is divided into four sections for quick reference.

The "Profile of Financial Support to Artists" is intended to give you an idea of the size and scope of the program. This section includes the total amount of funding and the value of in-kind support that the organization gives to individual artists, the total number of applications for funding that the organization receives from individual artists, the number of individuals that receive funding, and the dollar range of grants to individuals. At a glance, you are able to determine how many opportunities exist and how many people compete for them.

The "Direct Support Programs" section details fellowship, project support, professional development grants, emergency assistance, and residencies available to individual film and video artists. Equipment access grants, commissions, and arts-in-education programs may also be included here, depending on the scope of the program, the standardization of the application and selection process, and the availability of direct funds for independent producers. This section also outlines each program's eligibility requirements, scope and application/selection process. *When considering a particular grant, artists should consider how their projects correspond to the stated purpose of the program.* A careful examination of the information provided under the eligibility heading can save time and effort. Citizenship, residency, age, art forms, and other special requirements can all affect your eligibility. In the description of the application/selection process, you will find information on deadlines; the organization's preferred method for making an initial contact; the application procedure, including required support materials; the selection process; the notification process; and reporting requirements. The deadlines supplied here are subject to change, and you should always contact the organization to confirm dates.

The "Equipment Access" section describes low-cost or free access to production and/or post-production equipment for film and video in various formats. Discounted rates are usually reserved for producers working on noncommercial work, and further restrictions may apply. Restrictions are explained under the comments heading. Media centers frequently upgrade equipment, and many are adding Hi-8 video equipment; a phone call to check on any additions may be worthwhile. Producers interested in equipment access programs may also want to contact their local cable television companies. Many carry public-access channels that offer equipment usage and/or broadcast time for independent producers.

The "Technical Assistance Programs and Services" section encompasses a wide range of activities that benefit independent producers. These include fiscal sponsorship, artists' registries, screening opportunities, festivals, and arts-in-education programs. Also included in this section are workshops and seminars on equipment, aesthetic issues, and business-related matters. Most media centers charge fees or require membership for some technical assistance services, but many state and local arts agencies provide certain services for a nominal charge or free.

Many organizations confine their programs to artists living in certain areas or to specific types of support. Not all programs are for everyone. To help you find the programs for which you are eligible and which best match your needs and interests, we have provided four indices. The Alphabetical Index of Organizations lets you quickly locate the organizations you are most interested in researching. The Index of Organizations by Geographic Area lists the organizations according to the area served: listings include individual states, the U.S., Canada, and international service organizations. For practical reasons, most media centers are listed according to the state in which they are located, but many do not require residency in that state for equipment access programs. The Index of Organizations by Medium and Format allows you to determine which media centers have production or post-production equipment compatible with the film or video format you are using. Producers seeking equipment access should also consult the equipment access heading in the Index of Organizations by Types of Support: some organizations provide discounted rates at a variety of off-site facilities. The Index of Organizations by Types of Support lists organizations according to the services they provide:

- ART IN PUBLIC PLACES/COMMISSIONS. Organizations that commission work from film or video artists.

- ARTISTS' COLONIES/RESIDENCY OPPORTUNITIES. Organizations that provide a working retreat for artists. Some request that residents pay a fee, but offer stipends or full or partial fee waivers to artists in financial need. Though film and video equipment and facilities are generally limited, colonies can provide media artists with an opportunity to pursue pre-production activities, such as scripting.

- ARTS IN EDUCATION/COMMUNITY RESIDENCIES AND TOURING. Organizations that sponsor, administer, or select artists for school/community residency and visiting artist programs.

- DISTRIBUTION/MARKETING/PUBLIC RELATIONS. Organizations that offer information on or assistance with distribution, marketing, or publicity.

- EMERGENCY ASSISTANCE. Organizations that provide financial support for artists facing work-related or personal emergencies.

- EQUIPMENT ACCESS. Organizations that offer low-cost or free access to on-site and off-site production or post-production equipment and facilities.

- FELLOWSHIPS/AWARDS. Organizations that offer financial support to artists based on past accomplishments or on potential for future success. These grants generally carry few or no restrictions.

- FESTIVALS. Organizations that sponsor or coordinate film or video festivals. Producers are often charged an entry fee, but cash prizes are sometimes available.

- FINANCE. Organizations that provide information on or assistance with taxes, record keeping, accounting, or financial management.

- FISCAL SPONSORSHIP. Organizations that act as nonprofit fiscal agents for independent producers seeking funding from other sources.

- HEALTH. Organizations that offer group health plans for artists or information on health care options or art hazards.

- INTERNATIONAL OPPORTUNITIES/EXCHANGE PROGRAMS. Organizations that sponsor residencies or independent work or study abroad.

- INTERNSHIPS. Organizations that offer or coordinate internships.
- JOB OPPORTUNITIES/CAREER DEVELOPMENT. Organizations that maintain job banks, publicize employment opportunities, or conduct career development workshops.
- LEGAL ASSISTANCE AND ADVICE. Organizations that provide information or referrals on legal matters.
- PROFESSIONAL DEVELOPMENT/TECHNICAL ASSISTANCE GRANTS. Organizations that provide financial support for general professional development activities such as travel to conferences or seminars, consultation fees, and promotion efforts. Sometimes these grants may be used for the production or exhibition of work deemed critical to an artist's career.
- PROJECT SUPPORT. Organizations that offer grants for the development, production, or completion of a specific project.
- REGISTRIES. Organizations that maintain registries or directories of individual artists.
- SCREENINGS/EXHIBITIONS. Organizations that sponsor screenings, broadcasts, or exhibitions of independent works on a regular basis.
- STUDY GRANTS. Organizations that offer grants for independent study, workshop attendance, or study at an institution. Artists interested in study grants should also consult the Professional Development/Technical Assistance Grants heading.
- TRAVEL GRANTS. Organizations that offer grants for travel, often for project development or professional development purposes. Artists interested in travel grants should also consult the Professional Development/Technical Assistance Grants heading.

One last thing. You can help us and other artists by sharing what you have learned on your own. If you know of programs that aren't listed here, please complete and return the card inserted in this book so that we can include them in the next edition.

Good luck!

Suzanne Niemeyer
Editor

May 15, 1991

THE GUIDE

ACADEMY OF MOTION PICTURE ARTS AND SCIENCES/ACADEMY FOUNDATION

8949 Wilshire Boulevard
Beverly Hills, CA 90211
213-247-3000
CONTACT: GREG BEAL, PROGRAM COORDINATOR

PROFILE OF FINANCIAL SUPPORT TO ARTISTS
Total Funding/Value of In-Kind Support: $100,000 for FY 1989-90
Competition for Funding: Total applications, 2,900; total individuals funded/provided with in-kind support, 5
Grant Range: $20,000

DIRECT SUPPORT PROGRAMS
➤ **NICHOLL FELLOWSHIPS IN SCREENWRITING**
Purpose: To foster the development of the art of screenwriting
Eligibility:
Special Requirements: Previous recipients ineligible; professional screenwriters for theatrical films or applicants who have sold screen or television rights to any original story, treatment, screenplay, or teleplay are ineligible
Art Forms: Screenwriting for feature-length films
Type of Support: $20,000; recipients expected to complete a screenplay during fellowship year
Scope of Program: 5 awards in 1989-90
Application/Selection Process:
Deadline: June 1
Preferred Initial Contact: Write for application/guidelines; include SASE

Application Procedure: Submit application form, $25 fee, samples of work; finalists submit synopsis of proposed screenplay, resumé, biographical essay
Selection Process: Organization staff, jury of individuals from outside of organization, committee of Academy members
Notification Process: Letter 3-5 months after deadline
Formal Report of Grant Required: Yes

ALABAMA STATE COUNCIL ON THE ARTS (ASCA)

One Dexter Avenue
Montgomery, AL 36130
205-242-4076
CONTACT: RANDY SHOULTS, COMMUNITY DEVELOPMENT PROGRAM MANAGER

PROFILE OF FINANCIAL SUPPORT TO ARTISTS
Total Funding/Value of In-Kind Support: $56,750 for FY 1990-91
Competition for Funding: Total applications, 90; total individuals funded/provided with in-kind support, 21
Grant Range: $750-$5,000

DIRECT SUPPORT PROGRAMS
➤ FELLOWSHIPS
Purpose: To encourage professional development of individual Alabama artists
Eligibility:
  Citizenship: U.S.
  Residency: Alabama
  Special Requirements: Previous grantees ineligible for 3 years
  Art Forms: Dance, media/photography, music, literature, theater, visual arts/crafts
Type of Support: $2,500-$5,000
Scope of Program: 14 awards in FY 1990-91
Application/Selection Process:
  Deadline: May 1
  Preferred Initial Contact: Call or write for application/guidelines
  Application Procedure: Submit application form, samples of work, 3 reviews of work (when available)
  Selection Process: Professional advisory panel, ASCA council and staff
  Notification Process: 4 months after deadline
  Formal Report of Grant Required: Yes

➤ **TECHNICAL ASSISTANCE GRANTS**
Purpose: To provide funds for artists in need of assistance in marketing their work, establishing a portfolio, learning tax laws and accounting basics, grantseeking, or perfecting a particular artistic technique
Eligibility:
    Citizenship: U.S.
    Residency: Alabama
    Special Requirements: Artists may submit only 1 technical assistance application per grant period
    Art Forms: All disciplines
Type of Support: Up to $1,500 for attending workshops or seminars, studying under another artist, or other educational opportunities except for pursuit of a college degree
Scope of Program: Limited funds
Application/Selection Process:
    Deadline: While funds last (fiscal year begins October)
    Preferred Initial Contact: Call or write for application/guidelines
    Application Procedure: Submit application form, samples of work, 3 reviews of work (when available), project budget
    Selection Process: Professional advisory panel, ASCA council and staff
    Notification Process: 4 months after receipt of application
    Formal Report of Grant Required: Yes

ALASKA STATE COUNCIL ON THE ARTS (ASCA)

411 West 4th Avenue
Suite 1E
Anchorage, AK 99501-2343
907-279-1558
CONTACT: G. JEAN PALMER, GRANTS OFFICER

PROFILE OF FINANCIAL SUPPORT TO ARTISTS
Total Funding/Value of In-Kind Support: $47,880 for FY 1991
Competition for Funding: Total applications, 103; total individuals funded/provided with in-kind support, 33
Grant Range: Up to $5,000

DIRECT SUPPORT PROGRAMS
➤ **INDIVIDUAL ARTIST FELLOWSHIP GRANTS**
Purpose: To assist experienced, professional artists in the creation of original works of art and in the development of their careers

Eligibility:
  Residency: Alaska
  Special Requirements: No full-time students; previous grantees ineligible for 3 years, preference given to artists who have never received an ASCA fellowship; collaborative projects ineligible
  Art Forms: Visual arts, crafts, photography, traditional Native art eligible in odd-numbered years; music composition, choreography, media arts, literature eligible in even-numbered years
Type of Support: $5,000
Scope of Program: 6 awards in FY 1991
Application/Selection Process:
  Deadline: October 1
  Preferred Initial Contact: Call or write for application/guidelines
  Application Procedure: Submit application form, samples of work
  Selection Process: Peer panel of artists, board of directors
  Notification Process: By letter in late November
  Formal Report of Grant Required: Yes

➤ **ARTIST TRAVEL GRANTS**

Purpose: To enable individual artists to attend events that will enhance their artistic skills or professional standing
Eligibility:
  Residency: Alaska
  Special Requirements: Originating artists only; no full-time students; previous grantees ineligible for 1 year, preference given to artists who have never received Travel Grant
  Art Forms: Visual arts, photography, media arts, literary arts, musical composition, choreography, and other arts involving the creation of new works
Type of Support: Maximum $600 to cover up to two-thirds of travel costs to attend workshops, conferences, or seminars, or to undertake projects
Scope of Program: 22 grants, totalling $8,868, awarded in FY 1989
Application/Selection Process:
  Deadline: 30 days before departure; awards made on first-come, first-served basis (fiscal year begins in July)
  Preferred Initial Contact: Call or write for application/guidelines
  Application Procedure: Submit application form, resumé, samples of work
  Notification Process: Letter within 2 weeks of application's receipt
  Formal Report of Grant Required: Yes

TECHNICAL ASSISTANCE PROGRAMS AND SERVICES

Programs of Special Interest: Staff assistance is available for guidance on arts planning, artist promotion, project development, and grant application development.

ALBERTA CULTURE AND MULTICULTURALISM, ARTS BRANCH

10004 - 104 Avenue
11th Floor, CN Tower
Edmonton, Alberta
Canada T5J OK5
403-427-6315
CONTACT: BILL STEWART

PROFILE OF FINANCIAL SUPPORT TO ARTISTS

Total Funding/Value of In-Kind Support: $31,480 in production and study grants for FY 1988-89

Competition for Funding: Total applications, n/a; total individuals funded/provided with in-kind support, 19

Grant Range: n/a

DIRECT SUPPORT PROGRAMS

➤ **SHORT FILM/VIDEO PRODUCTION GRANT PROGRAM/ ARTS STUDY GRANTS**

Purpose: Production grants provide financial support for independent filmmakers and videomakers for short films and videos; study grants enable writers, publishers, and film/video artists to participate in short-term, noncredit, educational seminars and workshops

Eligibility:
  Citizenship: Canada (landed immigrants also eligible)
  Residency: Alberta
  Art Forms: Film, video, literary arts (study grants only)

Type of Support: Production grants, up to $5,000 to assist, not entirely underwrite, the cost of a project; study grants, up to $500

Scope of Program: 8 production grants, totalling $25,000, in FY 1988-89; 11 study grants, totalling $6,480, in FY 1988-89

Application/Selection Process:
  Deadline: May 15 (production grants), July 2 (study grants)
  Preferred Initial Contact: Call or write for information
  Application Procedure: Submit application form, letters of reference, samples of work (if available)
  Selection Process: Jury, board of directors
  Notification Process: Letter
  Formal Report of Grant Required: Yes

➤ **THE QUEBEC-ALBERTA TELEVISION PRIZE/ THE ALBERTA-QUEBEC CINEMA PRIZE**

Purpose: To award individuals or organizations for cultural excellence in Canadian television and cinema

Eligibility:
  Citizenship: Canada (landed immigrants also eligible)
  Art Forms: Film, video
Type of Support: $2,500
Scope of Program: 2 television prizes, 2 cinema prizes annually
Application/Selection Process:
  Deadline: April or May
  Preferred Initial Contact: Call or write for information
  Selection Process: Jury

TECHNICAL ASSISTANCE PROGRAMS AND SERVICES

Programs of Special Interest: Alberta Culture and Multiculturalism offers consultations and a variety of workshop and seminar programs relating to professional development. The National Screen Institute-Canada provides training and development programs for filmmakers (contact the National Screen Institute-Canada, 8540 - 109 Street, Suite 202, Edmonton, Alberta, Canada T6G 1E6; 403-439-8461).

THE AMERICAN FILM INSTITUTE (AFI)

2021 North Western Avenue
P.O. Box 27999
Los Angeles, CA 90027
213-856-7600

PROFILE OF FINANCIAL SUPPORT TO ARTISTS

Total Funding/Value of In-Kind Support: $728,100 for FY 1990
Competition for Funding: Total applications, 1,504; total individuals funded/provided with in-kind support, 47
Grant Range: Up to $20,000

DIRECT SUPPORT PROGRAMS

➤ **INDEPENDENT FILM AND VIDEOMAKER PROGRAM**
CONTACT: ANDREA ALSBERG, GRANTS COORDINATOR
Phone: 213-856-7787

Purpose: To encourage and support the continued development of the moving image as an art form through funding productions that emphasize creative use of the media
Eligibility:
  Citizenship: U.S. (permanent residents also eligible)
  Special Requirements: Professional artists only; no students
  Art Forms: Film, video

Type of Support: Up to $20,000

Scope of Program: 12 grants, totalling $228,100, in 1990

Application/Selection Process:

    Deadline: September 14

    Preferred Initial Contact: Call or write for application/guidelines

    Application Procedure: Submit application form, samples of work, script or treatment, resumé, project budget

    Selection Process: Individuals from outside of organization, peer panel of artists

    Notification Process: Phone call to recipients, letter to non-recipients 6-7 months after deadline

➤ **DIRECTING WORKSHOP FOR WOMEN**

CONTACT: TESS MARTIN, DIRECTOR, PRODUCTION TRAINING DIVISION
Phone: 213-856-7722

Purpose: To offer mid-career professional women in the media arts their first opportunities to direct a dramatic project

Eligibility:

    Citizenship: U.S. (permanent residents also eligible)

    Age: 18 or older

    Special Requirements: Women only; must have considerable professional experience in television, film, video, or the dramatic arts but not yet had the opportunity to direct dramatic films or television; must reside and work in the U.S. or its territories during grant period

    Art Forms: Video

Type of Support: $5,000 grant to direct 30-minute narrative videotape; 2 weeks of seminars and hands-on training before start of individual production; access to production equipment and editing facilities

Scope of Program: 12 grants, totalling $60,000, over last 18- to 24-month cycle

Application/Selection Process:

    Deadline: Spring

    Preferred Initial Contact: Write for application/guidelines

    Application Procedure: Submit application form, $50 fee, references, resumé

    Selection Process: Organization staff, peer panel of artists, individuals outside of organization and board of trustees

    Notification Process: Letter or phone call

➤ **AFI/ACADEMY INTERNSHIP PROGRAM**

CONTACT: TESS MARTIN, DIRECTOR, PRODUCTION TRAINING DIVISION
Phone: 213-856-7640

Purpose: To provide opportunities for promising new directors to observe established film and television directors at work during the production of a feature film, mini-series, or movie for television

Eligibility:
    Citizenship: U.S.
    Age: 21 or older
    Special Requirements: Must have directed at least 1 project on film or videotape; must demonstrate an understanding of the filmmaking process
    Art Forms: Film
Type of Support: Internship with $200-$250 weekly stipend
Scope of Program: 2-5 internships per year
Application/Selection Process:
    Deadline: June 30
    Preferred Initial Contact: Write for application/guidelines
    Application Procedure: Submit application form, references, resumé
    Selection Process: Organization staff, peer panel of artists, individuals outside of organization and board of trustees
    Notification Process: Phone call or letter

➤ **DANIEL MANDELL EDITING INTERNSHIP**
CONTACT: TESS MARTIN, DIRECTOR, PRODUCTION TRAINING DIVISION
Phone: 213-856-7640
Purpose: To provide emerging filmmakers who are committed to pursuing a career in editing with the opportunity to work with professional editors during the editing of a feature film, television series, or movie made for television
Eligibility:
    Citizenship: U.S. (permanent residents also eligible)
    Age: 21 or older
    Special Requirements: Must have edited at least 1 project for film or videotape
    Art Forms: Film, video
Type of Support: Internship with $200-$250 weekly stipend
Scope of Program: 3 internships per year
Application/Selection Process:
    Deadline: July 31
    Preferred Initial Contact: Write for application/guidelines
    Application Procedure: Submit application form, references, resumé
    Selection Process: Organization staff, peer panel of artists, individuals from outside of organization and board of trustees
    Notification Process: Phone call or letter

➤ **TELEVISION WRITERS SUMMER WORKSHOP**
CONTACT: TESS MARTIN, DIRECTOR, PRODUCTION TRAINING DIVISION
Phone: 213-856-7623
Purpose: To provide a learning environment for promising new talents to hone their scriptwriting skills and to apply what they have learned by developing a script
Eligibility:
   Citizenship: U.S. (permanent residents also eligible)
   Age: 18 or older
   Special Requirements: Preference to new writers with media or theater backgrounds who have no major commercial television writing credits
   Art Forms: Scriptwriting for television
Type of Support: Workshop ($450 fee; scholarships with $1,000 living stipend available)
Scope of Program: 3 scholarships per year
Application/Selection Process:
   Deadline: March or April
   Preferred Initial Contact: Call or write for application/guidelines
   Application Procedure: Submit application form, $35 fee, samples of work, references, resumé
   Selection Process: Organization staff, peer panel of artists, individuals from outside of organization and board of trustees
   Notification Process: Phone call or letter

TECHNICAL ASSISTANCE PROGRAMS AND SERVICES
Programs of Special Interest:.The AFI selects new feature-length comedy films to be screened at the annual Cinetex festival and conference (fees involved; contact 213-856-7675).

THE AMERICAN-SCANDINAVIAN FOUNDATION (ASF)

725 Park Avenue
New York, NY 10021
212-879-9779
CONTACT: DELORES DI PAOLA, DIRECTOR OF EXCHANGE

PROFILE OF FINANCIAL SUPPORT TO ARTISTS
Total Funding/Value of In-Kind Support: n/a
Competition for Funding: n/a
Grant Range: $2,000-$10,000

DIRECT SUPPORT PROGRAMS
➤ AWARDS FOR STUDY IN SCANDINAVIA

Purpose: To encourage advanced study and research in Scandinavia

Eligibility:
   Citizenship: U.S. (permanent residents also eligible)
   Special Requirements: Must have completed undergraduate education; language competence (as necessary), the special merit of pursuing the project in Scandinavia, and evidence of confirmed invitation or affiliation are important factors; conference attendance and study at English-language institutions are ineligible for support
   Art Forms: All disciplines and scholarly fields

Type of Support: $2,000 grants for short visit to Scandinavia; $10,000 fellowships for a full academic year of research or study

Scope of Program: $170,500 available for 1991-92

Application/Selection Process:
   Deadline: November 1
   Preferred Initial Contact: Call or write for application/guidelines
   Application Procedure: Submit application form, $10 fee, samples of work, resumé, project description
   Selection Process: Committee
   Notification Process: Letter by mid-April
   Formal Report of Grant Required: Yes

APPALSHOP, INC.

306 Madison Street
Whitesburg, KY 41858
606-633-0108
CONTACT: MIMI PICKERING

PROFILE OF FINANCIAL SUPPORT TO ARTISTS
Total Funding/Value of In-Kind Support: $47,000 for FY 1990

Competition for Funding: Total applications, 170; total individuals funded/provided with in-kind support, 18

Grant Range: $1,000-$6,000

DIRECT SUPPORT PROGRAMS
➤ SOUTHEAST MEDIA FELLOWSHIP PROGRAM (SEMFP)

Purpose: To assist independent media artists in the Southeast by providing grants for the production of personally conceived works in film and video

Eligibility:
   Citizenship: U.S.

Residency: Alabama, Florida, Georgia, Kentucky, Louisiana, Mississippi, North Carolina, South Carolina, Tennessee, Virginia, 1 year
Special Requirements: No full-time students; artist must have overall control of content and primary creative responsibility for project; no commercial or instructional projects
Art Forms: Film, video
Type of Support: Up to $8,000 for residents of Kentucky, Louisiana, Mississippi, North Carolina, South Carolina, Tennessee; up to $5,000 for residents of Alabama, Florida, Georgia, Virginia; Equipment Access Grants from South Carolina Arts Commission Media Arts Center available for 3/4" video production, 16mm film production, 3/4" video editing, 16mm film editing, S-VHS video production, computer graphics system, audio/electronic music studio; grantees must pay for shipping production equipment to and from their location
Scope of Program: 17 cash grants, totalling $47,000, in 1990; 8 equipment access grants available for 1991
Application/Selection Process:
  Deadline: February 1
  Preferred Initial Contact: Call or write for application/guidelines
  Application Procedure: Submit application form, $4 for return shipping, samples of work, resumé, project budget, support material (optional)
  Selection Process: Independent panel of artists and arts professionals
  Notification Process: Letter 4 months after deadline
  Formal Report of Grant Required: Yes

EQUIPMENT ACCESS

Film: Production and post-production for 16mm
Video: Production and post-production for 3/4" and VHS
Comments: Rates for facilities, equipment, and crews range from no charge to commercial rates, depending on the nature of the project. A recording studio is also available.

TECHNICAL ASSISTANCE PROGRAMS AND SERVICES

Programs of Special Interest: Appalshop exhibits and broadcasts independent films and videos, and provides fundraising and distribution assistance.

ARIZONA CENTER FOR THE MEDIA ARTS

P.O. Box 40638
Tucson, AZ 85717
602-628-1737

TECHNICAL ASSISTANCE PROGRAMS AND SERVICES
Programs of Special Interest: The center offers workshops on funding and new equipment; consultation services regarding funding, distribution, and festivals; and a screening facility.

ARIZONA COMMISSION ON THE ARTS

417 West Roosevelt Street
Phoenix, AZ 85003
602-255-5882
CONTACT: KRISTA ELRICK, VISUAL ARTS DIRECTOR

PROFILE OF FINANCIAL SUPPORT TO ARTISTS
Total Funding/Value of In-Kind Support: $73,900 for FY 1990

Competition for Funding: Total applications, 494; total individuals funded/provided with in-kind support, 18

Grant Range: $3,300-$5,000

DIRECT SUPPORT PROGRAMS
➤ VISUAL ARTS FELLOWSHIPS

Purpose: To allow individual artists to set aside time to work, to purchase supplies and materials, to achieve specific artistic career goals, and to further their professional development

Eligibility:
  Residency: Arizona
  Age: 18 or older
  Special Requirements: No students enrolled for more than 3 credit hours at college or university
  Art Forms: Visual arts (eligible media rotate on 3-year cycle among 3-dimensional (1991), 2-dimensional (1992), film/video/photography (1993))

Type of Support: $5,000-$7,500

Scope of Program: Varies; $60,000 budgeted for 1991 fellowships in creative writing, performing arts, and visual arts; budget divided among disciplines in proportion to number of applicants

Application/Selection Process:
  Deadline: September 14

Preferred Initial Contact: Call or write for application/guidelines
Application Procedure: Submit application form, samples of work, resumé, reviews of work (optional), miscellaneous documentation (optional)
Selection Process: Panel of out-of-state arts professionals
Notification Process: April

➤ **ARTIST PROJECTS**

Purpose: To support artist projects that allow the artist increased time to research and develop ideas or new works, that stretch the artist's work or seek to advance the artform, that bear relevance to the artist's community, or that involve interdisciplinary collaborations with other artists or non-artists

Eligibility:
  Residency: Arizona
  Age: 18 or older
  Special Requirements: No students enrolled in more than 3 credit hours at a college or university; previous grantees not eligible
  Art Forms: All disciplines, innovative work encouraged

Type of Support: Up to $5,000 for project-related costs

Scope of Program: $20,000 allotted for 1991

Application/Selection Process:
  Deadline: September 14
  Preferred Initial Contact: Call or write for application/guidelines
  Application Procedure: Submit application forms, biographies of artists involved, samples of work
  Selection Process: Panel of out-of-state artists
  Notification Process: April
  Formal Report of Grant Required: Yes

➤ **PROFESSIONAL DEVELOPMENT GRANTS**

Purpose: To provide Arizona artists and organizations representing artists assistance in attending out-of-state conferences that will contribute to their professional growth

Eligibility:
  Residency: Arizona
  Special Requirements: Artists usually limited to one Professional Development Grant per year; assistance usually not provided for artist to attend same conference for 2 successive years
  Art Forms: All disciplines

Type of Support: Up to $500

Scope of Program: $20,000 budget for 1991

Application/Selection Process:
  Deadline: 6 weeks before conference
  Application Procedure: Submit materials describing conference (if available) and letter of request outlining conference date and location, how attendance would be beneficial, total costs involved, amount and source of other financial assistance

TECHNICAL ASSISTANCE PROGRAMS AND SERVICES
Programs of Special Interest: Individuals may apply for inclusion on the selective Artists Roster, which provides information to community sponsors interested in the Artists in Residence: Schools; Artists in Residence: Communities; Bicultural Arts; and Traveling Exhibitions programs. The commission's Arts Services Program and Arts Resource Center furnish artists with information about business-related issues.

ARKANSAS ARTS COUNCIL (AAC)

The Heritage Center, Suite 200
225 East Markham
Little Rock, AR 72201
501-324-9337
CONTACT: SALLY A. WILLIAMS, ARTIST PROGRAMS COORDINATOR

TECHNICAL ASSISTANCE PROGRAMS AND SERVICES
Programs of Special Interest: The Individual Artist Directory links artists with professional opportunities. Film and video artists may apply for inclusion in the AAC's Artists-in-Education roster. The AAC assists artists who cannot afford legal services through referrals to the University of Arkansas at Little Rock Law School Legal Clinic. The Arts Council Library offers a wide selection of reference materials.

ARTISTS FOUNDATION

8 Park Plaza
Boston, MA 02116
617-227-2787
CONTACT: BARBARA BAKER, EXECUTIVE DIRECTOR

PROFILE OF FINANCIAL SUPPORT TO ARTISTS
Total Funding/Value of In-Kind Support: $389,000 for FY 1990
Competition for Funding: Total applications, 2,050; total individuals funded/provided with in-kind support, 112
Grant Range: $1,000-$10,000

DIRECT SUPPORT PROGRAMS
➤ **MASSACHUSETTS ARTISTS FELLOWSHIP PROGRAM**
CONTACT: KATHLEEN BRANDT, FELLOWSHIP DIRECTOR
Purpose: To nurture the work of Massachusetts' best individual artists by recognizing exceptional, completed work

Eligibility:
Residency: Massachusetts, 6 months
Age: 18 or older
Special Requirements: No undergraduate students; no graduate students enrolled in program related to category of application; previous grantees ineligible for 3 years
Art Forms: Disciplines rotate on 2-year cycle between artists' books/ choreography/crafts/drawing/film/interarts/music composition/ new genres/photography/printmaking/sculpture/video and design in the built environment/fiction/folk & ethnic arts/nonfiction/painting/playwriting/poetry
Type of Support: $10,000 fellowship awards, $1,000 finalist awards
Scope of Program: 17 fellowship awards, 50 finalist awards for FY 1991
Application/Selection Process:
Deadline: December
Preferred Initial Contact: Call or write for application/guidelines
Application Procedure: Submit application form, samples of work
Selection Process: Peer panel of artists
Notification Process: Letter in June
Formal Report of Grant Required: No

➤ **ARTISTS EMERGENCY ASSISTANCE PROGRAM**
Purpose: To provide loans or grants to artists confronted by medical emergencies, fire, or unexpected catastrophes, and to provide loans when emergency funds are needed to complete an arts project
Eligibility:
Residency: Massachusetts, 1 year
Special Requirements: Professional artists only; no students enrolled in degree-granting programs
Art Forms: Artists' books, choreography, crafts, drawing, film, interarts, music composition, new genres, photography, printmaking, sculpture, video, design in the built environment, fiction, folk & ethnic arts, nonfiction, painting, playwriting, poetry
Type of Support: Up to $500 grant or loan
Scope of Program: $5,000 revolving fund
Application/Selection Process:
Deadline: Funds distributed on first-come, first-served basis (fiscal year begins in July)
Preferred Initial Contact: Call to check on availability of funds
Application Procedure: Submit application form, references, proof of status as artist (e.g., samples of work, resumé, reviews)
Notification Process: 5 days after receipt of application

TECHNICAL ASSISTANCE PROGRAMS AND SERVICES

Programs of Special Interest: The Health Education Program provides publications and seminars on hazards in the arts; Volunteer Lawyers for the Arts are available for pro bono and reduced-rate legal services; Outreach/Technical Assistance for Professional Services focuses on furnishing assistance and information to minority and disabled artists and to artists outside the Greater Boston area.

ARTISTS SPACE

223 West Broadway
New York, NY 10013
212-226-3970
CONTACT: HENDRIKA TER ELST, SLIDE FILE/GRANT COORDINATOR

PROFILE OF FINANCIAL SUPPORT TO ARTISTS
Total Funding/Value of In-Kind Support: $42,000 for FY 1989-90
Competition for Funding: Total applications, 375; total individuals and groups funded/provided with in-kind support, 298
Grant Range: $50-$500

DIRECT SUPPORT PROGRAMS
➤ **ARTISTS GRANTS**
Purpose: To provide financial aid to artists for the public presentation of their work in noncommercial situations
Eligibility:
    Residency: New York State (out-of-state artists may apply for exhibitions taking place in New York State)
    Special Requirements: Applicant must have a scheduled date and place for exhibition
    Art Forms: Visual arts, architecture, landscape architecture, crafts, photography, media arts, interdisciplinary, multi-disciplinary
Type of Support: Up to $200 for individuals; up to $500 for groups
Scope of Program: $42,000 awarded to 298 individuals and groups in FY 1989-90
Application/Selection Process:
    Deadline: Multiple deadlines
    Preferred Initial Contact: Call or write for application/guidelines
    Application Procedure: Submit application form, project budget
    Selection Process: Organization staff
    Notification Process: Letter 2-3 weeks after deadline
    Formal Report of Grant Required: Yes

TECHNICAL ASSISTANCE PROGRAMS AND SERVICES
Programs of Special Interest: The Video Program offers continuous daily video screenings that emphasize the work of emerging artists

while including historically important work of established video-makers. Artists interested in submitting videotapes for review can mail their tapes (3/4" NTSC preferred) with resumé and SASE to the attention of the Film/Video Curator. Artists Space also presents video installations, film installations, and a number of evening events, including films. Proposals for these events are accepted throughout the season. Every artist who shows work receives an honorarium and financial assistance with materials and installation costs. New York State and New Jersey film and video artists may submit slides of their work to the Artists File, a computerized directory that serves as a primary resource for Artists Space exhibitions.

ARTISTS' TELEVISION ACCESS (ATA)

992 Valencia Street
San Francisco, CA 94110
415-824-3890

EQUIPMENT ACCESS
Video: Production and post-production for VHS
Comments: Equipment access is available at subsidized rates to artists, community organizations, and people on limited incomes.

TECHNICAL ASSISTANCE PROGRAMS AND SERVICES
Programs of Special Interest: ATA programs "Other Cinema," a weekly Saturday night film/video screening, and produces "Artists' Television" and "Ethnic Trip," weekly half-hour public access art and documentary film/video cablecasts. Guest curators program a weekly Friday night screening/performance series. Artists are not charged exhibition entry fees and are paid honoraria whenever possible. ATA coordinates an intern program with local colleges and universities.

ARTIST TRUST

512 Jones Building
1331 Third Avenue
Seattle, WA 98101
206-467-8734
CONTACT: DAVID MENDOZA, EXECUTIVE DIRECTOR

PROFILE OF FINANCIAL SUPPORT TO ARTISTS

Total Funding/Value of In-Kind Support: $65,000 for FY 1990

Competition for Funding: Total applications, 650; total individuals funded/provided with in-kind support, 50

Grant Range: $300-$5,000

DIRECT SUPPORT PROGRAMS

➤ **ARTIST TRUST FELLOWSHIPS**

Purpose: To allow individual artists time to create

Eligibility:
   Citizenship: U.S. (resident aliens eligible)
   Residency: Washington State, 1 year
   Special Requirements: Must be a Washington State registered voter (except resident aliens); no students; practicing professionals only; originating artists only
   Art Forms: Dance, design, theater, visual arts, crafts, literature, media (including screenwriting, film production, video, audio art), music composition

Type of Support: $5,000; recipient must participate in and report on a "Meet the Artist" activity outside of his or her community

Scope of Program: 16 awards (dance, 2; design, 2; theater, 2; visual arts, 2; crafts, 2; literature, 2; media, 2; music composition, 2)

Application/Selection Process:
   Deadline: Multiple deadlines depending on discipline
   Preferred Initial Contact: Call or write for application/guidelines
   Application Procedure: Submit application form, samples of work, resumé, copy of voter's registration card (except resident aliens), proof of residency (copy of driver's license or tax return)
   Selection Process: Peer panel of artists, board of directors
   Notification Process: Letter 8-12 weeks after deadline
   Formal Report of Grant Required: Yes

➤ **GAP (GRANTS FOR ARTIST PROJECTS)**

Purpose: To allow artists to pursue their own creative development through projects such as development, completion, or presentation of a new work; publication; travel for artistic research or to present or complete work; workshops for professional development

Eligibility:
   Residency: Washington State
   Special Requirements: No students
   Art Forms: All disciplines
Type of Support: $100-$750 for specific project
Scope of Program: 41 grants in FY 1990
Application/Selection Process:
   Deadlines: 2 per year, usually in spring and fall
   Preferred Initial Contact: Call or write for application/guidelines
   Application Procedure: Submit application form, samples of
   work, resumé, project budget
   Selection Process: Committee of artists and arts professionals
   Notification Process: Letter 8-12 weeks after deadline
   Formal Report of Grant Required: Yes

TECHNICAL ASSISTANCE PROGRAMS AND SERVICES

Programs of Special Interest: Artist Trust maintains an information clearinghouse of programs and services of interest to Washington State artists. Extensive data on healthcare options is available. A quarterly journal for artists is also available.

ARTPARK

Box 371
Lewiston, NY 14092
716-745-3377 (Oct-Mar)/716-754-9001 (Apr-Sep)
CONTACT: JOAN MCDONOUGH, PARK PROGRAMS DIRECTOR

PROFILE OF FINANCIAL SUPPORT TO ARTISTS

Total Funding/Value of In-Kind Support: $377,000 for FY 1990
Competition for Funding: Total applications, 600; total individuals funded/provided with in-kind support, 100
Grant Range: n/a

DIRECT SUPPORT PROGRAMS
➤ **ARTPARK RESIDENCIES**

Purpose: To offer artists opportunities to experiment, collaborate, and develop their work
Eligibility:
   Citizenship: U.S. (workshop visa holders also eligible)
   Special Requirements: Practicing professional artists only;
   no students

Art Forms: Visual arts (including film and video), crafts, performing arts

Type of Support: 1- to 6-week residencies including $450 weekly fee, $200 weekly living allowance, and allowances for travel and materials; residents work as project, craft, workshop, or performing artists

Scope of Program: 100-150 residencies per year

Application/Selection Process:
  Preferred Initial Contact: Call or write for guidelines
  Application Procedure: Submit $20 fee, resumé, samples of work (project, craft, and performing artists), description of proposed work or workshop (craft, workshop, and performing artists); project artist finalists make 1-day, expenses-paid site visit, then present project proposals
  Selection Process: ArtPark staff (craft, workshop, and performing artists); guest curator and ArtPark staff (project artists)
  Notification Process: Letter
  Formal Report of Grant Required: Yes

THE ARTS AND HUMANITIES COUNCIL OF TULSA (AHCT)

2210 South Main Street
Tulsa, OK 74114
918-584-3333
CONTACT: JOHN L. EVERITT

PROFILE OF FINANCIAL SUPPORT TO ARTISTS
Total Funding/Value of In-Kind Support: $11,000
Competition for Funding: n/a
Grant Range: n/a

DIRECT SUPPORT PROGRAMS
➤ **INDIVIDUAL ARTIST/HUMANITIES GRANTS**
CONTACT: GEORGIA WILLIAMS

Purpose: To allow artists, writers, and scholars to create new works, complete works in progress, or to pursue new avenues of artistic expression and scholarly endeavor

Eligibility:
  Residency: Tulsa metropolitan area, 1 year
  Art Forms: All disciplines in the arts and humanities

Type of Support: Up to $1,000

Scope of Program: $5,000 awarded annually

Application/Selection Process:
  Deadline: April 15

Preferred Initial Contact: Call or write for application/guidelines after March 1
Application Procedure: Submit application form, support material as requested
Selection Process: Board panel
Notification Process: Letter
Formal Report of Grant Required: Yes

ARTS AND SCIENCE COUNCIL OF CHARLOTTE/ MECKLENBURG, INC. (ASC)

214 North Church Street
Suite 100
Charlotte, NC 28203
704-372-9667
CONTACT: BECKY W. ABERNETHY, ASSOCIATE DIRECTOR, ARTS EDUCATION/GRANTS

PROFILE OF FINANCIAL SUPPORT TO ARTISTS
Total Funding/Value of In-Kind Support: $11,627 for FY 1991
Competition for Funding: Total applications, 22; total individuals funded/provided with in-kind support, 12
Grant Range: $227-$1,200

DIRECT SUPPORT PROGRAMS
➤ EMERGING ARTIST PROGRAM (EAP)
Purpose: To enable established, professional artists to further their careers and pursue their artistic goals
Eligibility:
   Residency: Mecklenburg County, 1 year
   Age: 18 or older
   Special Requirements: No students; previous grantees ineligible
   Art Forms: Dramatic arts, literary arts (includes screenwriting/ playwriting), music, dance, visual arts (includes media arts, photography), multi-disciplinary, interdisciplinary
Type of Support: $200-$1,200 to support project that furthers artist's career
Scope of Program: $10,000-$13,500 awarded annually
Application/Selection Process:
   Deadline: Late summer/early fall
   Preferred Initial Contact: Call or write for application/guidelines
   Application Procedure: Submit application form, samples of work, letters of recommendation

Selection Process: Panel of artists, ASC board and staff
Notification Process: Letter 2-3 months after application
Formal Report of Grant Required: No

TECHNICAL ASSISTANCE PROGRAMS AND SERVICES

Programs of Special Interest: ASC staff offer grantwriting assistance for ASC's Emerging Artist Program, North Carolina Arts Council grant programs, and other select local grant programs that the artist has researched; call at least 1 week in advance for appointment. The Cultural Education Research Handbook lists artists who are qualified to teach or perform in local schools; artists who live within a 200-mile radius of Charlotte/Mecklenburg are eligible for inclusion.

THE ARTS ASSEMBLY OF JACKSONVILLE, INC.

128 East Forsyth Street
3rd Floor
Jacksonville, FL 32202
904-358-3600
CONTACT: PAGE D. MANKIN, GRANTS AND SERVICES MANAGER

PROFILE OF FINANCIAL SUPPORT TO ARTISTS

Total Funding/Value of In-Kind Support: $25,000 for FY 1990-91
Competition for Funding: Total applications, 44; total individuals funded/provided with in-kind support, 11
Grant Range: $790-$3,500

DIRECT SUPPORT PROGRAMS

➤ **ART VENTURES FUND CAREER OPPORTUNITY GRANTS FOR ARTISTS**

Purpose: To assist artists in attaining the "next level" of their professional development by funding expenses such as materials, advanced study with a mentor, contracting professional services for a project, travel, equipment rental or purchase, living expenses during pursuit of a specific project

Eligibility:
  Citizenship: U.S.
  Residency: First Coast area of Florida (Duval, St. Johns, Baker, Clay, Nassau counties), 1 year
  Age: 18 or older
  Special Requirements: No students
  Art Forms: Visual arts, literary arts, film/video, music, performing arts

Type of Support: Up to $5,000

Scope of Program: 11 awards in FY 1990-91

Application/Selection Process:
> **Deadline:** June 1
> **Preferred Initial Contact:** Call or make appointment to seek technical assistance
> **Application Procedure:** Submit application form, samples of work, 2 letters of recommendation, resumé, project budget; evaluation panel may schedule on-site visits to applicants
> **Selection Process:** Panel of artists and staff member, Art Ventures Fund Advisory Committee
> **Notification Process:** By letter in September
> **Formal Report of Grant Required:** Yes

➤ **FLORIDA TIMES-UNION ARTS EDUCATION MATCHING GRANT PROGRAM**

Purpose: To provide matching funds for schools, PTAs, arts organizations, and artists who wish to provide Duval County school students with basic arts education experiences as a supplement to basic curriculum

Eligibility:
> **Citizenship:** U.S.
> **Residency:** Duval County
> **Special Requirements:** School principal must agree to present project; must have 1:1 matching funds
> **Art Forms:** All disciplines

Type of Support: Up to $500 matching grant

Scope of Program: 20 grants in 1991

Application/Selection Process:
> **Preferred Initial Contact:** Call or write for information
> **Application Procedure:** Attend workshops, meetings for program development
> **Selection Process:** Peer panel review
> **Notification Process:** Letter
> **Formal Report of Funding Required:** Yes

TECHNICAL ASSISTANCE PROGRAMS AND SERVICES

Programs of Special Interest: The Arts Assembly of Jacksonville administers an Artist in Residence program for Duval County schools and distributes to First Coast Schools a resource guide publicizing arts education programs available from individual artists. An annual arts education conference also provides a showcase opportunity for artists.

ARTS COUNCIL FOR CHAUTAUQUA COUNTY

116 East 3rd Street
Jamestown, NY 14701
716-664-2465
CONTACT: PATRICE DANIELSON, DIRECTOR OF ARTISTS SERVICES

PROFILE OF FINANCIAL SUPPORT TO ARTISTS
Total Funding/Value of In-Kind Support: $6,500 for FY 1990
Competition for Funding: Total applications, 11; total individuals funded/provided with in-kind support, 7
Grant Range: $500-$1,000

DIRECT SUPPORT PROGRAMS
➤ FUND FOR THE ARTS PROJECTS POOL FELLOWSHIPS/
DECENTRALIZATION GRANTS
CONTACT: SHARON BARTOO, ASSISTANT TO THE DIRECTOR
Purpose: Fellowships, awarded solely on the basis of creative excellence, assist the career development of Chautauqua County artists; decentralization grants expand and upgrade the arts and cultural programming in Chautauqua and Cattaraugus counties
Eligibility:
    Residency: Chautauqua County, 1 year (Cattaraugus County residents also eligible for decentralization grants)
    Age: 18 or older
    Special Requirements: Decentralization grant applicants must be sponsored by nonprofit organization; previous grantees ineligible for 1 year
    Art Forms: All disciplines
Type of Support: $1,000 fellowships, up to $3,000 decentralization grants
Scope of Program: 5 fellowships, 2 decentralization grants to individuals in FY 1990
Application/Selection Process:
    Deadline: October 17
    Preferred Initial Contact: Call or write for application/guidelines
    Application Procedure: Submit application form, samples of work, references, resumé, project budget, proof of residency
    Selection Process: Individuals outside of organization
    Notification Process: Letter after panel recommendations approved by board
    Formal Report of Grant Required: Yes

TECHNICAL ASSISTANCE PROGRAMS AND SERVICES

Programs of Special Interest: The council offers a Group Health Program for working artists and their families and a reference library and workshops that address artists' needs. The council refers artists to local organizations to hold workshops and lectures/demonstrations.

THE ARTS COUNCIL OF GREATER NEW HAVEN

110 Audubon Street
New Haven, CT 06511
203-772-2788

EQUIPMENT ACCESS

Media Arts Center
70 Audubon Street
New Haven, CT 06511

Video: Production for Hi-8, 3/4", VHS; post-production for Hi-8, 3/4", S-VHS

Comments: The Media Arts Center offers affordable equipment rental rates to members working on noncommercial projects. A $50 Access Membership provides access to in-house post-production equipment and some production equipment during regular business hours; a $150 Full Access Membership provides access to production and post-production equipment on a 24-hour basis.

TECHNICAL ASSISTANCE PROGRAMS AND SERVICES

Programs of Special Interest: The arts council offers group health insurance to individual artist members ($25 membership fee). The council's Media Arts Center provides workshops on media-related topics, screening and networking opportunities for local as well as national media artists, and festivals featuring both national and international works.

ARTS COUNCIL OF HILLSBOROUGH COUNTY

1000 North Ashley
Suite 316
Tampa, FL 33602
813-229-6547
CONTACT: SUSAN EDWARDS, DIRECTOR, PROGRAM SERVICES

PROFILE OF FINANCIAL SUPPORT TO ARTISTS
Total Funding/Value of In-Kind Support: $25,843 for FY 1990
Competition for Funding: Total applications, 75; total individuals funded/provided with in-kind support, 33
Grant Range: $250-$1,000

DIRECT SUPPORT PROGRAMS
➤ **EMERGING ARTIST GRANTS**
Purpose: To assist promising local artists and arts groups in advancing their careers
Eligibility:
   Residency: Hillsborough County
   Special Requirements: Previous grantees ineligible for 2 years
   Art Forms: All disciplines
Type of Support: Up to $1,500 for a specific project
Scope of Program: 33 awards in FY 1990
Application/Selection Process:
   Deadline: 2 per year
   Preferred Initial Contact: Call or write for application/guidelines
   Application Procedure: Submit application form, samples of work, resumé, project budget, supporting materials
   Selection Process: Panel of artists and arts professionals, board of directors
   Notification Process: Letter 5 weeks after deadline
   Formal Report of Grant Required: Yes

TECHNICAL ASSISTANCE PROGRAMS AND SERVICES
Programs of Special Interest: The council sponsors workshops for artists in areas such as basic business matters, marketing, public relations, fundraising, grantwriting, and taxes (artists pay nominal fees). The council also offers tax and insurance planning services and acts as a liaison between artists and those seeking their services and as an arts advocate in legislative and policy matters. The Arts Library holds a wide reference collection on arts issues, and the *Arts Directory* covers almost 200 arts organizations. The council administers an Artists in the Schools program.

ARTS COUNCIL OF INDIANAPOLIS (ACI)

47 South Pennsylvania
Suite 703
Indianapolis, IN 46204
317-631-3301
CONTACT: NORMAN BRANDENSTEIN, DIRECTOR OF SERVICES

PROFILE OF FINANCIAL SUPPORT TO ARTISTS
Total Funding/Value of In-Kind Support: $18,500 for FY 1990
Competition for Funding: Total applications, 59; total individuals
funded/provided with in-kind support, 7
Grant Range: $1,000-$5,000

DIRECT SUPPORT PROGRAMS
➤ **INDIVIDUAL ARTIST FELLOWSHIPS/RECOGNITION
GRANTS—VISUAL ARTS**
Purpose: To foster the professional development and recognition of
established and emerging artists living and working in Indianapolis/
Marion County
Eligibility:
  Residency: Marion County, 1 year
  Age: 18 or older
  Special Requirements: No students; previous grantees ineligible;
  3 years professional stature (fellowship); less than 3 years profes-
  sional experience (recognition grant)
  Art Forms: Painting, sculpture, work on paper, photography, per-
  formance art, crafts, design arts, visual folk arts, film, video, radio
Type of Support: $5,000 fellowship, $1,000 recognition grant;
recipients conduct community service activity and public forum
discussion of fellowship activities
Scope of Program: 1 fellowship, 1 recognition grant per year
Application/Selection Process:
  Preferred Initial Contact: Call or write for application/guidelines
  Application Procedure: Submit application form, samples of
  work, artist's statement, resumé, supporting materials (optional)
  Selection Process: Peer panel of artists
  Notification Process: Letter 7 weeks after deadline
  Formal Report of Grant Required: Yes

TECHNICAL ASSISTANCE PROGRAMS AND SERVICES
Programs of Special Interest: The council maintains the unjuried
Indianapolis Artist Registry and a project pool for artists.

ARTS COUNCIL OF SANTA CLARA COUNTY

4 North Second Street
Suite 505
San Jose, CA 95113
408-998-2787
CONTACT: LAWRENCE THOO, ASSOCIATE DIRECTOR

PROFILE OF FINANCIAL SUPPORT TO ARTISTS

Total Funding/Value of In-Kind Support: $9,000 for FY 1990

Competition for Funding: Total applications, n/a; total individuals funded/provided with in-kind support, 7

Grant Range: $1,000-$1,500

➤ **INDIVIDUAL ARTIST ACCOMPLISHMENT AWARDS**

Purpose: To secure for the South Bay a robust cultural environment equal to the dynamism, pluralism, and spirit of adventure that characterize life in Silicon Valley

Eligibility:
   Residency: Santa Clara County
   Age: 18 or older
   Art Forms: All; eligible disciplines rotate

Type of Support: $1,000-$1,500

Scope of Program: 7 awards in FY 1990

Application/Selection Process:
   Preferred Initial Contact: Call or write for application/guidelines
   Application Procedure: Submit application form, samples of work, financial statement, project budget
   Selection Process: Peer panel of artists

TECHNICAL ASSISTANCE PROGRAMS AND SERVICES

Programs of Special Interest: A registry of individual Santa Clara County artists is in development.

ARTS FOR GREATER ROCHESTER, INC. (AGR)

335 E. Main Street, Suite 200
Rochester, NY 14604
716-546-5602
CONTACT: GINNA MOSESON, PROGRAM DIRECTOR

PROFILE OF FINANCIAL SUPPORT TO ARTISTS

Total Funding/Value of In-Kind Support: n/a

Competition for Funding: n/a

Grant Range: n/a

DIRECT SUPPORT PROGRAMS
➤ **AGR DECENTRALIZATION GRANT PROGRAM**

Purpose: To enable nonprofit community organizations and arts groups to sponsor arts-related projects of community interest that are open to the public

Eligibility:
    Citizenship: U.S.
    Residency: Monroe County
    Age: 18 or older
    Special Requirements: Artists must apply through a Monroe County nonprofit organization
    Art Forms: All disciplines

Type of Support: Up to $5,000 for specific project

Scope of Program: 24 grants, totalling $39,300, awarded to organizations in 1990

Application/Selection Process:
    Deadline: Late August
    Preferred Initial Contact: Attend application seminar
    Application Procedure: Sponsor submits application form, financial statement, project budget, artist's resumé, samples of work
    Selection Process: Peer panel of artists and community representatives
    Notification Process: Letter 3-4 months after deadline
    Formal Report of Grant Required: Yes

TECHNICAL ASSISTANCE PROGRAMS AND SERVICES

Programs of Special Interest: AGR's Volunteer Lawyers for the Arts program provides legal assistance to Monroe County artists with annual incomes below $15,000 a year and nonprofit organizations who bring in less than $100,000 a year. AGR maintains an artist registry and a reference library, and offers group insurance for artists and networking opportunities through weekly breakfasts and an annual "artist to artist" event.

ARTS FOUNDATION OF MICHIGAN (AFM)

1553 Woodward Avenue
Suite 1352
Detroit, MI 48226
313-964-2244
CONTACT: KIMBERLY ADAMS, EXECUTIVE DIRECTOR

PROFILE OF FINANCIAL SUPPORT TO ARTISTS
Total Funding/Value of In-Kind Support: $27,170 for FY 1990

Competition for Funding: Total applications, n/a; total individuals funded/provided with in-kind support, 15

Grant Range: n/a

DIRECT SUPPORT PROGRAMS

➤ **MICHIGAN ARTS AWARDS/GENERAL GRANTS PROGRAM**

Purpose: Michigan Arts Awards recognize individual and groups of artists in Michigan for consistent dedication and vision in advancing standards of creativity and excellence in the fine and performing arts; General Grants fund new works by individual artists that demonstrate the quality, originality, and professional execution of the artist

Eligibility:

Residency: Michigan

Special Requirements: Professional artists only; must apply with nonprofit sponsoring organization (General Grants); project must be accessible to the public (General Grants); limit 1 General Grant per year to an artist or sponsoring organization; Michigan Arts Awards by nomination only

Art Forms: All disciplines

Type of Support: $5,000 Michigan Arts Awards (winner must give brief presentation at awards ceremony in Detroit); General Grants average $1,500 to fund salaries of artists working on specific project

Scope of Program: 3 Michigan Arts Awards in 1991; 10 General Grants, totalling $17,670, in 1990

Application/Selection Process:

Preferred Initial Contact: Call or write for information

Application Procedure: Michigan Arts Awards by nomination only (nominator submits nomination form, samples of artist's work, letters of recommendation); for General Grants, sponsoring organization submits application form, proof of nonprofit status, financial statement, project narrative and budget

Selection Process: Board of directors

Notification Process: Letter

Formal Report of Funding Required: Yes

TECHNICAL ASSISTANCE PROGRAMS AND SERVICES

Programs of Special Interest: AFM has copublished the Michigan Arts Resource Guide, which includes information on technical assistance, career development, sources of funding, internships, and fellowships. The Competition Program supplies funds for cash prizes to Michigan organizations sponsoring arts competitions.

ARTS INTERNATIONAL (AI)

Institute of International Education
809 United Nations Plaza
New York, NY 10017
212-984-5370

PROFILE OF FINANCIAL SUPPORT TO ARTISTS
Total Funding/Value of In-Kind Support: n/a
Competition for Funding: n/a
Grant Range: n/a

DIRECT SUPPORT PROGRAMS
➤ **READER'S DIGEST ARTISTS AT GIVERNY PROGRAM**
Purpose: To give U.S. artists an opportunity to live and work in Giverny, France, home of Claude Monet
Eligibility:
  Citizenship: U.S.
  Special Requirements: Bachelor's degree or equivalent professional experience; recipients may not hold other fellowships or a regular job in France during residency
  Art Forms: Visual arts (includes painting, sculpture, works on paper, photography, installation, video, textiles)
Type of Support: 6-month (April 1-September 30) residency including round-trip transportation, housing, studio space, use of a car, $2,000 stipend before departure, $1,500 monthly stipend, $1,600 upon return to U.S.
Scope of Program: 3 residencies per year
Application/Selection Process:
  Deadline: Early November
  Application Procedure: Submit application form, samples of work, references, proposal summary/career plans
  Selection Process: Jury of U.S. artists, critics, and historians; international panel
  Notification Process: 1 month after deadline

Arts United of Greater Fort Wayne

114 East Superior Street
Fort Wayne, IN 46802
219-424-0646
CONTACT: ROBERT BUSH, PRESIDENT

Profile of Financial Support to Artists

Total Funding/Value of In-Kind Support: n/a

Competition for Funding: Total applications, 18 in 1990; total individuals funded/provided with in-kind support, 6

Grant Range: Up to $1,000

Direct Support Programs

➤ **INDIVIDUAL ARTIST FELLOWSHIPS**

Purpose: To foster the development of northeast Indiana's artists by funding activities significant to an artist's professional growth and recognition or for creation or completion of a project

Eligibility:

Residency: Northeast Indiana (Adams, Allen, DeKalb, Huntington, LaGrange, Noble, Steuben, Wabash, Wells, Whitely counties), 1 year

Special Requirements: Previous grantees ineligible for 1 cycle; Master Fellowship applicants must have significant professional record of working, exhibiting, or performing in their art form

Art Forms: Eligible disciplines rotate on a 2-year cycle between dance/music/theater/literature/performing folk arts (1991-92) and visual arts/crafts/media arts/design arts/visual folk arts (1992-93)

Type of Support: Master Fellowships, up to $1,000; Associate Fellowships, up to $500

Scope of Program: 6 awards in 1990

Application/Selection Process:

Deadline: April 1

Application Procedure: Submit application form, samples of work, resumé, catalogs or reviews (if available)

Selection Process: Panel of experts in eligible disciplines, board of directors

Notification Process: 2 months after deadline

Formal Report of Grant Required: Yes

ASIAN CINEVISION

32 East Broadway
New York, NY 10002
212-925-8685
CONTACT: PETER CHOW, EXECUTIVE DIRECTOR

EQUIPMENT ACCESS

Video: Production for VHS, 3/4"; post-production (off-line) for
S-VHS and 3/4"
Comments: Selected video artists may have access to equipment
and facilities at low rates.

TECHNICAL ASSISTANCE PROGRAMS AND SERVICES

Programs of Special Interest: Asian Cinevision holds annual Asian-
American film and video festivals and maintains a video archive of
Asian-American films and videos.

ASSOCIATION OF INDEPENDENT VIDEO AND FILMMAKERS (AIVF)/FOUNDATION FOR INDEPENDENT VIDEO AND FILM (FIVF)

625 Broadway
Ninth Floor
New York, NY 10012
212-473-3400

PROFILE OF FINANCIAL SUPPORT TO ARTISTS

Total Funding/Value of In-Kind Support: $57,000 in 1990
Competition for Funding: n/a
Grant Range: $5,000-$10,000

DIRECT SUPPORT PROGRAMS

➤ **FIVF DONOR-ADVISED FILM AND VIDEO FUND**
Purpose: To support independently-produced social issue media
projects that combine intellectual clarity and journalistic quality
with creative filmmaking or videomaking
Eligibility:
  Special Requirements: Applicant must be affiliated with a
  nonprofit organization; institutional projects for internal or
  promotional use, public television station productions, and
  student productions are ineligible
  Art Forms: Film, video

Type of Support: $5,000-$10,000
Scope of Program: $57,000 granted in 1989
Application/Selection Process:
  Deadline: July
  Preferred Initial Contact: Call or write to check on availability of funds; FIVF does not administer this fund every year
  Application Procedure: Submit application form, additional materials as specified
  Selection Process: Peer review panel, donors
  Notification Process: 5 months after deadline
  Formal Report of Grant Required: No

TECHNICAL ASSISTANCE PROGRAMS AND SERVICES

Programs of Special Interest: AIVF offers reasonably priced group health, life, and disability insurance. The Festival Bureau maintains information on over 400 film and video festivals in the U.S. and around the world. AIVF's resource files contain sample proposals, contracts, and press kits, and information on funders, distributors, exhibitors, and television markets. The association maintains a library and sells hard-to-find books and pamphlets on topics ranging from feature film production to copyright law. Seminars and workshops address business, technological, and aesthetic issues. AIVF's magazine, the *Independent*, is a national publication devoted exclusively to independent production. (Some AIVF services are for members only; individual memberships are $45.)

ATHENS CENTER FOR FILM AND VIDEO

P.O. Box 388
Room 407
Athens, OH 45701
614-593-1330

EQUIPMENT ACCESS

Film: Production and post-production for 16mm
Video: Production and post-production (off-line) for 3/4"
Comments: The Athens Post Production Center gives independent media artists in Ohio, West Virginia, Kentucky, Indiana, Michigan, and the surrounding region access to equipment and facilities at a low cost. Projects must not be commercial or for academic credit. A reservation form must be filled out in advance.

TECHNICAL ASSISTANCE PROGRAMS AND SERVICES

Programs of Special Interest: The Athens International Film and Video Festival includes a competition for independent producers.

Bay Area Video Coalition (BAVC)

1111 17th Street
San Francisco, CA 94107
415-861-3282

Profile of Financial Support to Artists

Total Funding/Value of In-Kind Support: n/a
Competition for Funding: n/a
Grant Range: n/a

Direct Support Programs

➤ **THE INTERACT PROGRAM: THE JOHN D. AND CATHERINE T. MACARTHUR FOUNDATION FELLOWSHIPS IN INTERACTIVE VIDEODISC PRODUCTION**

Purpose: To produce interactive videodiscs for community organizations by training independent producers in multi-media production
Eligibility:
    Special Requirements: Must have background working with community organizations and 1 useful skill necessary to produce an interactive video (e.g., video production, graphic design)
    Art Forms: Level III interactive videodisc
Type of Support: Fellowship to work 10-15 hours per week over a 10-week period on a team producing interactive videodiscs
Scope of Program: 16 awards in 1991
Application/Selection Process:
    Deadline: May 10
    Preferred Initial Contact: Write for application information
    Application Procedure: Submit answers to application questions, resumé
    Selection Process: Panel review
    Notification Process: Letter
    Formal Report of Grant Required: No

Equipment Access

CONTACT: FACILITY MANAGER, OPERATIONS SUPERVISOR, EDUCATIONAL COORDINATOR, PROGRAM MANAGER, SYSTEMS COORDINATOR, OR EXECUTIVE DIRECTOR
Phone: 415-861-3280
Video: Production and post-production for 1", Betacam, 3/4", VHS
Comments: BAVC has a 2-tier rate system: standard rates for the general public and subsidized rates for BAVC members who have been accepted into the subsidized access program. BAVC's principal interest is in supporting independent video producers who create noncommercial innovative or experimental work aimed at a large audience. Applications can be approved on the same day they are submitted to any of the contacts listed above if an appointment is scheduled in advance.

Technical Assistance Programs and Services

Programs of Special Interest: BAVC maintains a job and networking bulletin board and a media library; offers workshops on business, production, and post-production subjects (fees involved); and acts as a nonprofit umbrella for local independent producers. Project consultation is available to subsidized access program members for $20/hour.

Black American Cinema Society

3617 Mont Clair Street
Los Angeles, CA 90018
213-737-3292

Profile of Financial Support to Artists

Total Funding/Value of In-Kind Support: $6,750

Competition for Funding: Total applications, n/a; total individuals funded/provided with in-kind support, 6

Grant Range: $250-$3,000

Direct Support Programs

➤ **BLACK FILMMAKERS GRANTS PROGRAM**

Purpose: To give cash awards to black film and video artists for completed or near-complete film or video

Eligibility:
   Special Requirements: Must be a black artist (independent and student producers are eligible)
   Art Forms: Film, video

Type of Support: $250-$3,000 award

Scope of Program: 6 awards annually

Application/Selection Process:
   Deadline: March
   Preferred Initial Contact: Call or write for application/guidelines (available in January)
   Application Procedure: Submit application form, sample of work, script (if work is in progress)
   Selection Process: Jury
   Notification Process: Recipients by phone, nonrecipients by mail

BLACK FILM INSTITUTE (BFI)

University of the District of Columbia
800 Mount Vernon Place, NW
Washington, DC 20009
202-727-2396

TECHNICAL ASSISTANCE PROGRAMS AND SERVICES
Programs of Special Interest: BFI exhibits independent and other films and videos focusing on black and Third World artists, and conducts free workshops for young filmmakers.

BOSTON FILM/VIDEO FOUNDATION (BF/VF)

1126 Boylston Street
Boston, MA 02215
617-536-1540
CONTACT: MARIE FRANCE ALDERMAN, ARTIST SERVICES COORDINATOR

PROFILE OF FINANCIAL SUPPORT TO ARTISTS
Total Funding/Value of In-Kind Support: $52,000 for FY 1991
Competition for Funding: Total applications, 130; total individuals funded/provided with in-kind support, 12
Grant Range: Up to $6,000 in cash and in-kind support

DIRECT SUPPORT PROGRAMS
➤ **NEW ENGLAND FILM/VIDEO FELLOWSHIP PROGRAM**
Purpose: To foster the production of independent film and video by New England media artists through funding works-in-progress and new works
Eligibility:
    Residency: Connecticut, Maine, Massachusetts, New Hampshire, Rhode Island, Vermont, 1 year
    Age: 18 or older
    Special Requirements: Artist must have complete creative control over project; commercial and instructional projects ineligible; no students; previous recipients ineligible for 2 years
    Art Forms: Film, video
Type of Support: Up to $6,000 in cash, equipment usage, or a combination of the two; grantees supply a copy of their completed work to the Boston Film/Video New England Film/Video Program Archives
Scope of Program: $45,000 cash, $7,000 in noncash equipment access available in 1991

Application/Selection Process:
Deadline: April 1
Preferred Initial Contact: Call or write for application/guidelines
Application Procedure: Submit application form, samples of work, resumé, project budget
Selection Process: Panel of artists and arts professionals
Notification Process: 2 months after deadline

EQUIPMENT ACCESS

CONTACT: MICHAEL KING, EQUIPMENT/FACILITIES MANAGER

Film: Production for 16mm, Super 8; post-production for 16mm
Video: Production for Hi-8, Video 8, VHS, S-VHS, 3/4"; post-production for VHS (off-line), 3/4" (off-line and on-line)
Comments: BF/VF facilities include an audio studio and an electronic arts studio. BF/VF also offers the Boston On-Line program, assisting independent producers with low-cost access to commercial post-production facilities for noncommercial projects. $30 Basic Membership provides eligibility for access to the Boston On-Line program; $50 Access Membership provides access to in-house facilities at reduced rates during BF/VF office hours; $150 Equipment Membership provides 24-hour access to in-house facilities and location equipment at the lowest rate. (Equipment Membership is by application and member must be certified.)

TECHNICAL ASSISTANCE PROGRAMS AND SERVICES

Programs of Special Interest: BF/VF conducts workshops on film and video production and post-production as well as financing, marketing, and legal issues (fees range from $5 to $250), and offers members technical assistance for fundraising and grantwriting for independent projects. The Screening Program provides a venue for alternative and independent film and video exhibition, and BF/VF copresents the New England Film and Video Festival. *Visions*, a quarterly magazine for independent media producers, includes networking information for job and distribution opportunities.

BRITISH COLUMBIA MINISTRY OF MUNICIPAL AFFAIRS, RECREATION AND CULTURE—CULTURAL SERVICES BRANCH (CSB)

800 Johnson Street
Sixth Floor
Victoria, British Columbia
Canada V8V 1X4
604-356-1728
CONTACT: KATE WILKINSON, CO-ORDINATOR, ARTS AWARDS PROGRAMS

PROFILE OF FINANCIAL SUPPORT TO ARTISTS
Total Funding/Value of In-Kind Support: n/a
Competition for Funding: Total applications, 700; total individuals funded/provided with in-kind support, 400
Grant Range: $200-$25,000 for FY 1991-92

DIRECT SUPPORT PROGRAMS
➤ **PROFESSIONAL DEVELOPMENT ASSISTANCE PROGRAM**
Purpose: To assist tuition and course-related costs for the purposes of upgrading and improving the skills of practicing professional artists or arts managers
Eligibility:
    Citizenship: Canada (landed immigrants also eligible)
    Residency: Preference to applicants who have resided in British Columbia for at least 1 year
    Special Requirements: Minimum 2 years professional experience; artists who are changing disciplines must have minimum 5 years professional experience; must provide Canadian social insurance number; limit 1 grant per year
    Art Forms: Arts administration, literature, dance (performance, choreography), film/video, multi-disciplinary, museological and conservation studies, music (performance, composition), book publishing studies, theater (acting, directing, technical), visual arts
Type of Support: Maximum $1,500 for up to 50% of tuition and course-related costs for concentrated period of study at recognized educational institution
Scope of Program: n/a
Application/Selection Process:
    Deadline: May 15, September 15, January 15
    Preferred Initial Contact: Consult with Arts Awards Coordinator before applying
    Application Procedure: Submit application form, letters of reference, letter of acceptance from institution, project description and budget, resumé

Selection Process: Organization staff
Notification Process: Letter 3 months after deadline
Formal Report of Grant Required: Yes

➤ **FILM AND VIDEO PRODUCTION ASSISTANCE PROGRAM**
CONTACT: THE KNOWLEDGE NETWORK,
475 West Georgia Street, Suite 300,
Vancouver, British Columbia,
Canada V6B 4M9
Phone: 604-660-2000
Purpose: To encourage the development of talented professional film and video artists through assistance with the project costs of films or videos
Eligibility:
    Citizenship: Canada (landed immigrants also eligible)
    Residency: British Columbia, 1 year
    Special Requirements: Emerging artists and first-time directors who have experience in other areas of film or video may apply for Level I funding; senior filmmakers who have directed at least 1 film or professional artists who have produced a body of work in video may apply for Level II funding; filmmakers must have total editorial control over proposed productions; productions intended primarily for commercial television, industrial productions, and instructional productions ineligible; priority given to projects that have received production assistance from other sources; no full-time students
    Art Forms: Film, video
Type of Support: Up to 50% of development and production costs of specific project (Level I maximum, $10,000; Level II maximum, $25,000)
Scope of Program: n/a
Application/Selection Process:
    Preferred Initial Contact: Call or write for information
    Application Procedure: Submit application form, project budget, sample of work, first draft and script synopsis (dramatic and animated films), full treatment (documentary films), resumé, 2 letters of appraisal
    Selection Process: Peer panel of artists
    Notification Process: Letter 3 months after deadline
    Formal Report of Grant Required: Yes

➤ **TRAVEL ASSISTANCE PROGRAM FOR MEDIA ARTISTS**
CONTACT: THE KNOWLEDGE NETWORK, 475 WEST GEORGIA STREET, SUITE 300, VANCOUVER, BRITISH COLUMBIA, CANADA V6B 4M9
Phone: 604-660-2000
Purpose: To promote British Columbia film and video productions by assisting filmmakers and video artists to attend recognized festivals

Eligibility:
   Citizenship: Canada (landed immigrants also eligible)
   Residency: British Columbia
   Special Requirements: Film/video artists who have received an official invitation to, or whose productions will be officially screened at, recognized festivals or showcases; attendance at film markets or trade shows ineligible; must have matching funds; projects designed exclusively for theatrical release or prime-time television are ineligible; commercial, industrial, community development, instructional, or sponsored productions ineligible
   Art Forms: Film, video
Type of Support: Up to 50% of total costs, including travel, registration, and per diem, to a maximum of $2,000
Scope of Program: n/a
Application/Selection Process:
   Deadline: 8 weeks before event
   Preferred Initial Contact: Call or write for information
   Application Procedure: Submit proof of invitation to festival or showcase, project budget

BRONX COUNCIL ON THE ARTS (BCA)

1738 Hone Avenue
Bronx, NY 10461
212-931-9500
CONTACT: BETTI-SUE HERTZ

PROFILE OF FINANCIAL SUPPORT TO ARTISTS
Total Funding/Value of In-Kind Support: $27,000 for FY 1990
Competition for Funding: Total applications, 190; total individuals funded/provided with in-kind support, 18
Grant Range: $1,500

DIRECT SUPPORT PROGRAMS
➤ **BRONX RECOGNIZES ITS OWN (BRIO)**
Purpose: To assist the career development of Bronx artists
Eligibility:
   Residency: Bronx County
   Age: 18 or older
   Special Requirements: No degree-seeking students; previous grantees ineligible for 1 year
   Art Forms: Architecture, choreography, crafts, fiction, film, interpretive performance, music composition, nonfiction literature,

painting, performing art/emergent forms, photography, playwriting/screenwriting, poetry, printmaking/drawing/artists' books, sculpture, video

Type of Support: $1,500; recipients must perform public service activity

Scope of Program: 16 awards in 1990

Application/Selection Process:
   Deadline: Mid-January
   Preferred Initial Contact: Call or write for application/guidelines
   Application Procedure: Submit application form, samples of work, resumé
   Selection Process: Peer panel of artists
   Notification Process: Letter in April
   Formal Report of Grant Required: Yes

➤ **COMMUNITY REGRANTS PROGRAM**
CONTACT: ED FRIEDMAN, DIRECTOR OF ARTS SERVICES

Purpose: To fund ongoing programs of local community-based organizations that meet high standards of artistic quality and provide needed community service, programs developed by arts and community organizations that reach unserviced or underserved areas of the Bronx, and programs that serve or sponsor individual artists

Eligibility:
   Special Requirements: Individual artists must find nonprofit organization to apply on their behalf
   Art Forms: All disciplines

Type of Support: $350-$3,000 awards to organizations in 1990

Scope of Program: $110,000 total funding in 1990

Application/Selection Process:
   Deadline: August 15
   Preferred Initial Contact: Call or write for application/guidelines
   Application Procedure: Sponsoring organization submits application form, financial statement, project budget, samples of artist's work, artist's resumé
   Selection Process: Individuals from outside of BCA
   Notification Process: Letter 5 months after deadline
   Formal Report of Grant Required: Yes

TECHNICAL ASSISTANCE PROGRAMS AND SERVICES

Programs of Special Interest: The council provides seminars in such areas as management, fundraising, marketing and public relations, and offers the arts constituency graphic and public relations services, fundraising assistance, computer services, and special mailing privileges.

THE MARY INGRAHAM BUNTING INSTITUTE OF RADCLIFFE COLLEGE

34 Concord Avenue
Cambridge, MA 02138
617-495-8212
CONTACT: CHIHO TOKITA, FELLOWSHIP COORDINATOR

PROFILE OF FINANCIAL SUPPORT TO ARTISTS

Total Funding/Value of In-Kind Support: $86,000 for FY 1991-92

Competition for Funding: Total applications, 138; total individuals funded/provided with in-kind support, 4

Grant Range: $21,500

DIRECT SUPPORT PROGRAMS

➤ BUNTING FELLOWSHIP PROGRAM

Purpose: To support women who wish to advance their careers through independent work in academic and professional fields and in the creative arts

Eligibility:

  Special Requirements: Women only; artists must demonstrate significant professional accomplishments (participation in group or one-person shows) and must reside in Cambridge/Boston area *during* residency

  Art Forms: Visual arts, film, video, performing arts, literary arts (scholars in any field also eligible)

Type of Support: 1-year residency including $21,500 stipend, studio space, access to most Harvard/Radcliffe resources; fellows present work-in-progress at public colloquia or in exhibitions

Scope of Program: 10 awards per year

Application/Selection Process:

  Deadline: October 15

  Preferred Initial Contact: Call or write for application/guidelines

  Application Procedure: Submit application form, $40 fee, samples of work, resumé, references

  Selection Process: Peer panel of artists, interdisciplinary final selection committee

  Notification Process: Letter in April

TECHNICAL ASSISTANCE PROGRAMS AND SERVICES

Programs of Special Interest: The Affiliation Program offers appointees the use of studio space and other resources available to Bunting Fellows for 1 year. Applicants must meet same eligibility requirements as Bunting Fellows.

THE BUSH FOUNDATION

E-900 First National Bank Building
332 Minnesota Street
St. Paul, MN 55101
612-227-0891
CONTACT: SALLY DIXON, DIRECTOR, BUSH ARTIST FELLOWSHIPS

PROFILE OF FINANCIAL SUPPORT TO ARTISTS

Total Funding/Value of In-Kind Support: $495,000 for FY 1989-90
Competition for Funding: Total applications, 460; total individuals funded/provided with in-kind support, 15
Grant Range: $33,000

DIRECT SUPPORT PROGRAMS

➤ **BUSH ARTIST FELLOWSHIPS**
Purpose: To allow Minnesota, North Dakota, South Dakota, and western Wisconsin artists a significant period of uninterrupted time for work in their chosen form
Eligibility:
  Residency: Minnesota, North Dakota, South Dakota, western Wisconsin
  Age: 25 or older
  Special Requirements: No students or nonprofessionals; previous grantees ineligible for 5 years
  Art Forms: Visual arts, film/video (eligible in even-numbered years only), choreography, music composition, literature
Type of Support: $26,000 total stipend for 12-18 months' work on projects outlined in applicant's proposal, plus up to $7,000 for production and travel costs
Scope of Program: Up to 15 awards
Application/Selection Process:
  Preferred Initial Contact: Call or write for application/guidelines
  Application Procedure: Submit application, samples of work, resumé, references
  Selection Process: Peer panel of artists, interdisciplinary panel
  Notification Process: Letter 1 week after panel deliberations
  Formal Report of Grant Required: Yes

CALIFORNIA ARTS COUNCIL (CAC)

2411 Alhambra Boulevard
Sacramento, CA 95817
916-739-3186

PROFILE OF FINANCIAL SUPPORT TO ARTISTS

Total Funding/Value of In-Kind Support: $1,912,925 for FY 1989-90
Competition for Funding: Total applications, 2,065; total individuals funded/provided with in-kind support, 273
Grant Range: n/a

DIRECT SUPPORT PROGRAMS

➤ **ARTISTS FELLOWSHIP PROGRAM**

CONTACT: ANNE BOURGET, PROGRAM ADMINISTRATOR

Purpose: To recognize and honor the work and careers of California artists who are primary creators of their art
Eligibility:
  Residency: California, 1 year
  Special Requirements: Professional artist with at least 5 years experience; no students enrolled in degree-granting programs; previous applicants ineligible for 3 years; previous grantees ineligible for 7 years; originating artists only
  Art Forms: Disciplines rotate on 4-year cycle among media arts/new genres (1991-92), literature (1992-93), visual arts (1993-94), performing arts (1994-95)
Type of Support: $5,000
Scope of Program: 63 fellowships in FY 1989-90
Application/Selection Process:
  Deadline: October
  Application Procedure: Submit application form, resumé, artist's statement (optional), samples of work
  Selection Process: Peer panel of artists and arts professionals
  Notification Process: Letter in July
  Formal Report of Grant Required: Yes

➤ **ART IN PUBLIC BUILDINGS (AIPB) PROGRAM**

CONTACT: CLAUDIA CHAPLINE, MANAGER

Purpose: To provide opportunities for artists to work with state architects on design and architecturally-integrated art for state building projects
Eligibility:
  Residency: U.S. (preference given to California residents)
  Special Requirements: Professional artist with at least 3 years experience; no students enrolled in studio art degree programs; previous recipients ineligible for 3 years

Art Forms: Visual arts, crafts, media arts

Type of Support: Commission ($1,500-$45,000 for FY 1989-90)

Scope of Program: 12 artists awarded $160,000 in commissions for FY 1989-90

Application/Selection Process:

    Deadline: October

    Preferred Initial Contact: Call or write for application/guidelines

    Application Procedure: Submit application form, samples of work, resumé, letter outlining approach to project

    Selection Process: AIPB program staff, state architect, state agencies, panel of architects, artists, and arts professionals

    Notification Process: Commissioned artists announced in March

➤ **ARTIST IN RESIDENCE PROGRAM**

CONTACT: BRENDA BERLIN, ARTISTS IN SCHOOLS; ANDREA S. TEMKIN, ARTISTS SERVING SPECIAL CONSTITUENTS; LUCERO ARELLANO, ARTISTS IN COMMUNITIES

Purpose: To offer long-term interaction of professional artists in many disciplines with the public in workshops sponsored by schools, nonprofit arts organizations, government units, and tribal councils

Eligibility:

    Special Requirements: Professional artists with at least 3 years experience; artist must apply with sponsor; no full-time students in degree programs

    Art Forms: All disciplines

Type of Support: 3- to 11-month residencies; artists earn $1,300 per month for 80 hours project time

Scope of Program: 185 residencies totalling $1,405,555 in FY 1989-90

Application/Selection Process:

    Deadline: February

    Preferred Initial Contact: Call or write for application/ guidelines; 30-minute Artist in Residence video available

    Application Procedure: Submit application form, artist's statement, sponsor organization statement, project description and budget, supporting materials (e.g., reviews, performance programs), letters of support, samples of work

    Selection Process: Peer panel of artists and arts professionals

    Notification Process: 4-6 months after deadline

CALIFORNIA COMMUNITY FOUNDATION

606 South Olive Street
Suite 2400
Los Angeles, CA 90014
213-413-4042
CONTACT: SUSAN FONG, PROGRAM OFFICER

PROFILE OF FINANCIAL SUPPORT TO ARTISTS

Total Funding/Value of In-Kind Support: $95,000 for FY 1989-90
Competition for Funding: Total applications, 626; total individuals funded/provided with in-kind support, 17
Grant Range: Up to $10,000

DIRECT SUPPORT PROGRAMS

➤ **J. PAUL GETTY TRUST FUND FOR THE VISUAL ARTS**

Purpose: To nurture the accomplishments of mid-career artists, particularly those whose work is reflective of the multicultural make-up of Los Angeles
Eligibility:
   Residency: Los Angeles County
   Age: Generally over 35
   Special Requirements: At least 15 years experience in field; no students
   Art Forms: Painting, sculpture, photography, crafts, printmaking, drawing, artists' books, experimental and independent film and video, performance art with original visual art as integral component, conceptual art, new genres
Type of Support: $15,000
Scope of Program: 5 awards for 1990-91
Application/Selection Process:
   Deadline: October 15
   Preferred Initial Contact: Call or write for application/guidelines
   Application Procedure: Submit application form, samples of work, resumé, supporting materials (e.g., reviews, references)
   Selection Process: Outside advisory panel, staff
   Notification Process: Phone call and follow-up letter
   Formal Report of Grant Required: Yes

➤ **BRODY ARTS FUND**

Purpose: To strengthen and encourage emerging artists representing communities often outside the mainstream
Eligibility:
   Residency: Los Angeles County
   Age: No undergraduate students or younger

Special Requirements: No students; preference given to ethnic and other minorities (e.g., disabled, gay)
Art Forms: Disciplines rotate on a 3-year cycle among literature/media arts (1991), visual arts (1992), performing arts (1993)
Type of Support: $2,500
Scope of Program: 10 awards in 1989-90
Application/Selection Process:
  Deadline: September 15
  Preferred Initial Contact: Call or write for application/guidelines
  Application Procedure: Submit application form, samples of work, resumé, supporting materials (e.g., reviews, references)
  Selection Process: Multi-disciplinary panels, staff
  Notification Process: Phone call and follow-up letter in December
  Formal Report of Grant Required: Yes

TECHNICAL ASSISTANCE PROGRAMS AND SERVICES
Programs of Special Interest: The California Community Foundation maintains the Funding Information Center, a collection focusing on regional grant and fellowship opportunities. Grantseekers should call for reservations.

THE CANADA COUNCIL/ CONSEIL DES ARTS DU CANADA (CC/CAC)

99 Metcalfe Street
P.O. Box 1047
Ottawa, Ontario
Canada K1P 5V8
613-598-4365
CONTACT: LISE ROCHON, INFORMATION OFFICER, COMMUNICATIONS SECTION

PROFILE OF FINANCIAL SUPPORT TO ARTISTS
Total Funding/Value of In-Kind Support: n/a
Competition for Funding: Total applications, n/a; total individuals funded/provided with in-kind support, 1,200
Grant Range: n/a

DIRECT SUPPORT PROGRAMS
➤ **FILM—ARTS GRANTS "A"/ARTS GRANTS "B"**
CONTACT: MONIQUE BÉLANGER, ARTS AWARDS SERVICE
Phone: 613-598-4312
Purpose: Arts Grants "A" support the creative work of artists whose contributions to their field have been recognized at a national or international level and whose work has attracted critical attention; Arts Grants "B" support personal creative activity

Eligibility:
Citizenship: Canada (permanent residents also eligible)
Age: 18 or older
Special Requirements: Filmmakers must have completed formal training and professionally directed at least 1 film; individuals whose work has been produced solely in an educational context ineligible; commercial, educational, and commissioned projects ineligible; previous applicants ineligible for 1 year
Art Forms: Film (filmmakers, scriptwriters, researchers, authors/playwrights, film technicians eligible)

Type of Support: Arts Grants "A" up to $32,000 for living expenses (up to $2,500 per month) and project costs, plus up to $2,800 travel allowance; Arts Grants "B" up to $18,000 for living expenses (up to $1,500 per month), project costs, and travel costs (Arts Grants "B" for 2 collaborative artists up to $25,000; for 3 artists up to $30,000)

Scope of Program: 1 Arts Grant "A", 9 Arts Grants "B" in FY 1989-90

Application/Selection Process:
Deadline: October 1, April 1 (Arts Grants "B" only)
Preferred Initial Contact: Call or write for guidelines; submit project description and resumé before applying
Application Procedure: Submit application form, samples of work, references, project budget, resumé, financial statement
Selection Process: Peer panel of artists, organization staff, board of directors
Notification Process: Letter 3-5 months after deadline

➤ **FILM—PROJECT GRANTS/TRAVEL GRANTS**
CONTACT: MONIQUE BÉLANGER, ARTS AWARDS SERVICE
Phone: 613-598-4312

Purpose: Project Grants support artists who need a short period of time in which to pursue their own creative work or artistic development; Travel Grants assist artists who need to travel on occasions important to their careers

Eligibility:
Citizenship: Canada (permanent residents also eligible)
Age: 18 or older
Special Requirements: Filmmakers must have completed formal training and professionally directed at least 1 film; individuals whose work has been produced solely in an educational context ineligible; commercial, educational, and commissioned projects ineligible; previous applicants ineligible for 1 year
Art Forms: Film (filmmakers, scriptwriters, researchers, authors/playwrights, film technicians eligible)

Type of Support: Project Grants up to $4,000 for living expenses (up to $1,500 per month) and project costs, plus travel allowance up to $2,800; Travel Grants up to $2,800 for travel, plus living and local transportation expenses up to $500

Scope of Program: 16 Project Grants, 7 Travel Grants in FY 1989-90

Application/Selection Process:

Deadline: March 15, September 15, December 15

Preferred Initial Contact: Call or write for guidelines; submit project description and resumé before applying

Application Procedure: Submit application form, samples of work, references, project budget, resumé, financial statement

Selection Process: Peer panel of artists, organization staff, board of directors

Notification Process: Letter 6-8 weeks after deadline

➤ **FILM PRODUCTION GRANTS**

CONTACT: FRANCOYSE PICARD, MEDIA ARTS OFFICER (FILM AND HOLOGRAPHY)

Phone: 613-598-4358

Purpose: To provide support to professional independent filmmakers for materials, salaries, equipment rental, and other costs involved in film production

Eligibility:

Citizenship: Canada (permanent residents also eligible)

Special Requirements: Filmmakers must have completed formal training and professionally directed at least 1 film (first-time filmmakers may apply for Explorations Program Grants; contact the Explorations Program, 613-598-4336); students and individuals whose work has been produced solely in an educational context are ineligible; commercial, educational, and commissioned projects ineligible; priority to projects that demonstrate an original, innovative, and experimental approach to filmmaking

Art Forms: Film

Type of Support: Up to $50,000; print of film must be submitted to the council

Scope of Program: 49 grants in FY 1989-90

Application/Selection Process:

Deadline: March 15, July 15, November 15

Preferred Initial Contact: Call or write for guidelines

Application Procedure: Submit application form, project budget, samples of work (applicants encouraged to apply to the Arts Awards Service of the council for grants to cover their subsistence costs during a period of research, scriptwriting, or storyboarding before they submit an application for a Film Production Grants)

Selection Process: Jury of filmmakers and film experts

Formal Report of Grant Required: Yes

➤ **VIDEO—ARTS GRANTS "A"/ARTS GRANTS "B"**

CONTACT: ANNE-MARIE HOGUE, ARTS AWARDS SERVICE

Phone: 613-598-4318

Purpose: Arts Grants "A" support the creative work of artists whose contributions to their field have been recognized at a national or international level and whose work has attracted critical attention; Arts Grants "B" support personal creative activity

Eligibility:
   Citizenship: Canada (permanent residents also eligible)
   Age: 18 or older
   Special Requirements: Must have completed formal training and have completed 1 or more nonindustrial video or be otherwise recognized as a professional; preference given to candidates who approach video in an original, innovative, or experimental way
   Art Forms: Video

Type of Support: Arts Grants "A" up to $40,000 for materials and services (up to $10,000) and living expenses (up to $2,500 per month); Arts Grants "B" up to $18,000 for living expenses (up to $1,500 per month), project costs, and travel costs (Arts Grants "B" for 2 collaborative artists up to $25,000; for 3 artists up to $30,000)

Scope of Program: 3 Arts Grants "A", 3 Arts Grants "B" in FY 1989-90

Application/Selection Process:
   Deadline: April 1 (Arts Grants "B" only), October 1
   Preferred Initial Contact: Call or write for guidelines; submit project description and resumé before applying
   Application Procedure: Submit application form, samples of work, references (Arts Grants "B" only), project budget, resumé, financial statement
   Selection Process: Peer panel of artists, organization staff, board of directors
   Notification Process: Letter 3-5 months after deadline

▶ **VIDEO—PROJECT GRANTS/TRAVEL GRANTS**
CONTACT: ANNE-MARIE HOGUE, ARTS AWARDS SERVICE
Phone: 613-598-4318

Purpose: Project Grants support artists who need a short period of time in which to pursue their own creative work or artistic development; Travel Grants assist artists who need to travel on occasions important to their careers

Eligibility:
   Citizenship: Canada (permanent residents also eligible)
   Age: 18 or older
   Special Requirements: Must have completed formal training and have completed 1 or more nonindustrial video or be otherwise recognized as a professional; preference given to candidates who approach video in an original, experimental, or innovative way
   Art Forms: Video

Type of Support: Project Grants up to $4,000 for living expenses (up to $1,500 per month) and project costs, plus travel allowance up to $2,800; Travel Grants up to $2,800 for travel, plus living and local transportation expenses up to $500

Scope of Program: 9 Project Grants, 8 Travel Grants in FY 1989-90

Application/Selection Process:
Deadline: January 15, May 15, October 1
Preferred Initial Contact: Call or write for guidelines; submit project description and resumé before applying
Application Procedure: Submit application form, samples of work, references, project budget, resumé, financial statement
Selection Process: Peer panel of artists, organization staff, board of directors
Notification Process: Letter 6-8 weeks after deadline

➤ **VIDEO PRODUCTION GRANTS**
CONTACT: JEAN GAGNON, MEDIA ARTS OFFICER (VIDEO AND AUDIO)
Phone: 613-598-4356

Purpose: To encourage and promote the development of video as a medium of artistic expression by providing support to professional video artists for materials, salaries, equipment rental, and other costs related to the production of works in video
Citizenship: Canada (permanent residents also eligible)
Special Requirements: Must have completed formal training and have completed 1 or more nonindustrial video or be otherwise recognized as a professional (first-time video producers may apply for Explorations Program Grants; contact the Explorations Program, 613-598-4336); no full-time students; promotional, corporate, and industrial videos ineligible; director must have total artistic control over project; priority to projects that demonstrate an original, innovative, and experimental approach to video
Art Forms: Video

Type of Support: Up to $35,000; copy of funded project must be submitted to the council

Scope of Program: 21 grants in FY 1989-90

Application/Selection Process:
Deadline: April 15, November 15
Application Procedure: Submit application form, samples of work, 2 letters of appraisal, project budget
Selection Process: Jury of video artists and experts

TECHNICAL ASSISTANCE PROGRAMS AND SERVICES
Programs of Special Interest: The Film and Holography Workshop Program enables film and holography organizations to invite professional artists from outside their region to give 3- to 5-day advanced workshops in filmmaking and holography. The Videotape Fund provides blank tapes to independent professional artists.

THE CENTER FOR NEW TELEVISION

912 South Wabash Avenue
Chicago, IL 60605
312-427-5446

PROFILE OF FINANCIAL SUPPORT TO ARTISTS

Total Funding/Value of In-Kind Support: $112,500 in 1990 (estimate)
Competition for Funding: Total applications, 322; total individuals funded/provided with in-kind support, 61
Grant Range: $359-$5,000

DIRECT SUPPORT PROGRAMS

➤ **NEA/AFI GREAT LAKES REGIONAL FELLOWSHIP PROGRAM: FILM AND VIDEO PRODUCTION GRANTS**
Purpose: To assist independent film and video artists whose personal work shows promise or excellence
Eligibility:
 Residency: Illinois, Indiana, Ohio, Michigan, 1 year
 Special Requirements: Full-time students ineligible; commercial and instructional projects and projects associated with a degree program ineligible; applicant must have overall control and primary creative responsibility for project; previous grantees must have completed projects or production stages for which they received funding
 Art Forms: Film, video
Type of Support: New Project Grants, up to $15,000 may be used for any stage of production of new projects with total budgets up to $60,000; Work in Progress Grants, up to $7,000 for projects where at least half the shooting is completed or the editing is underway; Encouragement Grants, up to $3,000 for new projects with total cash budgets up to $10,000 (Encouragement Grants targeted to emerging artists); recipients supply 1 copy of their finished work to the CNTV library for a 1-time screening and/or broadcast
Scope of Program: $20,260 in New Project Grants, $30,000 in Work in Progress Grants, $15,000 in Encouragement Grants available in 1991
Application/Selection Process:
 Deadline: May
 Preferred Initial Contact: Call or write for application/guidelines
 Application Procedure: Submit application form, $4 for return postage, samples of work, resumé, project description and budget
 Selection Process: Peer panel of artists and arts professionals
 Notification Process: Letter in October
 Formal Report of Grant Required: Yes

➤ **RETIREMENT RESEARCH FOUNDATION NATIONAL MEDIA AWARDS**

Purpose: To identify and promote the visibility of outstanding films, videotapes, and television programs for and about aging or aged people and to encourage excellence in media productions on issues related to aging

Eligibility:

Special Requirements: Work must have been produced in the U.S. and must deal primarily with concerns that are of specific interest to aging or aged people or those working in the field of aging; work that primarily promotes a particular organization, institution, or product is ineligible; completed work only

Art Forms: Independent films and videos, television and theatrical film fiction, television nonfiction, training films and videos

Type of Support: $500-$5,000 awards; recipients asked to donate a copy of their work to the Retirement Research Foundation National Media Awards Library for in-house use only and to attend an awards ceremony in Chicago or to designate a representative to attend

Scope of Program: Up to $33,000 available in 1991

Application/Selection Process:

Deadline: February 1

Preferred Initial Contact: Call or write for application/guidelines

Application Procedure: Submit application form, sample of work

Selection Process: CNTV staff, media professionals, specialists on aging, Retirement Research Foundation representatives

Notification Process: 2-3 months after deadline

➤ **NEW TELEVISION AWARDS**

CONTACT: ELLEN MEYERS

Purpose: To provide access to facilities in order to encourage independent videomakers to produce and complete projects

Eligibility:

Special Requirements: Project must be an independent production

Art Forms: Video

Type of Support: Access to the center's equipment

Scope of Program: $46,000 worth of equipment access available in 1991

Application/Selection Process:

Deadline: Fall

Preferred Initial Contact: Call or write for application/guidelines

Application Procedure: Submit application form, sample of work

Selection Process: Board committee

Notification Process: Letter

Formal Report of Grant Required: Yes

EQUIPMENT ACCESS

Video: Production for Hi-8, 3/4"; post-production for 3/4" (on-line and off-line), VHS (off-line)

Comments: CNTV equipment and facilities are available at low rates to independents and artists who are not working for a client. The videomaker must exercise complete creative control over the project and be a member of CNTV. Individual access memberships are $60.

TECHNICAL ASSISTANCE PROGRAMS AND SERVICES

Programs of Special Interest: Staff consultation on project development, equipment acquisition and maintenance, and other subjects is available to members for $25/hour.

CHANGE, INC.

P.O. Box 705
Cooper Station
New York, NY 10276
212-473-3742
CONTACT: DENISE LE BEAU, BOARD MEMBER

PROFILE OF FINANCIAL SUPPORT TO ARTISTS

Total Funding/Value of In-Kind Support: $37,500 for FY 1990

Competition for Funding: Total applications, 200; total individuals funded/provided with in-kind support, 75

Grant Range: $500

DIRECT SUPPORT PROGRAMS

➤ EMERGENCY ASSISTANCE

Purpose: To assist artists in need of emergency financial aid

Eligibility:
   Special Requirements: Professional artists only; no students; applicants must require emergency financial aid; no previous recipients
   Art Forms: All disciplines

Type of Support: $100-$500; medical treatment, including free hospitalization, also available for qualified applicants

Scope of Program: 75 recipients in 1990

Application/Selection Process:
   Deadline: None
   Preferred Initial Contact: Request guidelines by mail or phone, or write letter of application

Application Procedure: Submit letter detailing financial emergency, documentation of emergency (e.g., copies of eviction notice, outstanding bills), resumé, samples of work, reviews, 2 letters of recommendation from individuals in field verifying professional status
Selection Process: Board of directors
Notification Process: Letter within a few days if necessary
Formal Report of Grant Required: No

CHICAGO DEPARTMENT OF CULTURAL AFFAIRS

Cultural Grants
78 East Washington Street
Chicago, IL 60602
312-744-1742
CONTACT: MARY E. YOUNG, DIRECTOR OF CULTURAL GRANTS

PROFILE OF FINANCIAL SUPPORT TO ARTISTS
Total Funding/Value of In-Kind Support: $367,400 for FY 1990 (includes project support to small arts organizations)
Competition for Funding: Total applications, 483; total individuals funded/provided with in-kind support, 343
Grant Range: $1,000-$4,000

DIRECT SUPPORT PROGRAMS
➤ **COMMUNITY ARTS ASSISTANCE PROGRAM**
CONTACT: COMMUNITY ARTS ASSISTANCE STAFF
Phone: 312-744-6630
Purpose: To promote Chicago's new and emerging multi-ethnic artists and nonprofit arts organizations by funding technical assistance, professional, or organizational development projects that address a specific need or problem
Eligibility:
   Citizenship: U.S. (permanent residents also eligible)
   Residency: Chicago, 6 months
   Age: 21 or older
   Art Forms: All disciplines
Type of Support: Up to $1,500 for project
Scope of Program: 268 grants in FY 1990 (includes grants to organizations)
Application/Selection Process:
   Deadline: January
   Preferred Initial Contact: Call or write for application/guidelines

Application Procedure: Submit application form, samples of work, proof of residency
Selection Process: Panel of artists and arts professionals
Notification Process: Letter 4-5 months after deadline
Formal Report of Funding Required: Yes

➤ **NEIGHBORHOOD ARTS PROGRAM (NAP)**
CONTACT: NEIGHBORHOOD ARTS STAFF MEMBER
Phone: 312-744-6630
Purpose: To encourage and support the presentation of high-quality instructional arts projects that benefit young, elderly, and disabled participants in Chicago's low- and moderate-income neighborhoods
Eligibility:
    Citizenship: U.S. (permanent residents also eligible)
    Residency: Chicago, 6 months
    Age: 21 or older
    Special Requirements: 1 project per applicant per funding year
    Art Forms: All disciplines
Type of Support: Up to $4,000 for project materials, artists' salaries, and support services
Scope of Program: 75 grants in FY 1990
Application/Selection Process:
    Deadline: August
    Preferred Initial Contact: Call or write for application/guidelines
    Application Procedure: Submit application forms, samples of work, proof of residency
    Selection Process: Panel of artists and arts professionals
    Notification Process: Letter 4-5 weeks after deadline
    Formal Report of Funding Required: Yes

TECHNICAL ASSISTANCE PROGRAMS AND SERVICES

Programs of Special Interest: Arts Resource Workshops and Special Events, conducted by professional consultants, are offered to artists, students, and arts administrators for nominal fees or free. The Arts Technical Assistance Guide outlines local and regional nonprofit arts organizations that provide technical assistance and funding opportunities for artists and arts administrators.

CITY OF RALEIGH ARTS COMMISSION (CORAC)

305 South Blount Street
Raleigh, NC 27601
919-831-6234
CONTACT: ELAINE LORBER, EXECUTIVE DIRECTOR

PROFILE OF FINANCIAL SUPPORT TO ARTISTS

Total Funding/Value of In-Kind Support: n/a
Competition for Funding: Total applications, n/a; total individuals funded/provided with in-kind support, 10 for FY 1989-90
Grant Range: n/a

DIRECT SUPPORT PROGRAMS

➤ EMERGING ARTISTS PROGRAM

Purpose: To recognize and provide financial support for committed, accomplished artists in their formative years, enabling them to advance their work and careers as developing professionals
Eligibility:
  Residency: Wake County, 1 year
  Age: 18 or older
  Special Requirements: Previous grantees ineligible for 3 years
  Art Forms: All disciplines
Type of Support: $250-$1,000 for specific professional development projects (e.g., expenses for training, travel, space, supplies)
Scope of Program: 10 awards in 1989-90
Application/Selection Process:
  Deadline: November 8
  Preferred Initial Contact: Call for application/guidelines
  Application Procedure: Confer with executive director before applying; submit application form, project proposal and budget, resumé, letters of recommendation, references, samples of work, supporting materials (optional)
  Notification Process: Letter 6-7 weeks after deadline
  Formal Report of Grant Required: Yes

COLORADO COUNCIL ON THE ARTS AND HUMANITIES (CCAH)

750 Pennsylvania Street
Denver, CO 80203-3699
303-894-2619
CONTACT: DANIEL A. SALAZAR, DIRECTOR, INDIVIDUAL ARTIST PROGRAM

PROFILE OF FINANCIAL SUPPORT TO ARTISTS

Total Funding/Value of In-Kind Support: $62,000 for FY 1990

Competition for Funding: Total applications, 200; total individuals funded/provided with in-kind support, 26

Grant Range: Up to $4,000

DIRECT SUPPORT PROGRAMS

➤ **INDIVIDUAL ARTIST PROGRAM**

Purpose: To recognize outstanding accomplishments among creative artists

Eligibility:
    Citizenship: U.S.
    Residency: Colorado, 1 year
    Age: 18 or older
    Special Requirements: Originating artists only; no full-time students enrolled in degree programs; previous grantees ineligible for 1 round
    Art Forms: Choreography, music composition, visual arts, crafts, photography, media arts, interdisciplinary, folk arts, fiction, poetry, playwriting; eligible disciplines rotate on 3-year cycle

Type of Support: $4,000 and assistance in promoting work

Scope of Program: 12 awards in 1990

Application/Selection Process:
    Deadline: November 15
    Preferred Initial Contact: Call or write for application/guidelines
    Application Procedure: Submit application form, samples of work
    Selection Process: Panel of artists and arts professionals
    Notification Process: Letter
    Formal Report of Grant Required: Yes

➤ **COLORADO VISIONS PROJECT GRANTS FOR INDIVIDUAL ARTISTS (COVISIONS)**

Purpose: To provide direct financial support for artists to produce and showcase within their community artwork that reflects the community's culture, history, and architecture, that fosters respect for diverse cultures, and that explores contemporary social issues

Eligibility:
 Citizenship: U.S.
 Residency: Colorado
 Age: 18 or older
 Special Requirements: Originating artists only
 Art Forms: Media arts (film, video, audio), performing arts (dance choreography, music composition, performance art), visual arts (painting, drawing, printmaking, photography, sculpture, installation, crafts), design arts, folk arts, literature
Type of Support: Up to $2,000 project grant
Scope of Program: $20,000 budget for 1991
Application/Selection Process:
 Deadline: December 10
 Preferred Initial Contact: Call or write for application/guidelines
 Application Procedure: Submit application form, samples of work, project proposal and budget
 Selection Process: Community Arts Development panel including artists
 Notification Process: Letter in February
 Formal Report of Grant Required: Yes

TECHNICAL ASSISTANCE PROGRAMS AND SERVICES
Programs of Special Interest: The unjuried Colorado Artists Register (CAR) houses slides of work by professional Colorado artists. Artists accepted to the CCAH Resource List are eligible for 1-week to 5-month residencies in schools through the Artist in Residence Program (contact Patty Ortiz, Artists in Residence Program Director, Young Audiences, Inc., 1415 Larimer Street, Denver, CO 80202; 303-825-3650).

COMMONWEALTH COUNCIL FOR ARTS AND CULTURE (CCAC)

P.O. Box 553, CHRB
Saipan, MP 96950
670-322-9982/9983
CONTACT: ANA S. TEREGEYO, EXECUTIVE DIRECTOR

PROFILE OF FINANCIAL SUPPORT TO ARTISTS
Total Funding/Value of In-Kind Support: n/a
Competition for Funding: n/a
Grant Range: $200-$2,000

DIRECT SUPPORT PROGRAMS
➤ **GRANTS-IN-AID**

Eligibility:
  Citizenship: U.S.
  Residency: Northern Mariana Islands
  Art Forms: Dance, media arts, music (performance, composition), photography, theater, visual arts (general, painting, sculpture, printmaking), literature, folk arts

Type of Support: $200-$2,000

Scope of Program: 6-9 awards per year

Application/Selection Process:
  Deadline: 90 days before project begins
  Preferred Initial Contact: Call or write the CCAC main office on Saipan or CCAC board representatives for application/guidelines

THE COMMUNITY FILM WORKSHOP (CFW)

1130 South Wabash Avenue
Suite 400
Chicago, IL 60605
312-427-1245

PROFILE OF FINANCIAL SUPPORT TO ARTISTS

Total Funding/Value of In-Kind Support: $20,000 for 1990

Competition for Funding: Total applications, 30; total individuals funded/provided with in-kind support, 4

Grant Range: $2,000-$5,000 worth of equipment access

DIRECT SUPPORT PROGRAMS
➤ **BUILD ILLINOIS FILMMAKERS GRANTS**

Purpose: To encourage the production of independent films by offering grants to be applied to rentals of CFW's production and post-production equipment and facilities to emerging independent filmmakers

Eligibility:
  Residency: Illinois
  Special Requirements: Must be CFW member; students and projects associated with a degree program ineligible; commercial and instructional projects are ineligible; previous grantees must have completed funded projects; minority applicants encouraged to apply
  Art Forms: 16mm film

Type of Support: Up to $5,000 worth of equipment/facilities rental for 16mm production and post-production

Scope of Program: 4 awards in 1990

Application/Selection Process:
  Deadline: December 1
  Preferred Initial Contact: Call or write for application/guidelines
  Application Procedure: Submit application form, $30 membership fee (if not a member of CFW), project description and budget, resumé, samples of work
  Selection Process: Independent jury of artists and arts professionals
  Notification Process: January
  Formal Report of Grant Required: Yes

CONNECTICUT COMMISSION ON THE ARTS

227 Lawrence Street
Hartford, CT 06106
203-566-4770
CONTACT: LINDA DENTE, PROGRAM MANAGER

PROFILE OF FINANCIAL SUPPORT TO ARTISTS

Total Funding/Value of In-Kind Support: $100,000 for FY 1989-90

Competition for Funding: Total applications, 300; total individuals funded/provided with in-kind support, 20

Grant Range: $5,000

DIRECT SUPPORT PROGRAMS

➤ ARTIST GRANTS

Purpose: To provide financial support for artists to develop new work or to complete works in progress

Eligibility:
  Residency: Connecticut, 2 years
  Special Requirements: No students; previous recipients ineligible for 3 years
  Art Forms: Visual arts (sculpture, printmaking, painting, photography, crafts, performance art), poetry, playwriting, fiction, music composition, choreography, film, video, new genres (categories alternate each year between visual arts and other disciplines)

Type of Support: $5,000

Scope of Program: 20 awards in FY 1989-90

Application/Selection Process:
  Deadline: January 29
  Preferred Initial Contact: Call or write for application/guidelines

Application Procedure: Submit application form, samples of work, resumé, project budget
Selection Process: Peer panel of artists
Notification Process: Letter in May
Formal Report of Grant Required: Yes

TECHNICAL ASSISTANCE PROGRAMS AND SERVICES

Programs of Special Interest: The commission holds an annual competition for Connecticut film and video artists. The winning entries are broadcast on Connecticut Public Television. Artist residencies are available through the Arts-in-Education program. Connecticut Volunteer Lawyers for the Arts provides a variety of free services for eligible artists and holds an annual Arts Law conference.

CONTEMPORARY ARTS CENTER

900 Camp Street
P.O. Box 30498
New Orleans, LA 70190
504-523-1216
CONTACT: ELENA RONQUILLO

PROFILE OF FINANCIAL SUPPORT TO ARTISTS

Total Funding/Value of In-Kind Support: $30,400
Competition for Funding: Total applications, 75; total individuals funded/provided with in-kind support, 8
Grant Range: $1,500-$6,500

DIRECT SUPPORT PROGRAMS

➤ REGIONAL ARTISTS PROJECTS (RAP)

Purpose: To provide funding for experimental or multi-cultural projects that would not be considered in other arts discipline categories because they are new or nontraditional forms
Eligibility:
  Citizenship: U.S.
  Residency: Louisiana, Mississippi, Alabama, Arkansas
  Art Forms: Film, video, visual arts, dance, music, literature, interdisciplinary
Type of Support: $1,500-$6,500 project support
Scope of Program: $30,400 budget
Application/Selection Process:
  Deadline: December
  Preferred Initial Contact: Write for application/guidelines
  Application Procedure: Submit application form, project description, biographical information, samples of work

Selection Process: Peer panel of artists
Notification Process: Letter
Formal Report of Grant Required: Yes

TECHNICAL ASSISTANCE PROGRAMS AND SERVICES
CONTACT: M. K. WEGMANN

Programs of Special Interest: The center offers information services in a wide range of areas, including equipment/facilities, employment, competitions, marketing, fellowships, and project support.

CORPORATION FOR PUBLIC BROADCASTING (CPB)

901 E Street, NW
Washington, DC 20004-2006
202-879-9740
CONTACT: CHARLIE DEATON, TELEVISION PROGRAM FUND

PROFILE OF FINANCIAL SUPPORT TO ARTISTS
Total Funding/Value of In-Kind Support: n/a
Competition for Funding: n/a
Grant Range: n/a

DIRECT SUPPORT PROGRAMS
➤ GENERAL PROGRAM REVIEW

Purpose: To support television projects in the research and development, scripting, preproduction, or post-production stage, or any combination thereof

Eligibility:
  Special Requirements: Organizations and independent producers are eligible; emphasis on multi-cultural and children's programs; programs must be appropriate for national PBS schedule; projects may be submitted only once
  Art Forms: Film, video

Type of Support: Up to $250,000

Scope of Program: Proposals reviewed quarterly; CPB anticipates funding no more than 1 project per cycle

Application/Selection Process:
  Deadline: Ongoing; quarterly review
  Preferred Initial Contact: Call for application/guidelines
  Selection Process: Staff and director of Program Fund; panel of program managers, independent producers, and specialists in certain disciplines; PBS program staff
  Notification Process: Letter
  Formal Report of Grant Required: Yes

➤ **MULTI-CULTURAL PROGRAMMING SOLICITATION**

Purpose: To support programming by producers from the 5 ethnic minorities (African-American, Asian-American, Native American, Latino, and Pacific Islander) and on subjects that could be of special interest to their indigenous communities

Eligibility:

Special Requirements: Organizations and independent producers are eligible; producer and director of independent production teams must be ethnic minorities; priority to projects that have significant representation of minority personnel

Art Forms: Film, video

Type of Support: Grant for project support

Scope of Program: $2,000,000 available for each funding cycle

Application/Selection Process:

Deadline: April 15, August 15

Preferred Initial Contact: Call or write for application/guidelines

Selection Process: Outside readers, panel

Notification Process: Letter

Formal Report of Grant Required: Yes

➤ **CONTENT SPECIFIC SOLICITATIONS**

Purpose: To solicit from diverse sources high quality programs of a specific nature that may be broadly or narrowly defined and range from 1-hour documentaries on a particular theme to miniseries concepts

Eligibility:

Special Requirements: Organizations and independent producers are eligible; student, instructional, and industrial projects ineligible; priority to children's programming, news/outreach/public affairs, and arts and cultural programming; programs must be able to command a national public broadcasting audience and have the potential to be broadcast by a majority of PBS stations; other requirements vary

Art Forms: Film, video

Type of Support: Grant for project support

Scope of Program: n/a

Application/Selection Process:

Deadline: Announced when requests for proposals are issued

Preferred Initial Contact: Call or write for application/guidelines

Selection Process: Panel review

Notification Process: Letter

Formal Report of Grant Required: Yes

➤ **PROGRAM CHALLENGE FUND**

CONTACT: DON MARBURY

Purpose: To insure that high-visibility, prime-time limited series are available each year for the national PBS schedule

Eligibility:
  Special Requirements: Organizations and independent producers are eligible; priority to series with potential for above-average viewership and critical attention; series may be documentary or drama and should cover subjects of significance
  Art Forms: Film, video
Type of Support: Grant for project support
Scope of Program: $10,000,000 available annually
Application/Selection Process:
  Deadline: None
  Preferred Initial Contact: Call any senior programming staffer at PBS or CPB for general information
  Application Procedure: Send proposal or letter to Don Marbury at CPB and Jennifer Lawson, Public Broadcasting Service, 1320 Braddock Place, Alexandria, VA 22314-1698; producers can also call either of them beforehand to ascertain their interest
  Selection Process: Outside readers, staff review
  Notification Process: Phone call or letter
  Formal Report of Grant Required: Yes

TECHNICAL ASSISTANCE PROGRAMS AND SERVICES

Programs of Special Interest: The Employment Outreach Project (EOP) provides job information and resource services to people seeking careers in public broadcasting. The EOP Talent Bank contains resumés from people across the country and emphasizes identifying members of groups traditionally underrepresented in broadcasting. The EOP Job Line publicizes opportunities at public radio and television stations (call 800-582-8220 or 202-393-1045).

COUNCIL FOR INTERNATIONAL EXCHANGE OF SCHOLARS (CIES)

3007 Tilden Street, NW
Suite 5M
Washington, DC 20008-3009
202-686-6245
CONTACT: DR. KAREN C. ADAMS

PROFILE OF FINANCIAL SUPPORT TO ARTISTS

Total Funding/Value of In-Kind Support: n/a
Competition for Funding: Total applications, 108; total individuals funded/provided with in-kind support, 25 (for Fulbright Faculty and Professional Awards—Communications Awards)
Grant Range: n/a

DIRECT SUPPORT PROGRAMS

➤ **FULBRIGHT FACULTY AND PROFESSIONAL AWARDS—COMMUNICATIONS AWARDS**

Purpose: To support film, video, and journalism professionals or scholars who wish to pursue research or lecture opportunities abroad

Eligibility:
   Citizenship: U.S.
   Residency: Must not have lived outside the U.S. in the past 10 years
   Special Requirements: Must be a practicing professional or have an advanced degree
   Art Forms: Film, video, journalism (professionals or scholars)

Type of Support: Travel costs and monthly stipend for research or lecturing abroad; in some years a special film and television award worth up to $20,000 is available to professionals who wish to pursue opportunities in the United Kingdom

Scope of Program: 25 lecture and research awards in 1990

Application/Selection Process:
   Deadline: August 1
   Preferred Initial Contact: Call for application/guidelines
   Application Procedure: Submit application form, resumé, project description, 4 letters of recommendation
   Selection Process: Peer panel of artists, selection committees in the U.S. and abroad
   Notification Process: Letter
   Formal Report of Grant Required: No

CUMMINGTON COMMUNITY OF THE ARTS

Rural Route #1
Box 145
Cummington, MA 01026
CONTACT: LUCIUS PARSHALL, EXECUTIVE DIRECTOR

PROFILE OF FINANCIAL SUPPORT TO ARTISTS

Total Funding/Value of In-Kind Support: $120,000 for FY 1990

Competition for Funding: Total applications, 1,500; total individuals funded/provided with in-kind support, 120

Grant Range: n/a

DIRECT SUPPORT PROGRAMS
➤ **ARTIST RESIDENCIES**

Purpose: To encourage artistic innovation and development, a commitment that favors emerging artists and writers, particularly those who offer alternative voices based on sex, race, age, or class

Eligibility:
   Special Requirements: Previous residents ineligible for up to 3 years
   Art Forms: Visual arts, fiction, playwriting, poetry, music composition, film/video, photography, performance art/choreography

Type of Support: 2-week to 3-month residency including room, studio; residents pay $400-$500 per month and maintain the community, but no one turned away for lack of money

Scope of Program: 120 residencies in 1990

Application/Selection Process:
   Deadline: Multiple deadlines
   Preferred Initial Contact: Write for application/guidelines
   Application Procedure: Submit application form, $10 fee, samples of work, references, resumé, supporting materials (optional)
   Selection Process: Peer panel of artists
   Notification Process: Letter

D.C. COMMISSION ON THE ARTS AND HUMANITIES

410 8th Street, N.W.
Fifth Floor
Washington, DC 20004
202-724-5613
CONTACT: JANN DARSIE, PROGRAM COORDINATOR

PROFILE OF FINANCIAL SUPPORT TO ARTISTS
Total Funding/Value of In-Kind Support: $480,040 for FY 1990

Competition for Funding: Total applications, 743; total individuals funded/provided with in-kind support, 93

Grant Range: $2,500-$8,800

DIRECT SUPPORT PROGRAMS
➤ **ARTS-IN-EDUCATION GRANTS/COMPREHENSIVE ARTS DEVELOPMENT GRANTS/GRANTS-IN-AID FELLOWSHIPS/SPECIAL CONSTITUENCIES GRANTS**

Purpose: Arts-in-Education grants fund professional artists' residencies in District public schools; Comprehensive Arts Development grants fund arts activities in traditionally underserved areas of the city; Grants-in-Aid provide fellowships and general operating support; Special Constituencies grants fund arts programming for populations such as senior citizens, the homeless, or the physically challenged

Eligibility:
  Residency: District of Columbia
  Age: 18 or older
  Art Forms: Dance, music, opera, theater, visual arts, design arts, crafts, media arts, literature, interdisciplinary, multi-disciplinary

Type of Support: For FY 1990 individual artists received up to $8,800 Arts-in-Education grants; $2,500 for Comprehensive Arts Development projects; $5,000 Grants-in-Aid fellowships; up to $3,700 for Special Constituency projects

Scope of Program: For FY 1990 individual artists received 13 Arts-in-Education grants; 8 Comprehensive Arts Development grants; 68 Grants-in-Aid fellowships; 4 Special Constituency grants

Application/Selection Process:
  Preferred Initial Contact: Call or write for application/guidelines or call to explain project
  Application Procedure: Submit application form, samples of work, resumé, project budget
  Selection Process: Peer panel of artists
  Notification Process: Letter
Formal Report of Grant Required: Yes

DEKALB COUNCIL FOR THE ARTS, INC. (DCA)

P.O. Box 875
Decatur, GA 30031
404-299-7910
CONTACT: SONDRA D. DANGELO, ACCOUNTING MANAGER

PROFILE OF FINANCIAL SUPPORT TO ARTISTS

Total Funding/Value of In-Kind Support: $3,550 for FY 1990
Competition for Funding: Total applications, 11; total individuals funded/provided with in-kind support, 5
Grant Range: $250-$1,200

DIRECT SUPPORT PROGRAMS

➤ INDIVIDUAL ARTISTS PROGRAM

Purpose: To provide artists with financial assistance that will enable them to provide the citizens of DeKalb County with an arts service

Eligibility:
  Residency: DeKalb County, 1 year
  Art Forms: All disciplines

Type of Support: Up to $1,500
Scope of Program: 5 awards, totalling $3,550, in FY 1990
Application/Selection Process:
  Deadline: December 8
  Preferred Initial Contact: Call or write for application/guidelines
  Application Procedure: Submit application form, samples of
  work, resumé, financial statement, project budget
  Selection Process: Peer panel of artists, organization staff, board
  of directors
  Notification Process: Letter 2-3 months after deadline
  Formal Report of Grant Required: Yes

TECHNICAL ASSISTANCE PROGRAMS AND SERVICES
Programs of Special Interest: The DeKalb Cultural Resources Directory lists area cultural and arts organizations, individual artists,
and DCA members. Artists may make appointments for one-to-one
consultations with staff for information about marketing, contracts,
copyright, networking, tax matters, funding sources, and general
professional development. DCA's bulletin board posts notices of
competitions, grant opportunities, and events. Professional development workshops are conducted for individual artists. For some
services members pay up to $20 fee; nonmembers, up to $25.

DELAWARE STATE ARTS COUNCIL

State Office Building
820 North French Street
Wilmington, DE 19801
302-577-3540
CONTACT: BARBARA R. KING, VISUAL ARTS/INDIVIDUAL ARTIST
FELLOWSHIP COORDINATOR

PROFILE OF FINANCIAL SUPPORT TO ARTISTS
Total Funding/Value of In-Kind Support: $40,000 for FY 1990
Competition for Funding: Total applications, 76; total individuals
funded/provided with in-kind support, 11
Grant Range: $2,000-$5,000

DIRECT SUPPORT PROGRAMS
➤ **INDIVIDUAL ARTIST FELLOWSHIPS**
Purpose: To enable artists to set aside time, purchase materials,
and work in their fields with fewer financial constraints
Eligibility:
  Citizenship: U.S.
  Residency: Delaware

Special Requirements: No students; previous recipients in "established professional" category ineligible; previous recipients in "emerging professional" category ineligible for 3 years
Art Forms: All disciplines
Type of Support: $5,000 for established professional; $2,000 for emerging professional
Scope of Program: 6 established professional, 5 emerging professional awards in 1990
Application/Selection Process:
  Deadline: March 22
  Preferred Initial Contact: Call or write for application/guidelines
  Application Procedure: Submit application form, samples of work, resumé, project proposal and budget, supporting materials
  Selection Process: Individuals from outside of organization
  Notification Process: Letter in July
  Formal Report of Grant Required: Yes

TECHNICAL ASSISTANCE PROGRAMS AND SERVICES

Programs of Special Interest: The Arts in Education program publishes a directory of artists approved for residencies. The council maintains an Arts Resource Library and a Job Bank of job announcements and career resources in the arts.

EBEN DEMAREST TRUST

Mellon Bank, N.A.
Room 3845
1 Mellon Bank Center
Pittsburgh, PA 15258
412-234-5712
CONTACT: HELEN COLLINS, CONTROLLER, MELLON BANK

PROFILE OF FINANCIAL SUPPORT TO ARTISTS

Total Funding/Value of In-Kind Support: $9,100 for FY 1991-92
Competition for Funding: Total applications, 4; total individuals funded/provided with in-kind support, 1
Grant Range: $9,100

DIRECT SUPPORT PROGRAMS

➤ EBEN DEMAREST TRUST

Purpose: To allow a gifted artist or archeologist to pursue his or her work without dependence on public sale or approval of the work
Eligibility:
  Citizenship: Preference to U.S. citizens
  Age: Preference to mature artists

Special Requirements: Artist's income must be less than income accruing from the trust; application must be sponsored by an arts organization; no students
Art Forms: All arts disciplines and archeology
Type of Support: $9,100 grant in FY 1991-92
Scope of Program: 1 award per year
Application/Selection Process:
  Deadline: June 1
  Preferred Initial Contact: Arts organization requests forms or writes letter on behalf of artist
  Application Procedure: Arts organization submits letter/forms, references, financial statement; unsolicited applications from individuals not accepted
  Selection Process: Board of directors
  Notification Process: Phone call or letter in mid-June

DENVER COMMISSION ON CULTURAL AFFAIRS (CCA)

303 West Colfax
Suite 1600
Denver, CO 80204
303-640-2678
CONTACT: GREGORY J. GEISSLER, DIRECTOR

PROFILE OF FINANCIAL SUPPORT TO ARTISTS
Total Funding/Value of In-Kind Support: $125,000 for FY 1990 (includes New Works, Project Support, Arts Education Collaborations programs)
Competition for Funding: n/a
Grant Range: $750-$3,500

DIRECT SUPPORT PROGRAMS
➤ NEW WORKS PROGRAM
Purpose: To provide opportunities for artists to work in the community and contribute to Denver's cultural vitality, and to encourage creative innovation across the broad spectrum of arts endeavors
Eligibility:
  Residency: City or County of Denver
  Special Requirements: Must apply through Denver nonprofit organization; must have matching funds; limit 1 application per artist or sponsor per year; project must take place in Denver and must include public presentation

Art Forms: Music composition, choreography, visual arts, multi-disciplinary/performance art, media arts, playwriting, poetry, prose, fiction

Type of Support: Up to $4,000 matching grant for project; 1:1 match may be cash or in-kind support

Scope of Program: 12 grants, totalling $25,000, for FY 1990

Application/Selection Process:
   Deadline: November
   Preferred Initial Contact: Call or write for application/guidelines
   Application Procedure: Sponsor submits application form, artist's resumé, samples of artist's work, project description and budget
   Selection Process: Individuals outside of organization
   Notification Process: Letter
   Formal Report of Grant Required: Yes

DIVERSE WORKS

1117 East Freeway
Houston, TX 77002
713-223-8346
CONTACT: DEBORAH GROTFELDT

PROFILE OF FINANCIAL SUPPORT TO ARTISTS

Total Funding/Value of In-Kind Support: $30,000 for 1990

Competition for Funding: Total applications, 200; total individuals funded/provided with in-kind support, 12

Grant Range: $2,000-$5,000 average

DIRECT SUPPORT PROGRAMS

➤ **NEW FORMS REGIONAL INITIATIVE**

Purpose: To provide funds for works that challenge traditional art disciplines and explore new forms of art and culture

Eligibility:
   Residency: New Mexico, Texas, Arizona, Oklahoma
   Special Requirements: Individual artists and collaborating artists may apply; projects must challenge traditional definitions of art or culture; no students
   Art Forms: Projects may involve 1 or more of the following disciplines: visual arts, video, film, dance, music, theater, performance art, installations, text, sound art, environmental art

Type of Support: $2,000-$5,000 average

Scope of Program: 12 awards, totalling $30,000, in 1990

Application/Selection Process:
Deadline: May 1
Preferred Initial Contact: Call or write for application/guidelines
Application Procedure: Submit application form, resumé, sample of work
Selection Process: Panel review
Notification Process: Letter
Formal Report of Grant Required: Yes

ALDEN B. DOW CREATIVITY CENTER

Northwood Institute
Midland, MI 48640-2398
517-832-4478
CONTACT: CAROL B. COPPAGE, DIRECTOR

PROFILE OF FINANCIAL SUPPORT TO ARTISTS
Total Funding/Value of In-Kind Support: n/a
Competition for Funding: n/a
Grant Range: n/a

DIRECT SUPPORT PROGRAMS
➤ **RESIDENCY FELLOWSHIP PROGRAM**
Purpose: To provide individuals in all professions an opportunity to pursue innovative ideas having the potential for impact in their fields
Eligibility:
Special Requirements: Projects involving major expenses discouraged
Art Forms: All arts and sciences
Type of Support: 10-week summer residency including round-trip travel to center, room, board, project expenses, and stipend
Scope of Program: 4 residencies per year
Application/Selection Process:
Deadline: December 31
Preferred Initial Contact: Call or write for application/guidelines
Application Procedure: Submit application form, samples of work, resumé, project budget; finalists make expenses-paid visit to Midland for interview
Selection Process: Board of directors, professionals in applicant's field
Notification Process: April 1
Formal Report of Grant Required: Yes

DOWNTOWN COMMUNITY TELEVISION CENTER (DCTV)

87 Lafayette Street
New York, NY 10013
212-966-4510

EQUIPMENT ACCESS

Video: Production for S-VHS, VHS, Video-8, Hi-8; post-production for S-VHS, VHS, 3/4"

Comments: Through the Artist-in-Residence program, DCTV offers $500 worth of equipment use for approved projects by 10 emerging video artists and independent producers in New York State (application deadlines January 31, August 31). The Community Projects program offers free or low-cost equipment to members interested in producing tapes that would impact their communities in a positive way (membership fee $20). Applications for Community Projects are accepted on an ongoing basis. Production equipment for other approved projects is available at low rates. Post-production facilities are available to the public on a first-come, first-served basis. Internships are available in all areas of the center, and interns receive free access to equipment to work on individual projects.

TECHNICAL ASSISTANCE PROGRAMS AND SERVICES

Programs of Special Interest: DCTV maintains a resumé/job file for members and regularly screens works by new videomakers. Producers can submit tapes at any time for consideration. Call 212-941-1298 for information about screenings and tape submissions.

DURHAM ARTS COUNCIL (DAC)

120 Morris Street
Durham, NC 27701
919-560-2720
CONTACT: MARGARET J. DEMOTT, DIRECTOR OF ARTIST SERVICES

PROFILE OF FINANCIAL SUPPORT TO ARTISTS

Total Funding/Value of In-Kind Support: $13,800 for FY 1990-91
Competition for Funding: Total applications, 61; total individuals funded/provided with in-kind support, 21
Grant Range: $250-$1,000

DIRECT SUPPORT PROGRAMS
➤ EMERGING ARTISTS PROGRAM

CONTACT: ELLA FOUNTAIN PRATT, DIRECTOR AND GRANTS OFFICER
919-560-2742

Purpose: To support developing professionals by funding projects pivotal to the advancement of their work and careers as artists

Eligibility:
  Residency: Chatham, Durham, Granville, Orange, or Person counties, 1 year
  Age: 18 or older
  Special Requirements: No degree-seeking students; previous grantees ineligible for 1 year
  Art Forms: All disciplines

Type of Support: Up to $1,000 for projects such as promotion/presentation, travel, securing services, supplies, or training

Scope of Program: 21 awards, totalling $13,800, in FY 1990-91

Application/Selection Process:
  Deadline: November 1
  Preferred Initial Contact: Call or write for application/guidelines
  Application Procedure: Submit application form, samples of work, resumé, project budget, references (optional)
  Selection Process: Anonymous judges, organizational committee
  Notification Process: Phone call or letter
  Formal Report of Grant Required: Yes

TECHNICAL ASSISTANCE PROGRAMS AND SERVICES
Programs of Special Interest: The Artists Services program offers artists workshops on topics such as marketing and project support.

DUTCHESS COUNTY ARTS COUNCIL (DCAC)

39 Market Street
Poughkeepsie, NY 12601
914-454-3222
CONTACT: SHERRE WESLEY, EXECUTIVE DIRECTOR

PROFILE OF FINANCIAL SUPPORT TO ARTISTS
Total Funding/Value of In-Kind Support: $9,000 in FY 1990

Competition for Funding: Total applications, n/a; total individuals funded/provided with in-kind support, 3

Grant Range: n/a

DIRECT SUPPORT PROGRAMS

➤ INDIVIDUAL ARTISTS FELLOWSHIP PROGRAM

Purpose: To provide support to individuals who are in the developmental phase of their careers as creative artists

Eligibility:
　Citizenship: U.S.
　Residency: Dutchess County, 2 years
　Age: 18 or older
　Special Requirements: No students enrolled in degree programs
　Art Forms: Eligible disciplines change yearly

Type of Support: $3,000; recipients perform a public service activity

Scope of Program: 3 awards in 1990

Application/Selection Process:
　Deadline: Mid-May
　Preferred Initial Contact: Call or write for application/guidelines
　Application Procedure: Submit application form, resumé, proof of residency, samples of work
　Selection Process: Peer panel of artists, board of directors
　Notification Process: Letter
　Formal Report of Grant Required: Yes

➤ PROJECT GRANTS

Purpose: To support art and cultural projects of Dutchess County nonprofit organizations

Eligibility:
　Citizenship: U.S.
　Special Requirements: Artists must be sponsored by a Dutchess County nonprofit organization; project must take place in Dutchess County and be open to the public
　Art Forms: Dance, music, opera/musical theater, theater, visual arts, design arts, crafts, photography, media arts, literature, folk arts, humanities, multi-disciplinary

Type of Support: Up to $5,000 for specific project

Scope of Program: $20,000 budgeted for 1991

Application/Selection Process:
　Deadline: Mid-September
　Preferred Initial Contact: Sponsor attends an application workshop or discusses project with DCAC staff
　Application Procedure: Sponsor submits application form, board list, financial statement, proof of nonprofit status, project budget, support documentation (e.g, samples of artist's work, reviews), artist's resumé
　Selection Process: Panel of community leaders, artists, and arts professionals, board of directors
　Notification Process: Letter
　Formal Report of Grant Required: Yes

TECHNICAL ASSISTANCE PROGRAMS AND SERVICES
Programs of Special Interest: DCAC provides artist referrals and maintains an arts resource library and an artist registry. Workshops address topics such as grantwriting and marketing.

EL PASO ARTS RESOURCE DEPARTMENT (ARD)

2 Civic Center Plaza
El Paso, TX 79901-1196
915-541-4481
CONTACT: ALEJANDRINA DREW, DIRECTOR

PROFILE OF FINANCIAL SUPPORT TO ARTISTS
Total Funding/Value of In-Kind Support: $5,767 in FY 1991
Competition for Funding: Total applications, 4; total individuals funded/provided with in-kind support, 3
Grant Range: $505-$3,178

DIRECT SUPPORT PROGRAMS
➤ **INDIVIDUAL PROJECT SUPPORT PROGRAM**
Purpose: To provide funds for community-based arts/cultural projects that have specific goals, objectives, and short-term time horizons
Eligibility:
    Residency: El Paso
    Special Requirements: Artist must apply with nonprofit, government, or educational umbrella organization; applicant must have matching funds (up to 50% may be in-kind support)
    Art Forms: All disciplines
Type of Support: Matching grant for specific project
Scope of Program: 3 grants, totalling $5,767, in FY 1991
Application/Selection Process:
    Deadline: January 15
    Preferred Initial Contact: Attend funding workshop
    Application Procedure: Submit application form, project budget, subcontract with sponsor, proof of sponsor's nonprofit status, sponsor's board list, samples of artist's work (optional), references (optional), artist's resumé (optional)
    Selection Process: Organization staff, advisory board
    Notification Process: Letter in March
    Formal Report of Grant Required: Yes

➤ **EMERGENCY FUNDING PROGRAM**

Purpose: To provide limited funding to artists and groups in El Paso in the event of an emergency or an extraordinary opportunity that may arise outside of the regular funding cycle

Eligibility:

Residency: El Paso

Special Requirements: Artists must have a nonprofit sponsor and matching funds

Art Forms: All disciplines

Type of Support: Matching grant for a project emergency or extraordinary opportunity

Scope of Program: $8,700 granted to organizations in FY 1991

Application/Selection Process:

Deadline: 15th of each month

Application Procedure: Submit application form, project budget, proof of sponsor's nonprofit status; applicants may be asked to appear at ARD Advisory Board meeting and to submit a more detailed project budget or evidence of other forms of community support

Selection Process: Organization staff, advisory board

Formal Report of Grant Required: Yes

THE EMPOWERMENT PROJECT (EP)

1653 18th Street
Suite #3
Santa Monica, CA 90404
213-828-8807
CONTACT: DAVID KASPER

EQUIPMENT ACCESS

Video: Post-production (on-line and off-line) for VHS, 3/4", S-VHS
Comments: EP offers subsidized rates for post-production equipment for selected projects that have the potential to cause social and political change. Facilities include a screening room.

TECHNICAL ASSISTANCE PROGRAMS AND SERVICES

Programs of Special Interest: EP provides support for project development, fundraising, and promotion, and assists independent producers with distribution of completed films and videos. EP also exhibits films and videos. EP's technical assistance services are geared toward politically and socially progressive projects.

EZTV

8547 Santa Monica Boulevard
West Hollywood, CA 90069
213-657-1532

EQUIPMENT ACCESS

Video: Production for VHS, S-VHS, 3/4", Video 8, Hi-8; post-production (off-line) for VHS, S-VHS, 3/4"

TECHNICAL ASSISTANCE PROGRAMS AND SERVICES

Programs of Special Interest: EZTV exhibits video art and maintains a resource center.

FILM ARTS FOUNDATION (FAF)

346 Ninth Street
Second Floor
San Francisco, CA 94103
415-552-8760
CONTACT: GAIL SILVA, DIRECTOR

PROFILE OF FINANCIAL SUPPORT TO ARTISTS

Total Funding/Value of In-Kind Support: $51,000 in FAF grants for FY 1990
Competition for Funding: Total applications, 243; total individuals funded/provided with in-kind support, 23
Grant Range: $400-$5,000

DIRECT SUPPORT PROGRAMS

➤ **FAF GRANTS PROGRAM**
Purpose: To aid experimental and independent media artists who have little recourse to traditional funding sources, or whose projects are at a stage where a small grant can have a significant impact
Eligibility:
  Residency: 10-county San Francisco Bay Area (San Francisco, Marin, Sonoma, Napa, Solano, Alameda, Contra Costa, San Mateo, Santa Clara, Santa Cruz counties), 1 year
  Special Requirements: Applicant must have artistic control of project; no commercial projects; previous grantees ineligible for 2 years
  Art Forms: Film, video

Type of Support: $3,000 Personal Works awards for new, short personal works that can be completely realized within this budget (funded projects must be available for Film Arts Festival); $1,000 Development awards for projects in the development and fundraising stages; $5,000 Completion/Distribution awards for films or tapes that can be completed or distributed with this amount

Scope of Program: 13 Personal Works awards, 5 Development awards, 2 Completion/Distribution awards available in 1991

Application/Selection Process:
  Deadline: May
  Preferred Initial Contact: Call or write for application/guidelines
  Application Procedure: Submit application form, resumé, project description and budget; semi-finalists submit samples of work
  Selection Process: Independent panel of artists and arts professionals
  Notification Process: Letter 2-3 months after deadline
  Formal Report of Grant Required: Yes

EQUIPMENT ACCESS

Film: Production and post-production for Super 8, 16mm

Comments: Members receive low-cost access to equipment and editing facility for noncommercial projects ($35 membership fee).

TECHNICAL ASSISTANCE PROGRAMS AND SERVICES

Programs of Special Interest: FAF maintains a resource library whose collection focuses on distribution, fundraising, grantwriting, copyright and media law, and film/video festivals; a videotape library of members' works; a Skills File of information relating to members' backgrounds and interests; and listings of projects seeking interns and of members who are seeking internships. FAF exhibits independent film and video, and holds the annual Film Arts Festival. Seminars and workshops cover the art, technical processes, and business of independent film and video (fees involved). The Group Legal Plan includes initial office or telephone consultation at no charge for up to 30 minutes, and reduced rates thereafter. The Project Sponsorship program makes available nonprofit fiscal agent services to selected noncommercial film/video projects. Staff assistance is available for developing project proposals, fundraising, and exhibition/distribution plans. FAF's monthly newsletter provides comprehensive coverage of regional independent film and video activities. (Membership required for most FAF services.)

FILM IN THE CITIES (FITC)

2388 University Avenue
St. Paul, MN 55114
612-646-6104
CONTACT: MARGARET WEINSTEIN, ARTISTS GRANTS ADMINISTRATOR

PROFILE OF FINANCIAL SUPPORT TO ARTISTS
Total Funding/Value of In-Kind Support: $170,940 for FY 1990
Competition for Funding: Total applications, 208; total individuals
funded/provided with in-kind support, 35
Grant Range: Up to $11,000

DIRECT SUPPORT PROGRAMS
➤ REGIONAL FILM/VIDEO GRANTS PROGRAM
Purpose: To assist independent film and video artists whose
personal work shows promise of excellence
Eligibility:
    Residency: Minnesota, Iowa, Wisconsin, North Dakota, South
    Dakota
    Special Requirements: Artist must have creative control over
    project; commercial projects and projects associated with a
    degree program ineligible; no full-time students
    Art Forms: Film, video
Type of Support: Production Grants, up to $16,000; Work in
Progress Grants, up to $7,000; Encouragement Grants, up to $3,000
Scope of Program: $70,000 in Production Grants, $30,000 in Work in
Progress Grants, $15,000 in Encouragement Grants available in 1990
Application/Selection Process:
    Deadline: May
    Preferred Initial Contact: Call or write for application/guidelines
    Application Procedure: Submit application form, samples of
    work, project description and budget, resumé, screening notes
    Selection Process: 2 independent panels of artists and
    arts professionals
    Notification Process: Letter 2 months after deadline
    Formal Report of Grant Required: Yes

EQUIPMENT ACCESS
CONTACT: STEVE WESTERLUND, ACCESS MANAGER
Film: Production for 16mm, Super 8; post-production for 16mm
Video: Production and post-production for VHS
Comments: FITC's Media Access Center also houses a recording
studio. Equipment and facilities are available at inexpensive rates
to members working on noncommercial projects. Experienced,

independent media artists may submit a membership application form to the access manager. Yearly membership rates are $65 for Super 8, $100 for 16mm and video, and $125 for total use.

TECHNICAL ASSISTANCE PROGRAMS AND SERVICES

Programs of Special Interest: Film in the Cities offers a variety of information services, acts as a fiscal agent for projects, and screens films and videos.

FILM/VIDEO ARTS (F/VA)

817 Broadway at 12th Street
Second Floor
New York, NY 10003
212-673-9361

EQUIPMENT ACCESS

Film: Production and post-production for 16mm, 35mm
Video: Production for Hi-8, 3/4"; post-production for VHS, 3/4", Hi-8, S-VHS
Comments: Low equipment access rates are available to artists working on noncommercial projects. New York State artists may apply for week-long residencies at F/VA's Image Processing Studio.

TECHNICAL ASSISTANCE PROGRAMS AND SERVICES

Programs of Special Interest: F/VA screens independent works, makes grants to New York State nonprofit organizations to exhibit independent works, and offers beginning and advanced courses in production, editing, and fundraising.

FLORIDA DIVISION OF CULTURAL AFFAIRS/ FLORIDA ARTS COUNCIL

Department of State
The Capitol
Tallahassee, FL 32399-0250
904-487-2980
CONTACT: KATHY ENGERRAN

PROFILE OF FINANCIAL SUPPORT TO ARTISTS

Total Funding/Value of In-Kind Support: $195,000 for FY 1990-91
Competition for Funding: Total applications, 528; total individuals funded/provided with in-kind support, 39
Grant Range: $5,000

DIRECT SUPPORT PROGRAMS
➤ **FELLOWSHIP PROGRAM**
Purpose: To enable Florida artists to improve their artistic skills and enhance their careers
Eligibility:
    Residency: Florida, 1 year
    Age: 18 or older
    Special Requirements: Originating, professional artists only; no students pursuing degrees; previous grantees ineligible for 5 years
    Art Forms: Choreography, folk arts, literature (fiction, poetry, children's literature), media arts, music composition, theater (design, playwriting, mime), visual arts and crafts (includes photography)
Type of Support: $5,000
Scope of Program: 39 awards in 1990-91
Application/Selection Process:
    Deadline: February (except visual arts)
    Application Procedure: Submit application form, samples of work, support materials (optional)
    Selection Process: Panel of arts professionals
    Formal Report of Grant Required: Yes

TECHNICAL ASSISTANCE PROGRAMS AND SERVICES
Programs of Special Interest: The division is expanding its Individual Media Artists Fellowship program by offering equipment access opportunities, and is planning to further develop the program to include access and usage agreements with private industry studios and equipment providers. Call the division for more information about these opportunities.

FRAMELINE

P.O. Box 14792
San Francisco, CA 94114
415-861-5245

PROFILE OF FINANCIAL SUPPORT TO ARTISTS
Total Funding/Value of In-Kind Support: $7,000 in 1990
Competition for Funding: Total applications, 65; total individuals funded/provided with in-kind support, 4
Grant Range: Up to $5,000

DIRECT SUPPORT PROGRAMS
➤ FRAMELINE FILM/VIDEO COMPLETION FUND

Purpose: To support works-in-progress by lesbian and gay video and film artists who have demonstrated advanced and innovative skills

Eligibility:

Special Requirements: All independent producers and nonprofit corporations eligible; project must make unique statement about lesbians and gay men or about issues of concern to lesbians and gay men; project must be in final stages of completion at time of award notification; work must be accessible to an English-speaking audience

Art Forms: Film, video

Type of Support: Up to $5,000 for project completion (average $1,000-$2,000); work must be made available for screening at the San Francisco International Lesbian and Gay Film Festival

Scope of Program: $7,000 awarded in 1990

Application/Selection Process:

Deadline: October 15

Preferred Initial Contact: Call or write for application/guidelines

Application Procedure: Submit application form, $25 application fee, project description or synopsis, project budget, biographies of all personnel, sample of work-in-progress

Selection Process: Panel of artists and arts professionals

Notification Process: 2 months after deadline

Formal Report of Grant Required: Yes

TECHNICAL ASSISTANCE PROGRAMS AND SERVICES

Programs of Special Interest: Frameline presents the annual San Francisco International Lesbian and Gay Film Festival, distributes films and videos by and about gays and lesbians, and sponsors "Frameline Presents," a weekly cable program featuring lesbian and gay video from around the world. Frameline provides information services on working with theaters, organizations, and festivals.

THE FUNDING EXCHANGE

666 Broadway, #500
New York, NY 10012

PROFILE OF FINANCIAL SUPPORT TO ARTISTS

Total Funding/Value of In-Kind Support: $300,000 for FY 1991

Competition for Funding: Total applications, 400; total individuals funded/provided with in-kind support, 35

Grant Range: $5,000-$10,000 average

DIRECT SUPPORT PROGRAMS
➤ THE PAUL ROBESON FUND

Purpose: To support the production and distribution of independent film and video that focus on social issues, reach a broad audience, respect the intelligence of the viewers, and combine intellectual clarity with creative use of the medium

Eligibility:

Special Requirements: Must be affiliated with a tax-exempt organization; priority to projects on issues where there are local or national organizing efforts and issues that have received minimal coverage, and to distribution initiatives that seek to increase the use of social issue films and videos by institutional users, public interest and community-based groups, cable and satellite programmers; no purely personal projects or strictly sociological or anthropological explorations

Art Forms: Film, video, radio productions

Type of Support: Average $5,000-$10,000 for pre-production and the creation of samples/trailers, production, and post-production

Scope of Program: $300,000 granted in FY 1991

Application/Selection Process:

Deadline: December 1

Preferred Initial Contact: Write for application/guidelines (available after September 1); no phone calls please

Application Procedure: Submit application form, project budget and description, biographical sketches of key personnel; semifinalists submit samples of work

Selection Process: Staff, panel

Notification Process: 4 months after deadline

GEORGIA COUNCIL FOR THE ARTS (GCA)

2082 East Exchange Place
Suite 100
Tucker, GA 30084
404-493-5780
CONTACT: RICK GEORGE, GRANTS COORDINATOR

PROFILE OF FINANCIAL SUPPORT TO ARTISTS

Total Funding/Value of In-Kind Support: $158,105 for FY 1991

Competition for Funding: Total applications, 228; total individuals funded/provided with in-kind support, 70

Grant Range: $500-$5,000

DIRECT SUPPORT PROGRAMS
➤ **INDIVIDUAL ARTIST GRANTS**

Purpose: To provide income for artists whose work demonstrates artistic merit and whose careers will potentially benefit from the completion of a particular project

Eligibility:
    Residency: Georgia, 1 year
    Special Requirements: No full-time students; previous grantees ineligible for 2 years
    Art Forms: All disciplines

Type of Support: Up to $5,000 for a specific project that includes a public service component

Scope of Program: 70 awards in FY 1991

Application/Selection Process:
    Deadline: April 1
    Preferred Initial Contact: Call or write for application/guidelines
    Application Procedure: Submit application form, samples of work, resumé, project budget
    Selection Process: Multi-disciplinary panels
    Notification Process: Letter in June
    Formal Report of Grant Required: Yes

TECHNICAL ASSISTANCE PROGRAMS AND SERVICES

Programs of Special Interest: The Artist-in-Education (AIE) Program provides 3- to 18-week residencies in Georgia schools (contact 404-493-5789). The GCA maintains the Georgia Artists Registry, and the Georgia Touring Roster lists artists approved for Georgia Touring Grants activities. The services of Georgia Volunteer Accountants and Georgia Volunteer Lawyers for the Arts are available to eligible artists.

GREATER COLUMBUS ARTS COUNCIL (GCAC)

55 East State Street
Columbus, OH 43215
614-224-2606

PROFILE OF FINANCIAL SUPPORT TO ARTISTS

Total Funding/Value of In-Kind Support: $30,000 for FY 1990

Competition for Funding: Total applications, 130; total individuals funded/provided with in-kind support, 6

Grant Range: $5,000

DIRECT SUPPORT PROGRAMS
➤ **INDIVIDUAL ARTIST PROGRAM**
Purpose: To support artists in creating new works or advancing their careers
Eligibility:
    Residency: Franklin County, 1 year
    Special Requirements: Must be registered voter; no students
    Art Forms: Disciplines change yearly; film/video eligible in some years
Type of Support: $5,000
Scope of Program: 6 awards in 1990
Application/Selection Process:
    Deadline: July 15
    Application Procedure: Submit application form, other materials as requested
    Selection Process: Panel review
    Notification Process: Letter

TECHNICAL ASSISTANCE PROGRAMS AND SERVICES
Programs of Special Interest: The council maintains an Artists-in-Schools roster and provides information on funding for emergency work-related needs, equipment, facilities, materials, and project support.

JOHN SIMON GUGGENHEIM MEMORIAL FOUNDATION

90 Park Avenue
New York, NY 10016
212-687-4470

PROFILE OF FINANCIAL SUPPORT TO ARTISTS
Total Funding/Value of In-Kind Support: $4,355,000 for FY 1990 (includes grants to nonartists)
Competition for Funding: Total applications, 3,536 (includes nonartists); total individuals funded/provided with in-kind support, 166 (about 50 artists)
Grant Range: $15,000-$30,000

DIRECT SUPPORT PROGRAMS
Purpose: To further the development of scholars and artists by assisting them to engage in research in any field of knowledge and creation in any of the arts

Eligibility:
    Citizenship: U.S., Canada, Latin America, the Caribbean (permanent residents also eligible)
    Special Requirements: Artists must have already demonstrated exceptional creative ability
    Art Forms: All disciplines
Type of Support: $26,000 average grant for 1990
Scope of Program: About 50 artists funded in 1990
Application/Selection Process:
    Deadline: October 15 (U.S. and Canada), December 1 (Latin America and the Caribbean)
    Preferred Initial Contact: Write for application/guidelines
    Application Procedure: Submit application form, samples of work, references, 3 supplementary statements regarding career and proposed use of funds
    Selection Process: Juries of artists and arts professionals, Committee of Selection
    Notification Process: 5-6 months after deadline
    Formal Report of Grant Required: Yes

HALLWALLS CONTEMPORARY ARTS CENTER

700 Main Street
Buffalo, NY 14202
716-854-5828
CONTACT: MS. RENÉ BROUSSARD

PROFILE OF FINANCIAL SUPPORT TO ARTISTS

Total Funding/Value of In-Kind Support: $4,500 in grants to filmmakers in FY 1989-90
Competition for Funding: Total applications, 25; total individuals funded/provided with in-kind support, 6
Grant Range: $1,000-$5,000

DIRECT SUPPORT PROGRAMS

➤ **WESTERN NEW YORK FILM REGRANT**
Purpose: To assist filmmakers with the development, production, or post-production stage of a project
Eligibility:
    Residency: Western New York State, 1 year
    Special Requirements: Artists receiving direct production support from NYSCA ineligible
    Art Forms: Film
Type of Support: $500-$1,000

Scope of Program: 6-9 awards per year

Application/Selection Process:
  Deadline: May 31
  Preferred Initial Contact: Call or write for application/guidelines
  Application Procedure: Submit application form, samples of work, resumé
  Selection Process: Panel
  Notification Process: Letter
  Formal Report of Grant Required: Yes

EQUIPMENT ACCESS
CONTACT: ANDREW DEUTSCH

Video: Post-production for 3/4"

Comments: Independent videomakers receive access to post-production facilities at subsidized rates for approved projects ($15 annual access fee).

TECHNICAL ASSISTANCE PROGRAMS AND SERVICES
Programs of Special Interest: Hallwalls administers an Arts-in-Education program for western New York State schools and exhibits films and videos.

HEADLANDS CENTER FOR THE ARTS

944 Fort Barry
Sausalito, CA 94965
415-331-2787
CONTACT: JENNIFER DOWLEY, EXECUTIVE DIRECTOR

PROFILE OF FINANCIAL SUPPORT TO ARTISTS
Total Funding/Value of In-Kind Support: n/a
Competition for Funding: n/a
Grant Range: n/a

DIRECT SUPPORT PROGRAMS
➤ **REGIONAL RESIDENCIES/NATIONAL AND INTERNATIONAL RESIDENCY PROGRAM**

Purpose: To provide time for the incubation and investigation of new ideas and to nurture exchange among artists of all mediums

Eligibility:
  Residency: San Francisco Bay Area (regional residencies), Ohio, North Carolina, Minnesota, Philadelphia, Italy

Special Requirements: No students; previous grantees ineligible for 5 years

Art Forms: All disciplines

Type of Support: Long-term regional residencies, 11-month residency including studio space and $2,500 stipend; short-term regional residencies, 2- to 4-week residency including studio space, housing, $200 weekly stipend; national and international residencies, 2- to 5-month residency including studio space, housing, $200 weekly stipend, travel expenses

Scope of Program: 5 long-term regional residencies, 3 short-term regional residencies, 7 national and international residencies in 1991

Application/Selection Process:

  Deadline: September

  Preferred Initial Contact: Call or write for application/guidelines

  Application Procedure: Submit application form, samples of work, resumé, references; prospective residents interviewed when possible

  Selection Process: Organization staff, board of directors, peer panel of artists

  Notification Process: Recipients by phone; nonrecipients by letter

  Formal Report of Grant Required: No

HELENA PRESENTS

15 North Ewing
Helena, MT 59601
406-443-0287

PROFILE OF FINANCIAL SUPPORT TO ARTISTS

Total Funding/Value of In-Kind Support: $23,000 for 1991

Competition for Funding: Total applications, 160; total individuals funded/provided with in-kind support, 10

Grant Range: $1,000-$5,000

DIRECT SUPPORT PROGRAMS

➤ **NEW FORMS: REGIONAL INITIATIVE**

Purpose: To fund artists' projects that are innovative and adventurous, and that explore new definitions of art forms or cultural definitions

Eligibility:

  Residency: Colorado, Idaho, Montana, Nevada, Utah, Wyoming, 1 year

  Special Requirements: No students enrolled in degree programs; previous grantees ineligible for 1 cycle; projects that are solely traditional in intent are ineligible; intercultural projects must involve artists active in the ethnic traditions to be explored

Art Forms: Dance, music/sound, theater, visual arts, video, film, text, performance art, installations, environmental art, environmental performance works, interdisciplinary, multi-disciplinary
Type of Support: $1,000-$5,000 (most grants $3,500 and under); public presentation of work required
Scope of Program: $23,000 budget for 1991
Application/Selection Process:
Deadline: February 1
Application Procedure: Submit application form, project description and budget, biographies or resumés for key artistic personnel, samples of work, 2 reviews or 2 letters of support
Selection Process: Interdisciplinary, culturally diverse panel of artists and arts professionals
Notification Process: 7 months after deadline
Formal Report of Grant Required: Yes

IDAHO COMMISSION ON THE ARTS (ICA)

304 West State Street
Boise, ID 83720
208-334-2119
CONTACT: JACQUELINE S. CRIST, ARTIST SERVICES DIRECTOR

PROFILE OF FINANCIAL SUPPORT TO ARTISTS
Total Funding/Value of In-Kind Support: $40,000 for FY 1991
Competition for Funding: Total applications, 110; total individuals funded/provided with in-kind support, 18
Grant Range: $600-$3,000

DIRECT SUPPORT PROGRAMS
➤ FELLOWSHIP AWARDS/WORKSITES AWARDS/SUDDEN OPPORTUNITY AWARDS
Purpose: Fellowships recognize outstanding work of exceptionally talented individual artists; Worksites are awarded to artists seeking to work with a master, or to artists seeking an artist colony residency, time to develop new work or work-in-progress, or to travel to investigate ideas relevant to existing work or work-in-progress; Sudden Opportunity Awards support a professional opportunity that is uniquely available during a limited time
Eligibility:
Residency: Idaho, 1 year
Age: 18 or older
Special Requirements: No degree-seeking students; previous recipients ineligible for 5 years (Worksites)

Art Forms: Disciplines for Fellowships and Worksites alternate between literature/dance/music/theater/media arts (odd-numbered years) and visual arts/crafts/design arts (even-numbered years); all disciplines eligible for Sudden Opportunity Awards

Type of Support: Fellowships, $5,000; Worksites, up to $5,000; Sudden Opportunity Awards, up to $1,000

Scope of Program: 18 awards in FY 1991

Application/Selection Process:

Deadline: Mid-April (Fellowships, Worksites), quarterly (Sudden Opportunity Awards)

Preferred Initial Contact: Call or write for application/guidelines

Application Procedure: Submit application form, samples of work, resumé

Selection Process: Peer panel of artists and arts professionals

Notification Process: Phone call and letter

ILLINOIS ARTS COUNCIL (IAC)

100 West Randolph
Suite 10-500
Chicago, IL 60601
800-237-6994 (in Illinois) or 312-814-6750
TDD: 312-814-4831
CONTACT: B. ROSE PARISI, ARTISTS SERVICES COORDINATOR

PROFILE OF FINANCIAL SUPPORT TO ARTISTS

Total Funding/Value of In-Kind Support: $525,077 for FY 1990

Competition for Funding: Total applications, 1,460; total individuals funded/provided with in-kind support, 227

Grant Range: $250-$10,000

DIRECT SUPPORT PROGRAMS

➤ ARTISTS FELLOWSHIP PROGRAM

Purpose: To enable Illinois artists of exceptional talent to pursue their artistic goals

Eligibility:

Citizenship: U.S. (permanent residents also eligible)

Residency: Illinois

Special Requirements: No students; previous grantees ineligible for 1-3 years

Art Forms: Choreography, crafts, ethnic and folk arts, interdisciplinary/performance art, literature, media arts, music composition, photography, playwriting/screenwriting, visual arts

Type of Support: $5,000-$15,000 fellowships; $500 finalist awards

Scope of Program: 70 fellowship awards; 40 finalist awards in FY 1990

Application/Selection Process:

    Deadline: September 1

    Preferred Initial Contact: Call or write for application/guidelines

    Application Procedure: Submit application form, samples of work, proof of residency

    Selection Process: Panel of artists and arts professionals, IAC board

    Notification Process: Letter 3-4 months after deadline

    Formal Report of Grant Required: Yes

➤ SPECIAL ASSISTANCE GRANTS

Purpose: To assist artists with specific projects such as attendance at a conference, workshop, or seminar; consultant's fees for resolution of a specific artistic problem; exhibits, performances, or publications; materials, supplies, or services

Eligibility:

    Citizenship: U.S. (permanent residents also eligible)

    Residency: Illinois, 6 months

    Special Requirements: No students; low priority given to artists who have received Artists Fellowship or Special Assistance Grant in the same fiscal year

    Art Forms: All disciplines

Type of Support: Up to $1,500

Scope of Program: 81 grants in FY 1990

Application/Selection Process:

    Deadline: 8 weeks before beginning project

    Preferred Initial Contact: Consult IAC staff before applying

    Application Procedure: Submit application form, samples of work, resumé, project budget, proof of residency

    Selection Process: IAC staff and board

    Notification Process: 6-8 weeks after application

    Formal Report of Grant Required: Yes

TECHNICAL ASSISTANCE PROGRAMS AND SERVICES

Programs of Special Interest: The Partners in Purchase program provides matching funds to institutions to purchase completed works of living Illinois video or media artists. IAC maintains the unjuried Illinois Artists Registry. The Special Projects and Services to the Field program furnishes a wide variety of technical assistance to artists. The Arts-in-Education Residency program administers 5-day to 8-month school and community residencies.

IMAGE FILM/VIDEO CENTER

75 Bennett Street, NW
Suite M-1
Atlanta, GA 30309
404-352-4225
CONTACT: DEBBIE FRAKER, OPERATIONS MANAGER

EQUIPMENT ACCESS

Film: Production and post-production for Super 8, 16mm
Video: Production for VHS, S-VHS; post-production for VHS, 3/4"
Comments: IMAGE offers equipment access at low cost to independent media artists working on noncommercial projects. A $35 membership fee ($20 for senior citizens and students) and a $25 access fee are required. The On-Line Program provides access to local commercial production and post-production equipment and facilities at low cost. Members interested in the On-Line Program must submit a $25 application fee.

TECHNICAL ASSISTANCE PROGRAMS AND SERVICES

Programs of Special Interest: IMAGE acts as a fiscal agent for member independent producers and exhibits independent films and videos. The annual Atlanta Film and Video Festival features over 30 independent works and distributes cash awards and equipment prizes ($25 entry fee, January deadline; contact Claire Reynolds, Events Coordinator). IMAGE also sponsors the annual Southeastern Screenwriting Competition; winning screenplays are sent to story editors at major production companies in Los Angeles and New York ($25 entry fee, July deadline; residents of VA, FL, KY, SC, NC, GA, AL, MS, LA, and DC are eligible). IMAGE conducts workshops and seminars on topics such as film and video technology, production, fundraising, and budgeting (fees involved).

INDEPENDENT FEATURE PROJECT (IFP)

New York Branch:
Independent Feature Project
132 West 21st Street
Sixth Floor
New York, NY 10011
212-243-7777

Los Angeles Branch:
Independent Feature Project/West
5550 Wilshire Boulevard, #204
Los Angeles, CA 90036
213-937-4379

Minneapolis Branch:
Independent Feature Project/North
1401 Third Avenue South
Minneapolis, MN 55404
612-870-0156

San Francisco Branch:
Independent Feature Project, Northern California
P.O. Box 460278
San Francisco, CA 94146
415-826-0574

Chicago Branch:
Independent Feature Project, Midwest
P.O. Box 148026
Chicago, IL 60614
312-902-5339

TECHNICAL ASSISTANCE PROGRAMS AND SERVICES

Programs of Special Interest: IFP is a nonprofit, membership
organization that provides information, support, and education
programs to independent filmmakers. Services include seminars,
workshops, screenings, advice, and referrals.

INDIANA ARTS COMMISSION (IAC)

402 West Washington
Room 072
Indianapolis, IN 46204
317-232-1268
TDD: 317-233-3001
CONTACT: MEDIA ARTS PROGRAM SPECIALIST

PROFILE OF FINANCIAL SUPPORT TO ARTISTS

Total Funding/Value of In-Kind Support: $102,000
Competition for Funding: n/a
Grant Range: $100-$5,000

DIRECT SUPPORT PROGRAMS

➤ **INDIVIDUAL ARTIST FELLOWSHIPS (IAF)**

Purpose: To assist artists with activities significant to their professional growth and recognition, or with the creation or completion of a project

Eligibility:
 Residency: Indiana, 1 year
 Special Requirements: High school and undergraduate students ineligible
 Art Forms: Visual arts (including crafts, design arts, folk arts), media arts eligible in odd-numbered years; performing arts (including dance, theater, folk arts), literature eligible in even-numbered years

Type of Support: $2,000 Associate Fellowship; $5,000 Master Fellowship

Scope of Program: Approximately 25 fellowships per year

Application/Selection Process:
 Deadline: April 1
 Preferred Initial Contact: Call or write for application/guidelines
 Application Procedure: Submit application form, samples of work
 Selection Process: Panel of artists and arts professionals, board of directors
 Notification Process: Letter
 Formal Report of Grant Required: Yes

➤ **TECHNICAL ASSISTANCE (TA) GRANTS**

Purpose: To encourage the professional development of artists, arts professionals, and administrators through funding consultant services and conference/workshop fees

Eligibility:
 Residency: Indiana, 1 year

Special Requirements: High school and undergraduate students ineligible
Art Forms: All disciplines
Type of Support: Up to $500 for professional development activity
Scope of Program: n/a
Application/Selection Process:
  Deadline: 6 weeks before beginning of activity
  Preferred Initial Contact: Call or write for application/guidelines
  Application Procedure: Submit application form, conference/workshop materials, resumé
  Selection Process: Staff and commission committees
  Notification Process: Letter
  Formal Report of Grant Required: Yes

TECHNICAL ASSISTANCE PROGRAMS AND SERVICES

Programs of Special Interest: The Arts in Education (AIE) program places professional artists in educational settings throughout Indiana for 1- to 8-month residencies; the Visiting Artist Program (VAP) brings artists to educational settings to offer adults and children introductory arts experiences (contact Education Program Specialist). The Presenter Touring Program (PTP) brings Indiana artists to underfunded, underrepresented, urban, and rural areas of the state to present performances, exhibitions, or readings (contact Media Arts Program Specialist). IAC maintains an unjuried Artists Registry, and Program Specialists are available to consult with grant applicants.

INTERMEDIA ARTS

425 Ontario Street SE
Minneapolis, MN 55414
612-627-4444
CONTACT: AL KOSTERS, DIRECTOR OF ARTIST PROGRAMS

PROFILE OF FINANCIAL SUPPORT TO ARTISTS
Total Funding/Value of In-Kind Support: n/a
Competition for Funding: n/a
Grant Range: $500-$12,000

DIRECT SUPPORT PROGRAMS
➤ **MCKNIGHT INTERDISCIPLINARY ARTISTS FELLOWSHIP**
Purpose: To provide support for artists who have a track record of pursuing personal interdisciplinary work
Eligibility:
  Citizenship: U.S.

Residency: Iowa, Kansas, Minnesota, Nebraska, North Dakota, South Dakota, Wisconsin, 2 years
Special Requirements: No full-time students or projects for a degree program; noncommercial work only
Art Forms: All disciplines
Type of Support: $8,000-$12,000
Scope of Program: $70,000 available annually
Application/Selection Process:
   Deadline: Late fall or winter
   Preferred Initial Contact: Write for application/guidelines
   Application Procedure: Detailed in application workshops
   Selection Process: Independent panel review
   Notification Process: Letter
   Formal Report of Grant Required: Yes

➤ **DIVERSE VISIONS REGIONAL GRANTS PROGRAM**
Purpose: To support artists who are attempting to explore new definitions of, or boundaries between, cultures, arts disciplines, or traditions in their work
Eligibility:
   Citizenship: U.S.
   Residency: Iowa, Kansas, Minnesota, North Dakota, Nebraska, South Dakota, Wisconsin, 2 years
   Special Requirements: No full-time students or projects for a degree program; noncommercial work only
   Art Forms: Open
Type of Support: Up to $5,000 for established artists, up to $1,500 for emerging artists
Scope of Program: $24,000 available annually
Application/Selection Process:
   Deadline: Spring
   Preferred Initial Contact: Write for application/guidelines
   Application Procedure: Detailed in application workshops
   Selection Process: Panel review
   Notification Process: Letter 5 months after deadline
   Formal Report of Grant Required: Yes

➤ **JEROME INSTALLATION ART COMMISSIONS**
CONTACT: MASON RIDDLE
Purpose: To commission emerging artists to create art installations specifically for the Intermedia Arts Gallery
Eligibility:
   Citizenship: U.S.
   Residency: Minnesota
   Special Requirements: No full-time students or projects for a degree program; noncommercial work only
   Art Forms: Open

Type of Support: $2,000 commission; additional materials and equipment support

Scope of Program: 3 awards per year

Application/Selection Process:
  Deadline: Spring
  Preferred Initial Contact: Write for application/guidelines
  Application Procedure: Submit application form, additional materials as requested
  Selection Process: Panel review
  Notification Process: Letter
  Formal Report of Grant Required: Yes

➤ **VIDEOWALL COMMISSIONING PROJECT**

Purpose: To offer artists an opportunity to access high-end production equipment for individual or collaborative projects to be exhibited on 24- to 32-screen videowall

Eligibility:
  Residency: Minnesota, Illinois
  Special Requirements: No full-time students or projects for a degree program; noncommercial work only
  Art Forms: Video, interdisciplinary with video

Type of Support: $3,000 commission plus $2,500 for production expenses and in-kind support for production, post-production, and exhibition needs

Scope of Program: 2 awards per year (1 to a Minnesota artist, 1 to an Illinois artist)

Application/Selection Process:
  Deadline: Fall or winter
  Preferred Initial Contact: Write for application/guidelines
  Application Procedure: Submit application form, additional materials as requested
  Selection Process: Panel review
  Notification Process: Phone call
  Formal Report of Grant Required: Yes

➤ **MEDIA PRODUCTION AWARDS PROGRAM**

Purpose: To provide artists with access to Intermedia's equipment for noncommercial work

Eligibility:
  Art Forms: Video, audio, some interdisciplinary

Type of Support: $1,000-$5,000 worth of equipment/facilities access; artist submits documentation of project to Intermedia's archives

Scope of Program: 10-12 awards per year

Application/Selection Process:
  Deadline: February 1, May 1, August 1, November 1
  Preferred Initial Contact: Write for application/guidelines

Application Procedure: Submit application form, additional materials as requested
Selection Process: Peer panel of artists
Notification Process: Letter
Formal Report of Grant Required: No

EQUIPMENT ACCESS

Video: Production for VHS, 3/4"; post-production for VHS, S-VHS, 3/4"
Comments: Intermedia Arts Artist Affiliate Members ($75 fee) receive low-cost access to equipment and facilities.

TECHNICAL ASSISTANCE PROGRAMS AND SERVICES

Programs of Special Interest: Intermedia Arts acts as a fiscal agent for individual artist projects.

INTERNATIONAL CENTER FOR 8MM FILM AND VIDEO (IC8FV)

Until December 31, 1991:
10R Oxford Street
Somerville, MA 02143
617-666-3372

New address effective January 1, 1992:
P.O. Box 335
Rowley, MA 01969

TECHNICAL ASSISTANCE PROGRAMS AND SERVICES

Programs of Special Interest: IC8FV acts as an information center for artists who use 8mm, Super 8, or Single 8 film or small format video. Its staff directs artists to sources of funding, technical information, and other resources.

IOWA ARTS COUNCIL (IAC)

Department of Cultural Affairs
Capitol Complex
Executive Hills
1223 E Court
Des Moines, IA 50319
515-281-4006
CONTACT: BRUCE WILLIAMS, DIRECTOR OF CREATIVE ARTISTS AND VISUAL ARTS

PROFILE OF FINANCIAL SUPPORT TO ARTISTS

Total Funding/Value of In-Kind Support: $53,949+ for FY 1990
Competition for Funding: n/a
Grant Range: $200-$1,500

DIRECT SUPPORT PROGRAMS

➤ **MINI-GRANTS**
CONTACT: JULIE BAILEY, DIRECTOR OF PARTNERSHIP PROGRAMS
Phone: 515-281-4018
Purpose: To provide grants for project support, training, or technical assistance to individual artists, and to support emergency or educational grants to organizations
Eligibility:
    Citizenship: U.S.
    Residency: Iowa
    Special Requirements: Professional artists only
    Art Forms: All disciplines
Type of Support: Up to $500 for project support or technical assistance; up to $200 for training (e.g., attendance at workshops, seminars)
Scope of Program: $18,000 total budget for FY 1991
Application/Selection Process:
    Deadline: 6 weeks before project
    Preferred Initial Contact: Call or write for application/guidelines
    Application Procedure: Submit application, resumé, project budget, samples of work
    Selection Process: Organization staff
    Notification Process: Letter within 30 days of application
    Formal Report of Grant Required: Yes

➤ **TOURING ARTS TEAMS**
CONTACT: KATHLEEN HILL, DIRECTOR OF EXPANSION ARTS
Phone: 515-281-8352
Purpose: To bring the arts to rural Iowa communities with populations of less than 2,000

Eligibility:
Special Requirements: Artists must be on an IAC roster
Art Forms: All disciplines
Type of Support: $1,100 plus transportation expenses, food, and lodging for 12-day tour of 5 towns; artists conduct workshops and give performances
Scope of Program: 21 artists funded in FY 1991
Application/Selection Process:
Deadline: March 1
Preferred Initial Contact: IAC mails application to all rostered artists 2-3 months before deadline
Application Procedure: Submit application form, tentative workshop plans
Selection Process: Organization staff
Notification Process: Letter, follow-up phone call
Formal Report of Grant Required: Yes

➤ **INDIVIDUAL ARTISTS GRANTS**
CONTACT: BRUCE WILLIAMS, DIRECTOR OF CREATIVE ARTISTS AND VISUAL ARTS
Phone: 515-281-4006
Purpose: To support the creation of new work by Iowa artists
Eligibility:
Residency: Iowa or bordering towns, 1 year
Age: 18 or older
Special Requirements: No students; previous grantees ineligible for 1-2 years
Art Forms: Dance, music, opera/musical theater, visual arts, design arts, crafts, photography/holography, media arts, literature, interdisciplinary/collaborations, performance art
Type of Support: Grants of at least $500 (average $1,000-$2,000)
Scope of Program: n/a
Application/Selection Process:
Deadline: January 10
Preferred Initial Contact: Call or write for application/guidelines
Application Procedure: Submit application form, samples of work, resumé, financial statement, project budget
Selection Process: Individuals from outside of organization
Notification Process: Letter
Formal Report of Grant Required: Yes

TECHNICAL ASSISTANCE PROGRAMS AND SERVICES
Programs of Special Interest: IAC offers residency opportunities through its Artists in Schools/Communities, Special Constituencies, and Arts to Share programs (contact Kay Swan, Director of Arts Education, 515-281-4100).

JEROME FOUNDATION

W-1050 First National Bank Building
332 Minnesota Street
St. Paul, MN 55101
612-224-9431
CONTACT: CYNTHIA A. GEHRIG, PRESIDENT

PROFILE OF FINANCIAL SUPPORT TO ARTISTS
Total Funding/Value of In-Kind Support: n/a
Competition for Funding: Total applications, n/a; total individuals funded/provided with in-kind support, 42 in FY 1988-89
Grant Range: n/a

DIRECT SUPPORT PROGRAMS
➤ **NEW YORK CITY FILM AND VIDEO PROGRAM**
Purpose: To support emerging film and video artists who make creative use of their media and who have not had the support needed to fully display their work
Eligibility:
   Citizenship: U.S. (permanent residents also eligible)
   Residency: New York City metropolitan area
   Special Requirements: Must have completed formal education; preference to projects in their early stages and to personal, low budget work in which the artist exercises complete creative control over production; strong preference to projects with budgets under $50,000; previous applicants ineligible for 1 year
   Art Forms: Film, video
Type of Support: $8,000-$20,000
Scope of Program: 14 grants in 1988-89
Application/Selection Process:
   Deadline: Applications reviewed 3 times per year
   Preferred Initial Contact: Call or write for application/guidelines
   Application Procedure: Submit application form, project budget, resumé, excerpt of script (for works with major narrative element), samples of work
   Selection Process: Panel of artists and arts professionals, board of directors
   Formal Report of Grant Required: Yes
➤ **TRAVEL AND STUDY GRANTS**
Purpose: To allow artists significant time for professional development through artist-to-artist communication on aesthetic issues, the experience of seeing artistic work outside of Minnesota, time for reflection and individualized study, a chance to develop future work and collaborations, and opportunities for the presentation or development of their work in other locations

Eligibility:
Residency: Twin Cities 7-county metropolitan area of Minnesota, 1 year
Special Requirements: Professional artists or administrators only
Art Forms: All disciplines
Type of Support: $1,000-$5,000 for travel
Scope of Program: $90,000 available for FY 1990-91
Preferred Initial Contact: Call or write for application/guidelines
Application Procedure: Submit application form, resumé, samples of work (optional)
Selection Process: Panel of arts professionals, board of directors
Notification Process: Within 6 weeks of deadline
Formal Report of Grant Required: Yes

JUNEAU ARTS AND HUMANITIES COUNCIL

P.O. Box 020562
Juneau, AK 99802-0562
907-586-2787
CONTACT: GINA SPARTZ, ADMINISTRATIVE ASSISTANT

PROFILE OF FINANCIAL SUPPORT TO ARTISTS
Total Funding/Value of In-Kind Support: $6,350 for FY 1990
Competition for Funding: Total applications, 21; total individuals funded/provided with in-kind support, 10
Grant Range: $300-$1,000

DIRECT SUPPORT PROGRAMS
➤ INDIVIDUAL ARTISTS ASSISTANCE PROGRAM
Purpose: To enable experienced artists of exceptional talent to produce works of art or advance their careers
Eligibility:
Citizenship: U.S.
Residency: Juneau, 1 year
Special Requirements: Previous grantees ineligible for 2 years
Art Forms: All disciplines
Type of Support: Up to $1,000 for a specific activity
Scope of Program: 10 awards in 1990
Application/Selection Process:
Deadline: 2 deadlines per year
Preferred Initial Contact: Call or write for application/guidelines
Application Procedure: Submit application form, samples of work, resumé, financial statement, project budget, copies of other grant applications related to project

Selection Process: Organization staff, board of directors, individuals outside of organization, peer panel of artists
Notification Process: Phone and letter
Formal Report of Grant Required: Yes

TECHNICAL ASSISTANCE PROGRAMS AND SERVICES

Programs of Special Interest: JAHC maintains a resource library and works with other arts organizations to closely monitor legislation regarding the arts.

KANSAS ARTS COMMISSION (KAC)

Jayhawk Tower
700 Jackson
Suite 1004
Topeka, KS 66603-3714
913-296-3335
CONTACT: CONCHITA REYES, ARTS PROGRAM COORDINATOR

PROFILE OF FINANCIAL SUPPORT TO ARTISTS

Total Funding/Value of In-Kind Support: $25,000 for FY 1990
Competition for Funding: Total applications, 111; total individuals funded/provided with in-kind support, 10
Grant Range: $385-$5,000

DIRECT SUPPORT PROGRAMS
➤ **PROFESSIONAL DEVELOPMENT GRANTS**
Purpose: To encourage artists in the next step of their development as they create original works of art in any discipline
Eligibility:
  Residency: Kansas
  Special Requirements: Originating artists only; artists must match grant in cash or combination of cash and in-kind services; no students; no previous recipients
  Art Forms: All disciplines
Type of Support: $100-$1,000 matching grant for specific project
Scope of Program: $5,000 available for FY 1990-91
Application/Selection Process:
  Deadline: First-come, first-served basis (FY begins in July); funding must be received 2 months before project begins
  Preferred Initial Contact: Call or write to confirm availability of funds

Application Procedure: Submit application form, resumé, project description and budget, financial statement, samples of work, support materials (optional)
Selection Process: Staff, 2 experts in field, KAC commissioner
Notification Process: Letter; applications reviewed upon receipt
Formal Report of Grant Required: Yes

TECHNICAL ASSISTANCE PROGRAMS AND SERVICES

Programs of Special Interest: KAC administers an Arts in Education Artist in Residency Program; film and video artist residencies last 2 weeks to 9 months. A monthly bulletin and a quarterly newsletter supply information about arts events and opportunities.

KENTUCKY ARTS COUNCIL (KAC)

Berry Hill Mansion
Frankfort, KY 40601
502-564-3757
CONTACT: IRWIN PICKETT, DIRECTOR OF VISUAL ARTS

PROFILE OF FINANCIAL SUPPORT TO ARTISTS

Total Funding/Value of In-Kind Support: $130,000 for FY 1990
Competition for Funding: Total applications, 150; total individuals funded/provided with in-kind support, 42
Grant Range: $1,000-$5,000

DIRECT SUPPORT PROGRAMS

➤ **AL SMITH FELLOWSHIPS**

Purpose: To support individual Kentucky artists in developing their art forms
Eligibility:
    Citizenship: U.S.
    Residency: Kentucky
    Age: 18 or older
    Special Requirements: Previous grantees ineligible for 2 years
    Art Forms: Disciplines alternate yearly between visual arts/media arts/new genres (odd-numbered years) and writers/composers/choreographers (even-numbered years)
Type of Support: $5,000 fellowships, $1,000 assistance awards
Scope of Program: 22 fellowships, 20 assistance awards
Application/Selection Process:
    Preferred Initial Contact: Call to explain project and need for funding

Application Procedure: Submit application form, samples of work, resumé, project proposal
Selection Process: Organization staff, board of directors, peer panel of artists
Notification Process: Letter
Formal Report of Grant Required: No

KING COUNTY ARTS COMMISSION (KCAC)

1115 Smith Tower
506 Second Avenue
Seattle, WA 98104
206-296-7580
CONTACT: MAYUMI TSUTUKAWA, MANAGER, CULTURAL RESOURCES DIVISION

PROFILE OF FINANCIAL SUPPORT TO ARTISTS
Total Funding/Value of In-Kind Support: $40,500 for FY 1990
(New Works Projects)
Competition for Funding: Total applications, 180; total individuals funded/provided with in-kind support, 11
Grant Range: $1,000-$5,000

DIRECT SUPPORT PROGRAMS
➤ **NEW WORKS PROJECTS**
CONTACT: VICKY LEE, PERFORMING ARTS COORDINATOR
Purpose: To encourage experimentation and to support the creation of new works
Eligibility:
   Residency: King County
   Special Requirements: Professional, originating artists only; previous recipients ineligible for 2 years
   Art Forms: Literature, visual arts, media arts, performing arts, interdisciplinary
Type of Support: $1,000-$5,000
Scope of Program: 8-10 awards per year
Application/Selection Process:
   Deadline: Mid-January
   Preferred Initial Contact: Consult with staff before applying
   Application Procedure: Submit application form, samples of work, project narrative
   Selection Process: Peer panel of artists, commission members
   Formal Report of Grant Required: Yes

TECHNICAL ASSISTANCE PROGRAMS AND SERVICES

Programs of Special Interest: African-American, Latino, Asian-American/Pacific Islander, and Native American artists may apply for arts-in-education residencies through the Ethnic Artists-in-Residence program; the Disabled Artists-in-Residence places blind and visually-impaired, deaf and hearing-impaired, deaf-blind, or physically disabled artists in arts-in-education residencies (contact Robert Roth, Community Arts Coordinator).

LAKE REGION ARTS COUNCIL, INC. (LRAC)

112 W. Washington Avenue
P.O. Box 661
Fergus Falls, MN 56538-0661
218-739-5780
CONTACT: SONJA PETERSON, PROGRAM COORDINATOR

PROFILE OF FINANCIAL SUPPORT TO ARTISTS

Total Funding/Value of In-Kind Support: $2,000 for FY 1990
Competition for Funding: Total applications, 18; total individuals funded/provided with in-kind support, 5
Grant Range: $74-$500

DIRECT SUPPORT PROGRAMS

➤ **LRAC/MCKNIGHT INDIVIDUAL ARTISTS GRANT PROGRAM**
Purpose: To provide small but critical grants to artists for specific projects that contribute directly to their growth and development as professionals
Eligibility:
  Citizenship: U.S.
  Residency: Minnesota (Becker, Clay, Douglas, Grant, Otter Tail, Pope, Stevens, Traverse, and Wilkin counties)
  Special Requirements: No students
  Art Forms: All disciplines
Type of Support: Up to $500 for expenses such as production and presentation of work, training, supplies, or services
Scope of Program: $2,000 budget in FY 1990
Application/Selection Process:
  Deadline: February 5
  Preferred Initial Contact: Call or write for application/guidelines
  Application Procedure: Submit application form, samples of work, references, resumé, project budget
  Selection Process: LRAC board of directors
  Notification Process: Letter in April
  Formal Report of Grant Required: Yes

TECHNICAL ASSISTANCE PROGRAMS AND SERVICES

Programs of Special Interest: LRAC maintains an unjuried registry of artists, publishes a monthly newsletter, and holds grantwriting workshops.

THE LATINO COLLABORATIVE

280 Broadway
Suite 412
New York, NY 10007
212-732-1121

PROFILE OF FINANCIAL SUPPORT TO ARTISTS

Total Funding/Value of In-Kind Support: n/a
Competition for Funding: n/a
Grant Range: $500-$1,500

DIRECT SUPPORT PROGRAMS

➤ **PROJECT DEVELOPMENT REGRANT PROGRAM**

Purpose: To make grants to independent Latino producers to assist them in the development of projects to be submitted for public broadcast funding and programming for national broadcast

Eligibility:
    Residency: Northeast U.S., Puerto Rico
    Special Requirements: Producer must be Latino; projects already in production are ineligible; first-time producers collaborating with an experienced producer are encouraged to apply
    Art Forms: Film, video

Type of Support: $500-$1,500 for project development in 1991 (grant range expected to increase)

Scope of Program: $15,000 available in 1991 (expected to increase)

Application/Selection Process:
    Preferred Initial Contact: Call or write for application/guidelines
    Application Procedure: Submit project description, budget for grant, resumé, samples of work
    Selection Process: Panel of producers, critics, and others related to public television
    Notification Process: After panel meeting in June
    Formal Report of Grant Required: Yes

TECHNICAL ASSISTANCE PROGRAMS AND SERVICES

Programs of Special Interest: The Latino Collaborative publishes a newsletter and provides information services for artists.

LIGHT WORK

316 Waverly Avenue
Syracuse, NY 13244
315-443-1300
CONTACT: JEFFREY HOONE, DIRECTOR

PROFILE OF FINANCIAL SUPPORT TO ARTISTS

Total Funding/Value of In-Kind Support: $30,000 for FY 1990
Competition for Funding: Total applications, 350; total individuals funded/provided with in-kind support, 25
Grant Range: $1,200

DIRECT SUPPORT PROGRAMS

➤ **ARTIST-IN-RESIDENCE PROGRAM**

Purpose: To provide photographers with an opportunity to work, free of any distractions or obligations, on projects of their choice
Eligibility:
    Age: 18 or older
    Art Forms: Photography, video, audio, interdisciplinary
Type of Support: 1-month residency including housing, private darkroom, $1,200 stipend
Scope of Program: 12-15 residencies per year
Application/Selection Process:
    Deadline: None
    Preferred Initial Contact: Call or write for guidelines
    Application Procedure: Submit letter of intent, resumé, samples of work, supporting material
    Selection Process: Organization staff
    Notification Process: Letter or phone call
    Formal Report of Grant Required: No

LONG BEACH MUSEUM OF ART/LBMA—VIDEO

5373 East Second Street
Long Beach, CA 90803
213-439-0751
CONTACT: JOE LEONARDI, GENERAL MANAGER, VIDEO ANNEX

PROFILE OF FINANCIAL SUPPORT TO ARTISTS

Total Funding/Value of In-Kind Support: n/a
Competition for Funding: Total applications, 110; total number of individuals/nonprofit organizations funded/provided with in-kind support, 12
Grant Range: $2,000 cash grants

DIRECT SUPPORT PROGRAMS

➤ **OPEN CHANNELS: VIDEO PRODUCTION GRANT PROGRAM**

Purpose: To support new video art pieces less than 15 minutes in length

Eligibility:
  Residency: California
  Special Requirements: No full-time students; preference to works not already in progress and to applicants who have not received this grant before
  Art Forms: Video

Type of Support: $2,000, supply of tape stock, 8 days access to production and post-production facilities at a local cable studio (participating facilities typically provide an ENG production package or a 3-camera studio, and access to 3/4" editing)

Scope of Program: 4 grants per year

Application/Selection Process:
  Deadline: Spring
  Preferred Initial Contact: Call or write for application/guidelines
  Application Procedure: Submit application form, resumé, samples of work
  Selection Process: Panel of independent jurors and staff
  Notification Process: Letter
  Formal Report of Grant Required: No

➤ **VIDEO ACCESS PROGRAM (VAP)**

Purpose: To provide production and post-production facility access grants to Southern California artists, noncommercial independent producers, and nonprofit organizations for the creation or completion of new works

Eligibility:
  Residency: Southern California
  Art Forms: Video

Type of Support: 5 days of production and post-production from LBMA Video Annex; grantees must provide 3/4" copy of completed project for LBMA Video Collection and must provide LBMA Video with nonexclusive exhibition, cable, and broadcast rights

Scope of Program: 8 awards per year

Application/Selection Process:
  Deadline: October
  Preferred Initial Contact: Call or write for application/guidelines
  Application Procedure: Submit application form, project description, resumé, samples of work
  Selection Process: Jury
  Notification Process: Letter
  Formal Report of Grant Required: No

EQUIPMENT ACCESS

Video: Production for S-VHS, 3/4"; post-production for VHS, S-VHS, 3/4"

Comments: LBMA's facilities include production studios. Artists receive access to facilities and equipment at subsidized rates.

TECHNICAL ASSISTANCE PROGRAMS AND SERVICES

Programs of Special Interest: The LMBA exhibits single-channel video and video installations. The cable television series "Viewpoints on Video" showcases video art.

LOS ANGELES CONTEMPORARY EXHIBITIONS (LACE)

1804 Industrial Street
Los Angeles, CA 90021
213-624-5650

PROFILE OF FINANCIAL SUPPORT TO ARTISTS

Total Funding/Value of In-Kind Support: n/a
Competition for Funding: n/a
Grant Range: n/a

➤ **ARTISTS' PROJECTS GRANTS**

Purpose: To encourage innovative projects that push the boundaries of contemporary art and challenge traditional formats

Eligibility:
  Residency: California (south of, but not including, Fresno), Hawaii
  Special Requirements: No full-time students; artists of diverse backgrounds encouraged to apply; individual artists and collaborating artists are eligible
  Art Forms: Single-disciplinary or interdisciplinary innovative projects

Type of Support: Cash grant

Scope of Program: 5-8 grants, totalling $30,250, available in 1991

Application/Selection Process:
  Deadline: April 15
  Application Procedure: Submit application form, samples of work, project description and budget, biographies of key artistic personnel
  Selection Process: Independent panel of artists and arts professionals
  Notification Process: August

EQUIPMENT ACCESS

CONTACT: VIDEO COORDINATOR

Comments: Artists working on noncommercial video and audio projects may apply to the On-line program, which offers access to professional post-production and recording facilities and technicians at reduced rates (membership fee and administrative fee required; contact the Video Coordinator). LACE also guides artists to sources of production equipment rentals and inexpensive off-line editing.

TECHNICAL ASSISTANCE PROGRAMS AND SERVICES

Programs of Special Interest: LACE maintains a listing of grants for video and audio artists and a bulletin board of festival and other announcements. LACE screens work by emerging and established artists from Los Angeles and elsewhere. Workshops and consultations on technical subjects are also available. (Membership and administrative fees apply to some services.)

LOS ANGELES CULTURAL AFFAIRS DEPARTMENT

433 South Spring Street
10th Floor
Los Angeles, CA 90013
213-485-2433
CONTACT: GRANTS DEPARTMENT, 213-620-9445

PROFILE OF FINANCIAL SUPPORT TO ARTISTS

Total Funding/Value of In-Kind Support: $538,215 for FY 1990-91
Competition for Funding: Total applications, 566; total individuals funded/provided with in-kind support, 77
Grant Range: $4,000-$7,000 average

DIRECT SUPPORT PROGRAMS

➤ COMMUNITY ARTS PROGRAM—CULTURAL GRANTS
Phone: 213-620-8635

Purpose: To offer arts experiences within a community setting to nonprofessional artists and to bring professional artists in direct contact with the public

Eligibility:
   Residency: City or County of Los Angeles
   Special Requirements: Artist must submit a letter of agreement with proposed host venue to produce the project if funded; project must take place in the City of Los Angeles in a nontraditional community site with public access

Art Forms: Dance, interdisciplinary, multi-disciplinary, literature, media arts, music, theater, urban and design arts, traditional and folk arts, visual arts

Type of Support: $1,500-$15,000 for project

Scope of Program: n/a

Application/Selection Process:
   Deadline: Fall
   Preferred Initial Contact: Call or write for application/guidelines
   Application Procedure: Submit application form, materials as outlined in guidelines
   Selection Process: Peer panel of artists
   Notification Process: Letter 5-6 months after deadline
   Formal Report of Grant Required: Yes

LOUISIANA DIVISION OF THE ARTS (DOA)

900 Riverside North
Baton Rouge, LA 70802
504-342-8180

CONTACT: ANN RUSSO, DIRECTOR, VISUAL ARTS AND ARTS IN EDUCATION PROGRAMS

PROFILE OF FINANCIAL SUPPORT TO ARTISTS

Total Funding/Value of In-Kind Support: $74,000 for FY 1991

Competition for Funding: Total applications, 185; total individuals funded/provided with in-kind support, 16

Grant Range: $3,400-$5,000

DIRECT SUPPORT PROGRAMS

➤ **ARTIST FELLOWSHIPS**

Purpose: To enable artists of exceptional talent to pursue their artistic goals

Eligibility:
   Residency: Louisiana, 2 years
   Special Requirements: Professional artists only; no students; previous grantees ineligible
   Art Forms: Crafts, dance, design arts, folk arts, literature, media arts, music, theater, visual arts

Type of Support: $5,000

Scope of Program: 10 awards in 1991

Application/Selection Process:
   Deadline: March 1
   Preferred Initial Contact: Write for application/guidelines

Application Procedure: Submit application form, samples of work, resumé
Selection Process: Individuals outside of organization
Notification Process: Letter 5 months after deadline
Formal Report of Grant Required: Yes

➤ **INDIVIDUAL ARTIST PROJECTS: FISCAL AGENTS**
Purpose: To support projects of exceptional merit initiated by individual artists
Eligibility:
   Residency: Louisiana, 2 years
   Special Requirements: Must be practicing artist; no students enrolled in arts-related degree or certificate-granting programs; must apply through a nonprofit organization; there should be a reasonable relationship between the project type and the primary purpose of the nonprofit, but the project must clearly be an individual artist project
   Art Forms: Visual arts, performing arts, folk arts, design arts, media arts
Type of Support: Up to $2,000
Scope of Program: n/a
Application/Selection Process:
   Deadline: March 1
   Preferred Initial Contact: Call or write for application/guidelines
   Application Procedure: Submit application form, other materials as requested
   Selection Process: Advisory panel, council
   Notification Process: Letter
   Formal Report of Grant Required: Yes

TECHNICAL ASSISTANCE PROGRAMS AND SERVICES
Programs of Special Interest: The Louisiana Artist Roster lists artists approved for Arts in Education residencies and projects.

LOWER MANHATTAN CULTURAL COUNCIL (LMCC)

42 Broadway
New York, NY 10004
212-269-0320
CONTACT: GRETA GUNDERSON, ASSOCIATE DIRECTOR

PROFILE OF FINANCIAL SUPPORT TO ARTISTS
Total Funding/Value of In-Kind Support: n/a
Competition for Funding: Total applications, n/a; total individuals funded/provided with in-kind support, 100+
Grant Range: $500-$7,500

DIRECT SUPPORT PROGRAMS
➤ MANHATTAN COMMUNITY ARTS FUND

Purpose: To support projects by small arts groups that have not yet received funding from traditional government sources

Eligibility:
  Special Requirements: Artists must apply under the aegis of a nonprofit sponsor not receiving DCA, NYSCA, or NEA support; previous grantees ineligible for 3 years
  Art Forms: Dance (ethnic, modern), music (new, ethnic, jazz, popular), theater (general), visual arts, design arts (architecture, urban/metropolitan), media arts, literature (fiction), inter-disciplinary, multi-disciplinary

Type of Support: Up to $3,000 for a specific project

Scope of Program: $64,940 awarded to organizations in FY 1988-89

Application/Selection Process:
  Preferred Initial Contact: Call or write for information
  Application Procedure: Sponsor submits letter of intent, project budget, artist's resumé, samples of work
  Notification Process: Letter or phone call within 6 weeks

LYNDHURST FOUNDATION

Tallan Building
Suite 701
. 100 West M. L. King Boulevard
Chattanooga, TN 37402

PROFILE OF FINANCIAL SUPPORT TO ARTISTS

Total Funding/Value of In-Kind Support: $660,000 in FY 1989
Competition for Funding: Total applications, n/a; total individuals funded/provided with in-kind support, 24
Grant Range: n/a

DIRECT SUPPORT PROGRAMS
➤ LYNDHURST PRIZE/YOUNG CAREER PRIZE

Purpose: Lyndhurst Prize enables individuals who have made distinctive contributions in the arts, particularly writing and photography, and in community service and leadership to carry forth their interests over an extended period of time without financial pressure; Young Career Prize supports young adults whose work in public service and the arts shows passion and promise but is not likely to attract substantial financial award

Eligibility:
  Art Forms: All disciplines

Type of Support: 3-year stipend (Lyndhurst Prize); 2-year stipend (Young Career Prize)

Scope of Program: 24 individuals received $660,000 in FY 1989

Application/Selection Process:
Awards granted solely at initiative of the board of trustees. No applications or nominations accepted.

JOHN D. AND CATHERINE T. MACARTHUR FOUNDATION

140 South Dearborn Street
Chicago, IL 60603

PROFILE OF FINANCIAL SUPPORT TO ARTISTS

Total Funding/Value of In-Kind Support: n/a

Competition for Funding: n/a

Grant Range: n/a

DIRECT SUPPORT PROGRAMS
➤ **GENERAL PROGRAM**

Purpose: To support projects related to the foundation's programmatic interests in the world environment and resources, peace and international cooperation, education, mental health, and world population

Eligibility:
Art Forms: Broad range of arts and humanities activities including film and video

Type of Support: Cash for project support

Scope of Program: n/a

Application/Selection Process:
Deadline: None; applications reviewed monthly
Preferred Initial Contact: Write for guidelines
Application Procedure: Submit 2- to 3-page letter of inquiry describing project and type of funding desired; staff review letters and request more information if project is of interest to the foundation
Selection Process: Staff review
Notification Process: Letter
Formal Report of Grant Required: Yes

THE MACDOWELL COLONY

100 High Street
Peterborough, NH 03458
603-924-3886
CONTACT: SHIRLEY BEWLEY, ADMISSIONS COORDINATOR

PROFILE OF FINANCIAL SUPPORT TO ARTISTS

Total Funding/Value of In-Kind Support: $803,000 for FY 1989
Competition for Funding: Total applications, 1,150; total
individuals funded/provided with in-kind support, 208
Grant Range: n/a

DIRECT SUPPORT PROGRAMS
➤ ARTIST RESIDENCY PROGRAM

Purpose: To provide a place where creative artists can find freedom
to concentrate on their work

Eligibility:
Special Requirements: Professional artists and emerging artists
of recognized ability; previous applicants ineligible for 1 year
Art Forms: Music composition, literature, visual arts, architecture,
film/video, mixed media, interdisciplinary

Type of Support: Residency including room, board, and studio for up
to 2 months; funds available to defray travel costs to and from colony;
artists who have financial resources pay on a voluntary basis

Scope of Program: 200+ residencies averaging 6 weeks

Application/Selection Process:
Deadline: January 15 (Summer), April 15 (Fall-Winter),
September 15 (Winter-Spring)
Preferred Initial Contact: Call or write for application/guidelines
Application Procedure: Submit application form, samples of
work, references, resumé, $20 fee
Selection Process: Peer panel of artists
Notification Process: Letter 2 months after deadline
Formal Report of Grant Required: No

MAINE ARTS COMMISSION (MAC)

55 Capitol Street
Station 25
Augusta, ME 04333-0025
207-289-2724
CONTACT: KATHY ANN JONES, MUSEUM/VISUAL ARTS ASSOCIATE

PROFILE OF FINANCIAL SUPPORT TO ARTISTS

Total Funding/Value of In-Kind Support: $18,000 for FY 1991
(excluding apprenticeships)

Competition for Funding: Total applications, 109; total individuals
funded/provided with in-kind support, 6

Grant Range: $3,000

DIRECT SUPPORT PROGRAMS

➤ **INDIVIDUAL ARTIST FELLOWSHIPS**

Purpose: To provide financial support for artists to advance
their careers

Eligibility:
  Residency: Maine
  Age: 18 or older
  Special Requirements: No students
  Art Forms: Awards rotate on a 3-year cycle among visual arts
  (1990), writing/design arts (1991), performing/traditional/media
  arts (1992)

Type of Support: $3,000

Scope of Program: 6 awards in 1991

Application/Selection Process:
  Deadline: September 1
  Preferred Initial Contact: Call for application/guidelines
  Application Procedure: Submit application form, samples of
  work, resumé, statement of intent (optional)
  Selection Process: Individuals from outside of organization
  Notification Process: Phone call and follow-up letter to
  recipients in November; letter to nonrecipients
  Formal Report of Grant Required: Yes

TECHNICAL ASSISTANCE PROGRAMS AND SERVICES

Programs of Special Interest: The Artist in Residence Program offers ten-day to year-long residencies in schools and other nonprofit
institutions. The commission administers Contemporary Exhibition
Aid to nonprofit organizations for exhibitions that promote the
work of contemporary visual, media, and design artists in Maine.

MANITOBA ARTS COUNCIL (MAC)

525-93 Lombard Avenue
Winnipeg, Manitoba
Canada R3B 3B1
204-945-4537
CONTACT: KALVIN ASMUNDSON, VISUAL ARTS ASSOCIATE CONSULTANT

PROFILE OF FINANCIAL SUPPORT TO ARTISTS
Total Funding/Value of In-Kind Support: $1,028,617 for FY 1988-89
Competition for Funding: Total applications, 800; total individuals funded/provided with in-kind support, n/a
Grant Range: n/a

DIRECT SUPPORT PROGRAMS
➤ **FILM PROJECT GRANTS/VIDEO PROJECT GRANTS**
Purpose: To assist independent Manitoba filmmakers in the creation and production of high quality, innovative films
Eligibility:
  Citizenship: Canada (landed immigrants also eligible)
  Residency: Manitoba, 1 year
  Special Requirements: Professional artists only; must have completed basic training; no students; principal creator/director of film/video must apply; applicant must retain artistic control and rights; commissioned, instructional, promotional, and industrial projects ineligible; pilots for commercial or educational television ineligible
  Art Forms: Film, video
Type of Support: Up to $6,000
Scope of Program: 12 grants, totalling $45,800, in FY 1988-89
Application/Selection Process:
  Deadline: April 1, October 1
  Preferred Initial Contact: Consult with Visual Arts Associate Consultant before applying
  Application Procedure: Submit application form, project proposal and budget, resumé, filmography/videography, synopsis and draft script (dramatic works), outline (documentaries), storyboard (animated works), film/video treatment, shooting script, samples of work
  Selection Process: Jury of independent professionals in the visual arts
  Notification Process: 2 months after deadline
  Formal Report of Grant Required: Yes

➤ **SHORT TERM PROJECT GRANTS FOR FILM/SHORT-TERM PROJECT GRANTS FOR VIDEO**

Purpose: To assist professional Manitoba filmmakers and videomakers with projects and programs of short-term duration such as short-term study or master classes, participation in workshops or seminars outside the province, work-related travel, and material costs where the need is immediate

Eligibility:
    Citizenship: Canada (landed immigrants also eligible)
    Residency: Manitoba, 1 year
    Special Requirements: Professional artists only; must have completed basic training; no students; previous recipients ineligible for 1 year; commissioned, instructional, promotional, and industrial projects ineligible; pilots for commercial or educational television ineligible
    Art Forms: Film, video

Type of Support: Up to $750

Scope of Program: 4 film grants, totalling $2,666, in FY 1988-89

Application/Selection Process:
    Deadline: 1 month before project begins
    Preferred Initial Contact: Consult with Visual Arts Associate Consultant before applying
    Application Procedure: Submit application form, project proposal and budget, resumé, filmography/videography, written confirmation of event (if applicable), samples of work
    Selection Process: Independent professional in the visual arts
    Notification Process: 1 month after application
    Formal Report of Grant Required: Yes

➤ **FILM PRODUCTION GRANTS/VIDEO PRODUCTION GRANTS**

Purpose: To assist independent Manitoba film and video artists in the creation and production of high quality, innovative work

Eligibility:
    Citizenship: Canada (landed immigrants also eligible)
    Residency: Manitoba, 1 year
    Special Requirements: Professional artists only; must have completed basic training; no students; principal creator/director of film/video must apply; applicant must retain artistic control and rights; commissioned, instructional, promotional, and industrial projects ineligible; pilots for commercial or educational television ineligible
    Art Forms: Film, video

Type of Support: Up to $20,000

Scope of Program: 5 grants, totalling $80,000, in FY 1988-89

Application/Selection Process:
    Deadline: April 1, October 1

Preferred Initial Contact: Consult with Visual Arts Associate Consultant before applying

Application Procedure: Submit application form, project proposal and budget, resumé, filmography/videography, synopsis and draft script (dramatic works), outline (documentaries), storyboard (animated works), film/video treatment, shooting script, samples of work

Selection Process: Jury of independent professionals in the visual arts

Notification Process: 2 months after deadline

Formal Report of Grant Required: Yes

➤ **FILM SCRIPT DEVELOPMENT GRANTS/VIDEO SCRIPT DEVELOPMENT GRANTS**

Purpose: To assist independent Manitoba film and video artists or writers in the creation of scripts for film or video

Eligibility:
　Citizenship: Canada (landed immigrants also eligible)
　Residency: Manitoba, 1 year
　Special Requirements: Professional artists only; must have completed basic training; no students; applicant must retain artistic control over script; scripts for commissioned, instructional, promotional, and industrial projects ineligible
　Art Forms: Film scripts, video scripts

Type of Support: Up to $6,000

Scope of Program: n/a

Application/Selection Process:
　Deadline: April 1, October 1
　Preferred Initial Contact: Consult with Visual Arts Associate Consultant before applying
　Application Procedure: Submit application form, project proposal and budget, resumé, filmography/videography, outline of script, samples of work
　Selection Process: Jury of independent professionals in the visual arts
　Notification Process: 2 months after deadline
　Formal Report of Grant Required: Yes

➤ **ARTVENTURES "A" GRANTS**

CONTACT: JAMIE HUTCHISON

Purpose: To support developmental and innovative programs in the arts

Eligibility:
　Residency: Manitoba
　Art Forms: All disciplines

Type of Support: Up to $5,000

Scope of Program: 2 grants, totalling $10,000, to individual film/video artists in FY 1988-89

Application/Selection Process:
Deadline: May 1, October 1
Preferred Initial Contact: Call or write for application/guidelines
Application Procedure: Submit application form, additional materials as requested
Selection Process: Peer review panel, jury decision
Notification Process: Letter
Formal Report of Grant Required: Yes

TECHNICAL ASSISTANCE PROGRAMS AND SERVICES
Programs of Special Interest: The Artists in the Schools Program maintains a roster of professional artists eligible for short-term and long-term residencies in Manitoba schools (contact Ann Atkey, Arts Education Consultant, 204-945-2978).

MARYLAND STATE ARTS COUNCIL (MSAC)

15 West Mulberry Street
Baltimore, MD 21201
301-333-8232
TDD: 301-333-6926
CONTACT: CHARLES CAMP, GRANTS OFFICER

PROFILE OF FINANCIAL SUPPORT TO ARTISTS
Total Funding/Value of In-Kind Support: $345,000 for FY 1991
Competition for Funding: Total applications, 900; total individuals funded/provided with in-kind support, 125
Grant Range: $2,500 to $6,000

DIRECT SUPPORT PROGRAMS
➤ **INDIVIDUAL ARTIST AWARDS**
Purpose: To identify, develop, and sustain artistic excellence in Maryland
Eligibility:
Citizenship: U.S.
Residency: Maryland
Age: 18 or older
Special Requirements: No students; previous grantees ineligible for 1 year
Art Forms: Choreography, fiction, media arts, music composition, new genres (collaborations, installations, interdisciplinary, multi-media, performance art), playwriting, poetry, crafts, painting, sculpture, works on paper, mixed media, photography
Type of Support: $2,500-$6,000

Scope of Program: 25 awards in 1991
Application/Selection Process:
  Deadline: November 9
  Preferred Initial Contact: Call or write for application/guidelines
  Application Procedure: Submit application form, samples of work
  Selection Process: Peer panel of artists, MSAC board
  Notification Process: Letter in May or June
  Formal Report of Grant Required: Yes

TECHNICAL ASSISTANCE PROGRAMS AND SERVICES
Programs of Special Interest: The MSAC maintains an artist registry.

MEDIA ALLIANCE

356 West 58th Street
New York, NY 10019
212-560-2919

EQUIPMENT ACCESS
Comments: The ON-LINE Program gives professional producers creating noncommercial artistic projects and documentaries access to state-of-the-art production and post-production services at commercial facilities in New York State at rates 50%-80% lower than commercial rates. Participating companies include Broadway Video, C.G.I., Editel, G.B.S. Video, LRP Video, Manhattan Transfer/Edit/ Digital, Technisphere, and TV-R Mastercolor. ($30 membership fee and $35 per project administrative fee required.)

TECHNICAL ASSISTANCE PROGRAMS AND SERVICES
Programs of Special Interest: Media Alliance maintains a mailing list of independent producers, publishes a bimonthly newsletter, and conducts workshops on managing and marketing the media arts. (Some services for members only; individual membership fees $20-$30; additional fees required for workshops.)

MEDIA NETWORK/ALTERNATIVE MEDIA INFORMATION CENTER

121 Fulton Street
Fifth Floor
New York, NY 10038
212-619-3455

TECHNICAL ASSISTANCE PROGRAMS AND SERVICES

Programs of Special Interest: Media Network acts as a nonprofit umbrella organization for independent film and video artists whose work addresses social, political, or cultural issues; screens selected works sponsored by the New York State Council on the Arts; and maintains a computer database and publishes catalogs of media works that address social issues.

METROPOLITAN REGIONAL ARTS COUNCIL (MRAC)

413 Wacouta Street
Suite 300
St. Paul, MN 55102
612-292-8010

PROFILE OF FINANCIAL SUPPORT TO ARTISTS

Total Funding/Value of In-Kind Support: n/a
Competition for Funding: n/a
Grant Range: n/a

DIRECT SUPPORT PROGRAMS

➤ ARTS PROJECT SUPPORT/MANAGEMENT ASSISTANCE

Purpose: To support nonprofit organizations or groups of 3 or more artists to undertake time-specific activities that produce art or provide services; Management Assistance grants fund projects intended to lead to the development of a formal arts organization
Eligibility:
    Special Requirements: Individual artists must apply in groups of 3 or more; project must take place in St. Paul metropolitan area; applicants must have matching funds; projects must not be exclusively for or by student organizations or schools
    Art Forms: All disciplines
Type of Support: Maximum $7,500 for up to 50% of project or program (match may include in-kind support)
Scope of Program: $260,000 budget for 1991

Application/Selection Process:
Deadline: January 31
Preferred Initial Contact: Call or write for information

MICHIANA ARTS AND SCIENCES COUNCIL, INC. (MASC)

P.O. Box 1543
South Bend, IN 46634
219-284-9160
CONTACT: LESLIE J. CHOITZ, ARTS PROGRAM DIRECTOR

PROFILE OF FINANCIAL SUPPORT TO ARTISTS

Total Funding/Value of In-Kind Support: $2,000 for FY 1990-91
Competition for Funding: Total applications, 10; total individuals funded/provided with in-kind support, 2
Grant Range: $1,000

DIRECT SUPPORT PROGRAMS

➤ **INDIVIDUAL ARTIST FELLOWSHIP PROGRAM**
Purpose: To foster the development of individual artists by funding the creation or completion of a project or activities significant to the artist's professional growth and recognition
Eligibility:
   Residency: St. Joseph, Elkhart, LaPorte, Kosciusko counties, 1 year
   Special Requirements: Must be emerging artist with less than 3 years professional stature; no high school or undergraduate students; Indiana Arts Commission fellowship recipients ineligible for 1 year
   Art Forms: All disciplines
Type of Support: $1,000
Scope of Program: 2 awards in FY 1990-91
Application/Selection Process:
   Deadline: Fall
   Preferred Initial Contact: Call or write for application/guidelines
   Application Procedure: Submit application form, samples of work, resumé, supporting materials (e.g., reviews)
   Selection Process: Peer panel of artists, board of directors
   Notification Process: Letter 6-8 weeks after deadline
   Formal Report of Funding Required: Yes

TECHNICAL ASSISTANCE PROGRAMS AND SERVICES

Programs of Special Interest: MASC maintains a resource library for the arts and a job bank, and sponsors workshops on funding and employment opportunities.

MICHIGAN COUNCIL FOR THE ARTS (MCA)

1200 Sixth Street
Detroit, MI 48226-2461
313-256-3731
TDD: 313-256-3734
CONTACT: BETTY BOONE, PROGRAM MANAGER

PROFILE OF FINANCIAL SUPPORT TO ARTISTS

Total Funding/Value of In-Kind Support: $595,000 for FY 1991

Competition for Funding: Total applications, 631; total individuals funded/provided with in-kind support, 88

Grant Range: $2,500-$10,000

DIRECT SUPPORT PROGRAMS

➤ **CREATIVE ARTISTS GRANTS**

Purpose: To enable Michigan artists to create new work or complete works-in-progress by providing funds that may be used for living expenses, materials, rent, presentation and documentation costs, and other expenses involved in producing original art

Eligibility:
  Residency: Michigan
  Special Requirements: Originating artists only; no students; previous grantees ineligible for 2 years
  Art Forms: All disciplines

Type of Support: Up to $10,000

Scope of Program: 88 awards, averaging $6,761, in FY 1991

Application/Selection Process:
  Deadline: April 5
  Preferred Initial Contact: Call or write for application/guidelines
  Application Procedure: Submit application form, samples of work, resumé, project budget
  Selection Process: Peer panel of artists, board of directors
  Notification Process: Letter
  Formal Report of Grant Required: Yes

TECHNICAL ASSISTANCE PROGRAMS AND SERVICES

Programs of Special Interest: MCA maintains a listing of Michigan artists.

MID ATLANTIC ARTS FOUNDATION

11 East Chase Street
Suite 2A
Baltimore, MD 21202
301-539-6656
TDD: 301-539-4241
CONTACT: HEATHER TUNIS, DIRECTOR OF VISUAL ARTS

TECHNICAL ASSISTANCE PROGRAMS AND SERVICES
Programs of Special Interest: Mid Atlantic Arts Foundation develops periodic technical assistance projects and schedules focus groups and networking sessions in conjunction with regional conferences, showcases, festivals, and exhibitions. The Arts Information Exchange Program (AIEX) database includes a Visual Arts Residencies: Sponsor Organization directory that profiles organizations that host visual and media artist residencies. The Visual Arts Residency Program supports two-week to three-month residencies by individual artists, including media artists, and professional art critics.

MILLENNIUM FILM WORKSHOP

66 East 4th Street
New York, NY 10003
212-673-0090

EQUIPMENT ACCESS
Film: Production and post-production for 16mm, Super 8
Comments: Equipment and facilities, including a production studio, are available at low cost to independent filmmakers, artists, and students. ($10 6-month membership fee and $20 monthly workshop fee required.)

TECHNICAL ASSISTANCE PROGRAMS AND SERVICES
Programs of Special Interest: Millennium screens independent films and offers low-cost workshops and seminars on film and video.

MILWAUKEE ARTS BOARD (MAB)

809 North Broadway
P.O. Box 324
Milwaukee, WI 53202
414-223-5790

PROFILE OF FINANCIAL SUPPORT TO ARTISTS
Total Funding/Value of In-Kind Support: n/a
Competition for Funding: n/a
Grant Range: n/a

DIRECT SUPPORT PROGRAMS
➤ **NEIGHBORHOOD ARTS PROGRAM**
Purpose: To assist nonprofit, neighborhood-based organizations in Milwaukee to strengthen their capacity to work with local artists and to provide local arts programming
Eligibility:
　　Residency: Preference given to Milwaukee artists
　　Special Requirements: Artists must apply with nonprofit sponsor organization that serves a particular Milwaukee neighborhood and whose governing board is composed primarily of community residents; project must serve a Milwaukee neighborhood; grant must be matched 1:1 (in-kind matches acceptable for first-time applicants)
　　Art Forms: All disciplines
Type of Support: Up to $7,000 matching grant
Scope of Program: n/a
Application/Selection Process:
　　Deadline: May 1
　　Preferred Initial Contact: Call or write for application/guidelines
　　Application Procedure: Sponsor submits application form, project budget, financial statement, artist's resumé
　　Selection Process: Peer panel of artists, individuals outside of organization, board of directors
　　Notification Process: Letter
　　Formal Report of Grant Required: Yes

TECHNICAL ASSISTANCE PROGRAMS AND SERVICES
Programs of Special Interest: MAB is developing a technical assistance workshop series.

MINNESOTA STATE ARTS BOARD

432 Summit Avenue
St. Paul, MN 55102
612-297-2603
CONTACT: KAREN MUELLER, ARTIST ASSISTANCE PROGRAM ASSOCIATE

PROFILE OF FINANCIAL SUPPORT TO ARTISTS
Total Funding/Value of In-Kind Support: $274,395 for FY 1990
Competition for Funding: Total applications, 730; total individuals funded/provided with in-kind support, 72
Grant Range: $400-$6,000

DIRECT SUPPORT PROGRAMS
➤ **ARTIST ASSISTANCE PROGRAM—FELLOWSHIPS/ CAREER OPPORTUNITY GRANTS**
Purpose: Fellowships support artists by providing time, materials, or living expenses; Career Opportunity Grants help artists take advantage of impending, concrete opportunities that will significantly advance their work or careers
Eligibility:
    Citizenship: U.S.
    Residency: Minnesota, 6 months
    Age: 18 or older
    Special Requirements: Professional artists only; previous fellowship recipients ineligible for 2 years; previous Career Opportunity Grant recipients ineligible for 1 year
    Art Forms: All disciplines
Type of Support: $6,000 fellowships; $100-$1,000 Career Opportunity Grants for specific project
Scope of Program: 34 fellowships for FY 1991; $20,000 a year available for Career Opportunity Grants
Application/Selection Process:
    Deadline: Mid-September for visual and media arts fellowships; quarterly for Career Opportunity Grants
    Preferred Initial Contact: Call or write for application/guidelines
    Application Procedure: Submit application form, samples of work, resumé, project proposal, project budget (Career Opportunity Grants only)
    Selection Process: Organization staff, board of directors, individuals outside of organization, peer panel of artists
    Notification Process: Letter 2 weeks after board or committee meeting
    Formal Report of Grant Required: Yes

TECHNICAL ASSISTANCE PROGRAMS AND SERVICES

Programs of Special Interest: Minnesota artists may apply through the arts board for 5-month residencies at the Headlands Center for the Arts in Sausalito, California. Artists with school residency experience may apply for inclusion in the Artists in Education Roster of Artists.

MISSISSIPPI ARTS COMMISSION

239 North Lamar Street
Suite 207
Jackson, MS 39201
601-359-6030
CONTACT: CINDY JETTER, PROGRAM ADMINISTRATOR

PROFILE OF FINANCIAL SUPPORT TO ARTISTS

Total Funding/Value of In-Kind Support: $25,000 for FY 1990

Competition for Funding: Total applications, 20; total individuals funded/provided with in-kind support, 5

Grant Range: $1,250-$5,000 in FY 1991

DIRECT SUPPORT PROGRAMS

➤ ARTIST FELLOWSHIPS

Purpose: To encourage and support the creation of new art and to recognize the contributions of artists of exceptional talent

Eligibility:
  Citizenship: U.S.
  Residency: Mississippi
  Age: 18 or older
  Special Requirements: No students; professional artists and folk artists only; previous grantees ineligible for 5 years
  Art Forms: Disciplines rotate on 3-year cycle among creative writing/music composition/folk arts (1990-1991); visual arts/choreography/film/video/media installations (1991-1992); and crafts/playwriting/screenwriting/new genres (1992-1993)

Type of Support: Up to $5,000 in 1991

Scope of Program: 5 awards in 1991

Application/Selection Process:
  Deadline: March 1
  Preferred Initial Contact: Call or write for application/guidelines
  Application Procedure: Submit application form, samples of work, resumé

Selection Process: Peer panel of artists, board of directors
Notification Process: Letter in early July
Formal Report of Grant Required: Yes

TECHNICAL ASSISTANCE PROGRAMS AND SERVICES

Programs of Special Interest: The Mississippi Arts Commission maintains an Arts in Education Residency Program Artist Roster (contact AIE Program Director). The commission's Arts Management Library holds books and periodicals covering a broad range of subjects relating to the arts and arts management and is open to the public.

MISSOURI ARTS COUNCIL

Wainwright Office Complex
111 North 7th Street
Suite 105
St. Louis, MO 63101-2188
314-340-6845

PROFILE OF FINANCIAL SUPPORT TO ARTISTS

Total Funding/Value of In-Kind Support: n/a
Competition for Funding: n/a
Grant Range: n/a

DIRECT SUPPORT PROGRAMS

➤ **CREATIVE ARTISTS' PROJECT**

CONTACT: PROGRAM ADMINISTRATOR

Purpose: To foster the creation of significant original work and to foster meaningful collaborations between creative artists and organizations interested in the development of such work

Eligibility:
   Residency: Missouri, 2 years
   Special Requirements: Originating artists only; no students in degree-granting programs; project must include a public component; artist must apply through a nonprofit sponsor; sponsors may submit only 1 application per year
   Art Forms: Music composition, choreography, literature, visual arts, film/video

Type of Support: Up to $5,000 matching grant for artists' fees not to exceed 50% of project cost (match may be any combination of cash and in-kind support)

Application/Selection Process:
   Deadline: January

Application Procedure: Sponsor submits application form, financial statement, project budget, artist's statement, samples of artist's work, artist's resumé
Selection Process: Organization staff, board of directors, advisory panel
Notification Process: After July 1
Formal Report of Grant Required: Yes

TECHNICAL ASSISTANCE PROGRAMS AND SERVICES
Programs of Special Interest: Artists selected for the Missouri Touring Program roster are eligible to tour Missouri communities to present arts-related activities including exhibitions, lecture-demonstrations, and residencies. The arts council hosts the annual Missouri Arts Conference, which includes a variety of technical assistance workshops for artists and arts organizations.

MONTANA ARTS COUNCIL (MAC)

48 North Last Chance Gulch
Helena, MT 59620
406-444-6430
CONTACT: JULIE SMITH, DIRECTOR OF ARTISTS SERVICES

PROFILE OF FINANCIAL SUPPORT TO ARTISTS
Total Funding/Value of In-Kind Support: $257,500 for FY 1990
Competition for Funding: Total applications, 200; total individuals funded/provided with in-kind support, 77
Grant Range: $2,000-$6,200

DIRECT SUPPORT PROGRAMS
➤ INDIVIDUAL ARTIST FELLOWSHIP PROGRAM
Purpose: To recognize, reward, and encourage outstanding professional artists in Montana
Eligibility:
  Residency: Montana
  Age: 18 or older
  Special Requirements: No students; previous grantees ineligible
  Art Forms: Dance, music, opera/musical theater, theater, visual arts, crafts, photography, media arts, literature (alternate years only)
Type of Support: $2,000
Scope of Program: 8 awards in 1990
Application/Selection Process:
  Deadline: May 1

Preferred Initial Contact: Call or write for application/guidelines
Application Procedure: Submit application form, samples of work, resumé, support materials (optional)
Selection Process: Peer panel of artists, board of directors
Notification Process: Phone call to recipients in early July; letter to nonrecipients
Formal Report of Grant Required: Yes

TECHNICAL ASSISTANCE PROGRAMS AND SERVICES
Programs of Special Interest: MAC provides technical assistance through telephone consultation and office visits, maintains a database of individual artists, and publishes *ArtistSearch*, a monthly bulletin describing competitions, job openings, and workshops. The council administers an Artists in Schools/Communities program that offers 1-week to 10-month residencies.

NATIONAL ENDOWMENT FOR THE ARTS, INTERNATIONAL ACTIVITIES OFFICE

Nancy Hanks Center
1100 Pennsylvania Avenue, NW
Washington, DC 20506
202-682-5422

CONTACT: GARY O. LARSON, PROGRAM OFFICER
Phone: 202-682-5562

PROFILE OF FINANCIAL SUPPORT TO ARTISTS
Total Funding/Value of In-Kind Support: $150,000 for FY 1991
Competition for Funding: Total applications, n/a; total individuals funded/provided with in-kind support, 5
Grant Range: n/a

DIRECT SUPPORT PROGRAMS
➤ **UNITED STATES/JAPAN ARTIST EXCHANGE FELLOWSHIP PROGRAM**
Purpose: To enable American artists to enrich their art by living and working in Japan, to observe Japanese artistic developments in their fields of interest, and to meet with their professional counterparts and pursue opportunities for artistic growth
Eligibility:
Citizenship: U.S. (permanent residents also eligible)
Special Requirement: No students; artists who have previously spent more than a total of 3 months in Japan are generally ineligible; artists may not earn additional income in Japan for lectures or demonstrations of their work

Art Forms: All disciplines

Type of Support: 6-month residency in Japan including 400,000 yen monthly living stipend, 100,000 yen monthly housing supplement, up to 100,000 yen monthly for professional support services, roundtrip travel for artist, spouse, and children; stipend for Japanese language study in U.S. available if necessary

Scope of Program: 5 residencies per year

Application/Selection Process:
  Deadline: November for media arts
  Preferred Initial Contact: Contact appropriate discipline program for application/guidelines (media arts contact Susan Lively 202-682-5452)
  Application Procedure: Submit application form, samples of work, references, resumé, financial statement, project budget to appropriate discipline program
  Selection Process: Discipline panels, American Selection Committee of artists and arts managers, Japanese Agency for Cultural Affairs
  Notification Process: Letter
  Formal Report of Grant Required: Yes

NATIONAL ENDOWMENT FOR THE ARTS, MEDIA ARTS PROGRAM

Nancy Hanks Center
1100 Pennsylvania Avenue, NW
Room 720
Washington, DC 20506
202-682-5452

PROFILE OF FINANCIAL SUPPORT TO ARTISTS

Total Funding/Value of In-Kind Support: $1,135,000 in Film/Video Production and Radio/Audio Production grants to individuals and organizations for 1990

Competition for Funding: Total applications, 559; total individuals and organizations funded/provided with in-kind support, 72

Grant Range: $3,000-$35,000 for individuals

DIRECT SUPPORT PROGRAMS

➤ **FILM/VIDEO PRODUCTION GRANTS**

CONTACT: MARY SMITH, PROGRAM SPECIALIST

Purpose: To support the creation or completion of film or video artworks of the highest quality

Eligibility:
   Citizenship: U.S. (permanent residents also eligible)
   Special Requirements: Must have substantial professional experience; instructional, promotional, and student projects ineligible; documentation or simple recordings of performances or events for archival purposes are ineligible
   Art Forms: Film, video
Type of Support: $10,000-$35,000 grants for individual producers
Scope of Program: $835,000 granted to individuals and organizations in 1990
Application/Selection Process:
   Deadline: November 1
   Preferred Initial Contact: Call or write for application/guidelines
   Application Procedure: Submit application form, samples of work, project description and budget, screenplay or treatment (if available), reviews (optional)
   Selection Process: Peer panel, National Council on the Arts, NEA chair
   Notification Process: Letter in July
   Formal Report of Grant Required: Yes

NATIONAL ENDOWMENT FOR THE ARTS, VISUAL ARTS PROGRAM

Nancy Hanks Center
1100 Pennsylvania Avenue, NW
Room 729
Washington, DC 20506
202-682-5448
CONTACT: SILVIO LIM, PROGRAM SPECIALIST

PROFILE OF FINANCIAL SUPPORT TO ARTISTS
Total Funding/Value of In-Kind Support: $2,130,000 for FY 1990
Competition for Funding: Total applications, 5,353; total individuals funded/provided with in-kind support, 177
Grant Range: $5,000-$20,000

DIRECT SUPPORT PROGRAMS
Purpose: To encourage the creative development of professional artists, enabling them to pursue their work
Eligibility:
   Citizenship: U.S. (permanent residents also eligible)

Special Requirements: Professional artists only; no students pursuing undergraduate or graduate degrees; previous recipients who received $15,000 or more ineligible for 2 cycles; artists may apply in only 1 fellowship area per cycle

Art Forms: Eligible media rotate on 2-year cycle; new genres (includes conceptual, performance, video), painting, works on paper (includes printmaking, drawing, artists' books) eligible in odd-numbered years; photography, sculpture, crafts eligible in even-numbered years

Type of Support: $15,000 fellowships in 1991-92

Scope of Program: $2,130,000 awarded to 177 artists in FY 1990

Application/Selection Process:

Deadline: January-March (exact date depends on medium)

Preferred Initial Contact: Call or write for application/guidelines

Application Procedure: Submit application form, samples of work, resumé

Selection Process: Peer panel of artists, National Council on the Arts, NEA chair

Notification Process: Letter in September

Formal Report of Grant Required: Yes

NATIONAL ENDOWMENT FOR THE HUMANITIES, MEDIA PROGRAM

1100 Pennsylvania Avenue, NW
Washington, DC 20506
202-786-0278

PROFILE OF FINANCIAL SUPPORT TO ARTISTS

Total Funding/Value of In-Kind Support: $9,000,000 for FY 1990 (includes grants to organizations)

Competition for Funding: Total applications, 253; total individuals funded/provided with in-kind support, 45

Grant Range: Up to $600,000

DIRECT SUPPORT PROGRAMS

➤ HUMANITIES PROJECTS IN MEDIA

Purpose: To provide support for the planning, scripting, or production of film, television, and radio programs on humanities subjects

Eligibility:

Citizenship: U.S. (permanent residents also eligible)

Special Requirements: Projects must involve humanities subjects and be suited for a national audience; projects must involve collaborations among humanities scholars and experienced producers, directors, and writers

Art Forms: Film, video, radio
Type of Support: Planning grants, up to $20,000; scripting grants, $20,000-$60,000; production grants, $150,000-$600,000
Scope of Program: $9,000,000 awarded annually
Application/Selection Process:
    Deadline: Mid-September, Mid-March
    Preferred Initial Contact: Call or write for information
    Notification Process: Letter or phone call
    Formal Report of Grant Required: Yes

NATIONAL FOUNDATION FOR ADVANCEMENT IN THE ARTS (NFAA)

3915 Biscayne Boulevard
4th Floor
Miami, FL 33137
305-573-0490
CONTACT: WILLIAM H. BANCHS, PH.D., VICE PRESIDENT, PROGRAMS

PROFILE OF FINANCIAL SUPPORT TO ARTISTS
Total Funding/Value of In-Kind Support: $193,000 for FY 1990
Competition for Funding: Total applications, 5,200; total individuals funded/provided with in-kind support, 111
Grant Range: $500-$5,000

DIRECT SUPPORT PROGRAMS
➤ **CAREER ADVANCEMENT OF VISUAL ARTISTS (CAVA)**
Purpose: To provide unencumbered work time, an opportunity to travel and work in a different environment, and professional exposure for young artists who have completed their formal education
Eligibility:
    Citizenship: U.S. (permanent residents eligible)
    Age: 19-39
    Special Requirements: Must have completed formal education at least 1 year ago
    Art Forms: Visual arts, photography, media arts
Type of Support: 4-month residencies in Miami including transportation, living and studio facilities, supplies, and $1,000 monthly stipend; residents' work exhibited at Bass Museum of Art, Miami Beach; residencies renewable annually for up to 3 years
Scope of Program: 3 new residencies per year
Application/Selection Process:
    Deadline: October 1

Preferred Initial Contact: Call or write for application/guidelines
Application Procedure: Submit application form, samples of work
Selection Process: Individuals outside of organization
Notification Process: Letter in mid-November

NATIVE AMERICAN PUBLIC BROADCASTING CONSORTIUM, INC.

P.O. Box 83111
Lincoln, NE 68501
402-472-3522
CONTACT: MATTHEW L. JONES

PROFILE OF FINANCIAL SUPPORT TO ARTISTS
Total Funding/Value of In-Kind Support: n/a
Competition for Funding: Total applications, 143; total individuals funded/provided with in-kind support, 25
Grant Range: $2,500-$50,000

DIRECT SUPPORT PROGRAMS
➤ NATIVE AMERICAN PROGRAM GRANTS
Purpose: To support film and video projects that address Native American subjects
Eligibility:
    Age: 21 or older
    Special Requirements: Work should address Native American issues
    Art Forms: Film, video
Type of Support: $2,500-$50,000
Scope of Program: 25 awards
Application/Selection Process:
    Preferred Initial Contact: Call for application form
    Application Procedure: Submit application form, additional materials as requested
    Selection Process: Panel review

Nevada State Council on the Arts (NSCA)

329 Flint Street
Reno, NV 89501
702-688-1225
Contact: Kirk Robertson, Program Director

Profile of Financial Support to Artists

Total Funding/Value of In-Kind Support: $73,145 for FY 1990
(includes Artist-in-Residence program)
Competition for Funding: Total applications, 80; total individuals
funded/provided with in-kind support, 43
Grant Range: $250-$5,000

Direct Support Programs

➤ **FELLOWSHIPS/MINI-GRANTS**

Purpose: Fellowships assist artists' efforts to advance their careers
by supporting the creation of new works; mini-grants provide short-
term project support to meet immediate needs
Eligibility:
  Citizenship: U.S. (resident aliens also eligible)
  Residency: Nevada, 1 year
  Special Requirements: No students
  Art Forms: All disciplines
Type of Support: $2,000-$10,000 fellowships; up to $1,000
mini-grants
Scope of Program: $20,000 in fellowships, $20,000 in mini-grants
awarded annually
Application/Selection Process:
  Deadline: May 15 (fellowships), 90 days before project
  (mini-grants)
  Preferred Initial Contact: Call or write for application/guidelines
  Application Procedure: Submit application form, samples of
  work, references, resumé, project budget
  Selection Process: Peer panel of artists, board of directors (fellow-
  ship); executive director, chairman (mini-grants)
  Notification Process: Letter
  Formal Report of Grant Required: Yes

Technical Assistance Programs and Services

Programs of Special Interest: The Artist-in-Residence program
provides residencies for practicing, professional artists in a variety
of settings.

New Brunswick Department of Tourism, Recreation and Heritage—Arts Branch

P.O. Box 12345
Fredericton, New Brunswick
Canada E3B 5C3
506-453-2555
CONTACT: ARTS BRANCH STAFF

Profile of Financial Support to Artists

Total Funding/Value of In-Kind Support: $363,700 for 1991
Competition for Funding: n/a
Grant Range: Up to $10,000

Direct Support Programs

➤ **TRAVEL PROGRAM**

Purpose: To increase participation in regional, national, and international festivals, fairs, and competitions, and to increase exposure of New Brunswick arts products

Eligibility:
  Citizenship: Canada (landed immigrants also eligible)
  Residency: New Brunswick, 2 of past 4 years
  Age: 18 or older
  Special Requirements: Must have received recognized honor at the provincial level or provide a letter of invitation
  Art Forms: All disciplines

Type of Support: Maximum $5,000 for up to 30% of costs

Scope of Program: $25,000 annual budget

Application/Selection Process:
  Deadline: March 15, September 15 (at least 60 days before event)
  Application Procedure: Submit application form, supporting materials as specified
  Selection Procedure: Multi-disciplinary jury of professional artists
  Notification Process: Letter 2 months after deadline
  Formal Report of Grant Required: Yes

➤ **PRODUCTION AND CREATION GRANTS**

Purpose: To support research and development or approved projects by artists or curators

Eligibility:
  Citizenship: Canada (landed immigrants also eligible)
  Residency: New Brunswick, 2 of past 4 years
  Art Forms: All disciplines

Type of Support: $1,000-$6,000 grants

Scope of Program: $182,000 annual budget
Application/Selection Process:
  Deadline: January 15, July 15
  Application Procedure: Submit application form, supporting materials as specified
  Selection Process: Multi-disciplinary jury of professional artists
  Notification Process: Letter 2 months after deadline
  Formal Report of Grant Required: Yes

➤ **EXCELLENCE AWARDS**

Purpose: To reward and honor excellence in the arts
Eligibility:
  Citizenship: Canada (landed immigrants also eligible)
  Residency: New Brunswick, 2 of past 4 years
  Special Requirements: Must be nominated by an individual or group
  Art Forms: Visual arts, literature, crafts, performing arts, cinematic arts
Type of Support: Cash prize
Scope of Program: $35,000 distributed according to jury's discretion
Application/Selection Process:
  Deadline: September 15 for nominations
  Application Procedure: Nominator submits nomination form, supporting materials as specified
  Selection Process: Multi-disciplinary jury of professional artists
  Notification Process: Letter 2 months after deadline
  Formal Report of Grant Required: No

NEW ENGLAND FOUNDATION FOR THE ARTS (NEFA)

678 Massachusetts Avenue
Suite 801
Cambridge, MA 02139
617-492-2914
CONTACT: MS. BJ LARSON-BREWER, PROGRAM COORDINATOR

PROFILE OF FINANCIAL SUPPORT TO ARTISTS

Total Funding/Value of In-Kind Support: $111,000 for FY 1989 (for fellowships only)
Competition for Funding: Total applications, 691; total individuals funded/provided with in-kind support, 33
Grant Range: Up to $5,000

Direct Support Programs
➤ NEW FORMS REGIONAL INITIATIVE

Purpose: To support projects by lesser-known artists whose work explores new definitions of cultures, artistic disciplines, or traditions and is not easily defined by historical Western-European fine arts traditions

Eligibility:
  Citizenship: U.S. (permanent residents also eligible)
  Residency: Connecticut, Maine, Massachusetts, New Hampshire, Rhode Island, Vermont
  Special Requirements: No students
  Art Forms: Experimental work that is innovative in form or content, collaborative or traditional work that explores new forms or contexts (eligible projects include performance art, multi-media, installations, dance, environmental work, textiles, theater work)

Type of Support: $2,000-$5,000 for project support

Scope of Program: 6-12 awards available in FY 1990-91

Application/Selection Process:
  Deadline: January 31
  Preferred Initial Contact: Call or write for application/guidelines
  Application Procedure: Submit application form, samples of work, resumé, project budget and description
  Selection Process: Peer panel of artists
  Notification Process: Letter

➤ MIXED SIGNALS CABLE TELEVISION SERIES

Purpose: To bring the work of outstanding film and video artists to New England audiences
  Art Forms: Film, video

Type of Support: Work broadcast on Mixed Signals, a New England cable television series; artists paid $30 per running minute

Scope of Program: 16-20 recipients per year

Application/Selection Process:
  Deadline: Fall, Spring
  Preferred Initial Contact: Call for application/guidelines
  Application Procedure: Submit film or video (up to 56 minutes in length)
  Selection Process: Curator
  Notification Process: Letter

Technical Assistance Programs and Services
Programs of Special Interest: Through the Exhibition Touring Program, the foundation sponsors the circulation of visual and media arts exhibits in New England and nationwide.

NEW HAMPSHIRE STATE COUNCIL ON THE ARTS (NHSCA)

40 North Main Street
Concord, NH 03301
603-271-2789
TDD: 603-225-4033
CONTACT: AUDREY SYLVESTER, ARTIST SERVICES COORDINATOR

PROFILE OF FINANCIAL SUPPORT TO ARTISTS

Total Funding/Value of In-Kind Support: $23,000 for FY 1991
Competition for Funding: Total applications, 125; total individuals funded/provided with in-kind support, 16
Grant Range: $500-$2,000

DIRECT SUPPORT PROGRAMS

➤ **INDIVIDUAL ARTIST FELLOWSHIPS**

Purpose: To recognize artistic excellence and professional commitment
Eligibility:
　　Residency: New Hampshire, 1 year
　　Age: 19 or older
　　Special Requirements: Must demonstrate professional commitment; no full-time students; previous recipients ineligible for 1 year
　　Art Forms: All disciplines
Type of Support: $1,000-$2,000 Fellowships; finalists eligible to apply for up to $500 matching cash Artist Opportunity Grant for professional development project; Fellowship winners asked to make public presentation of their work
Scope of Program: 10 Fellowships, 6 Artist Opportunity Grants in FY 1991
Application/Selection Process:
　　Deadline: May 1
　　Preferred Initial Contact: Call or write for application/guidelines
　　Application Procedure: Submit application form, samples of work, resumé
　　Selection Process: Peer panel of artists
　　Notification Process: Letter or phone call in October
　　Formal Report of Grant Required: Yes

TECHNICAL ASSISTANCE PROGRAMS AND SERVICES

Programs of Special Interest: NHSCA maintains a roster of professional artists eligible for Arts in Education residencies (contact Arts in Education Coordinator).

NEW JERSEY STATE COUNCIL ON THE ARTS (NJSCA)

4 North Broad Street
CN 306
Trenton, NJ 08625
609-292-6130
CONTACT: KATHI R. LEVIN, DIRECTOR OF FUNDING AND ARTS
MANAGEMENT SERVICES

PROFILE OF FINANCIAL SUPPORT TO ARTISTS

Total Funding/Value of In-Kind Support: $498,000 for FY 1991

Competition for Funding: Total applications, 1,072; total individuals funded/provided with in-kind support, 68

Grant Range: $5,000-$12,000

DIRECT SUPPORT PROGRAMS

➤ FELLOWSHIP AWARDS

Purpose: To enable experienced, professional artists to set aside time and to purchase materials to create original works of art

Eligibility:
   Residency: New Jersey
   Special Requirements: No students; previous grantees ineligible for 3 years
   Art Forms: Choreography, crafts, design arts, experimental art, film, graphics, interdisciplinary, music composition, painting, photography, playwriting, prose, poetry, sculpture, video

Type of Support: $5,000 to $15,000

Scope of Program: 68 awards, averaging $7,000, in 1991

Application/Selection Process:
   Deadline: March
   Preferred Initial Contact: Call or write for application/guidelines
   Application Procedure: Submit application form, samples of work, resumé
   Selection Process: Peer panel of artists
   Notification Process: Letter 6 months after deadline
   Formal Report of Grant Required: Yes

TECHNICAL ASSISTANCE PROGRAMS AND SERVICES

Programs of Special Interest: The Artists-in-Education (AIE) program determines artists' eligibility for 4-day to 4-month residencies in schools, communities, and correctional facilities.

NEW LANGTON ARTS

1246 Folsom
San Francisco, CA 94103
415-626-5416

PROFILE OF FINANCIAL SUPPORT TO ARTISTS

Total Funding/Value of In-Kind Support: $44,000

Competition for Funding: Total applications, 225; total individuals funded/provided with in-kind support, 13

Grant Range: $3,000-$5,000

DIRECT SUPPORT PROGRAMS

➤ NEW FORMS REGIONAL INITIATIVE

Purpose: To support individual artists working on interdisciplinary or collaborative projects

Eligibility:
  Residency: Northern California, Oregon, Washington State, Alaska
  Art Forms: Dance, literature, performance art, film, video, visual arts

Type of Support: $3,000-$5,000

Scope of Program: 9-13 awards per year

Application/Selection Process:
  Deadline: Early Spring
  Preferred Initial Contact: Write for application after November 1 (include SASE)
  Application Procedure: Submit application form, samples of work, project budget, supporting documentation
  Selection Process: Independent review panel of artists
  Notification Process: Letter
  Formal Report of Grant Required: Yes

TECHNICAL ASSISTANCE PROGRAMS AND SERVICES

Programs of Special Interest: New Langton Arts maintains a video screening room for exhibitions.

NEW LIBERTY PRODUCTIONS (NLP)

3500 Lancaster Avenue
Philadelphia, PA 19104
215-387-2296

EQUIPMENT ACCESS
Film: Production and post-production for 16mm
Video: Post-production for VHS (off-line)
Comments: NLP provides artists with low-cost access to equipment.

TECHNICAL ASSISTANCE PROGRAMS AND SERVICES
Programs of Special Interest: NLP serves as a fiscal sponsor for media artists.

NEW MEXICO ARTS DIVISION

224 East Palace Avenue
Santa Fe, NM 87501
505-827-6490

PROFILE OF FINANCIAL SUPPORT TO ARTISTS
Total Funding/Value of In-Kind Support: n/a
Competition for Funding: n/a
Grant Range: n/a

DIRECT SUPPORT PROGRAMS
➤ ARTS PROJECTS—CULTURALLY DIVERSE ARTS PROJECTS/OTHER ARTS PROJECTS
CONTACT: GRANTS AND SERVICES OFFICE STAFF
Purpose: Culturally Diverse Arts Projects recognize culturally specific and multi-cultural arts in New Mexico by procuring short-term arts services from those who practice such arts; Other Arts Projects support projects in all disciplines that do not meet eligibility requirements for Folk Arts or Culturally Diverse Arts
Eligibility:
  Residency: Projects involving New Mexico artists encouraged
  Special Requirements: Artists must apply with a nonprofit organization that agrees to act as a fiscal agent; project must be publicly presented in New Mexico; Other Arts Project applicants must provide 1:1 cash match of grant; Culturally Diverse Arts Projects applicants must provide cash matches after 2 years of funding; Culturally Diverse Arts Projects must be by and for

culturally specific groups (Hispanic, American Indian, African-American, Asian-American artists encouraged to apply)
Art Forms: All disciplines
Type of Support: Up to $5,000
Scope of Program: n/a
Application/Selection Process:
  Deadline: March 1
  Preferred Initial Contact: Consult with Grants and Services Office staff
  Application Procedure: Fiscal agent submits application forms, samples of artist's work, artist's resumé, project budget
  Selection Process: Peer panel of artists, commission
  Notification Process: July
  Formal Report of Grant Required: Yes

TECHNICAL ASSISTANCE PROGRAMS AND SERVICES

Programs of Special Interest: Artists selected for the Arts in Education (AIE) program's Resource Directory for Presenters and Artists are eligible for residencies in community, rural, and institutional settings (contact AIE staff, 505-827-6490). The Southwest Arts Conference, which takes place in Scottsdale, Arizona, each March, offers workshops for artists.

NEW ORLEANS VIDEO ACCESS CENTER (NOVAC)

2010 Magazine Street
New Orleans, LA 70130-5018
504-524-8626

EQUIPMENT ACCESS

Video: Production and post-production for 3/4", S-VHS
Comments: NOVAC equipment and facilities are available at low rates to independent producers working on original projects that evidence innovation or experimentation, or that deal with subject matter not traditionally supported by commercial financing. ($15 annual membership required.)

TECHNICAL ASSISTANCE PROGRAMS AND SERVICES

Programs of Special Interest: NOVAC is a membership organization that offers basic and advanced video workshops, fiscal sponsorship, internships, information on resources and opportunities, and a bimonthly newsletter that includes job listings for video professionals. NOVAC exhibits the works of local and international artists. (Fees required for some services.)

NEW YORK CITY DEPARTMENT OF CULTURAL AFFAIRS (DCA)

2 Columbus Circle
New York, NY 10019
212-974-1150

PROFILE OF FINANCIAL SUPPORT TO ARTISTS
Total Funding/Value of In-Kind Support: n/a
Competition for Funding: n/a
Grant Range: n/a

DIRECT SUPPORT PROGRAMS
➤ **MATERIALS FOR THE ARTS (MFA)**
CONTACT: SUSAN GLASS, DIRECTOR, MATERIALS FOR THE ARTS, 410 WEST 16TH STREET, FOURTH FLOOR, NEW YORK, NY 10011
Phone: 212-255-5924
Purpose: To link materials donations from both private and governmental sources to nonprofit cultural organizations and individual artists involved in public projects
Eligibility:
Special Requirements: Must be working with a registered, nonprofit cultural organization on a specific project in a public setting in New York City
Art Forms: All disciplines
Type of Support: Donated equipment, furniture, and supplies
Scope of Program: Over $1,000,000 in goods distributed to 819 organizations in FY 1989
Application/Selection Process:
Application Procedure: Submit resumé, proposal, letter from 1 sponsoring organization

TECHNICAL ASSISTANCE PROGRAMS AND SERVICES
Programs of Special Interest: The Arts Apprenticeship Program (AAP) assists young artists, students, and arts administrators to bridge the gap between their education and careers by promoting professional experience through training with artists and nonprofit cultural organizations.

NEW YORK FOUNDATION FOR THE ARTS (NYFA)

5 Beekman Street, #600
New York, NY 10038
212-233-3900
CONTACT: DAVID GREEN, DIRECTOR, COMMUNICATIONS

PROFILE OF FINANCIAL SUPPORT TO ARTISTS

Total Funding/Value of In-Kind Support: $1,647,000 for FY 1990
Competition for Funding: Total applications, 7,000; total individuals funded/provided with in-kind support, 241
Grant Range: $7,000

DIRECT SUPPORT PROGRAMS

➤ **ARTISTS' FELLOWSHIPS**

CONTACT: PENELOPE DANNENBERG, DIRECTOR, ARTISTS' FELLOWSHIPS

Purpose: To support individual, originating artists from diverse cultures and at all stages of professional development
Eligibility:
  Residency: New York State, 2 years
  Age: 18 or older
  Special Requirements: Originating artists only; no students; previous grantees ineligible for 3 years
  Art Forms: Fiction, nonfiction literature, playwriting/screenwriting, poetry, crafts, film, photography, printmaking/drawing/artists' books, music composition, painting, sculpture, architecture, choreography, performance art/emergent forms, video
Type of Support: $7,000
Scope of Program: 241 awards in FY 1990
Application/Selection Process:
  Deadline: September-October, depending on discipline
  Preferred Initial Contact: Call or write for application/guidelines
  Application Procedure: Submit application form, samples of work, resumé
  Selection Process: Peer panel of artists
  Notification Process: Letter in early April
  Formal Report of Grant Required: Yes

TECHNICAL ASSISTANCE PROGRAMS AND SERVICES

Programs of Special Interest: The Artists' New Works sponsorship program helps independent film and video artists find funding for projects (contact Lynda Hansen, Director, Artists' New Works). American Independents and Features Abroad (AIFA) represents independently-made American film and video at the Berlin Film Festival, its European Film Market, and other international film festivals and markets. The foundation's Communications Program holds workshops, conferences, and seminars to educate artists about advocacy and lobbying efforts and opportunities for fellowships, project support, residencies in schools, sponsorship, and emergency financial assistance for personal needs. The Artists in Residence Program awards matching grants to organizations to support school and community residencies. The annual Common Ground conference addresses the concerns of arts councils, individual artists, and educators. The free quarterly newsletter *FYI* contains information on career opportunities and grants deadlines.

NEW YORK STATE COUNCIL ON THE ARTS (NYSCA)

915 Broadway
New York, NY 10010
212-614-2900 (general)/212-614-3988 (Individual Artists Program)
CONTACT: LINDA EARLE, DIRECTOR, INDIVIDUAL ARTISTS PROGRAM

PROFILE OF FINANCIAL SUPPORT TO ARTISTS
Total Funding/Value of In-Kind Support: $1,557,982 for FY 1990
Competition for Funding: Total applications, 1,021; total individuals funded/provided with in-kind support, 146
Grant Range: $2,500-$25,000

DIRECT SUPPORT PROGRAMS
➤ **INDIVIDUAL ARTISTS PROGRAM**
Purpose: To provide financial support that allows artists to create, develop, and present new work
Eligibility:
   Residency: New York State
   Age: 18 or older
   Special Requirements: No students; artists must find a sponsoring nonprofit organization to submit an application on their behalf
   Art Forms: Visual arts (including photography and crafts), music composition, theater commissions (directing, playwriting, design), film, electronic media (including video art and audio art)
Type of Support: Up to $25,000 for project
Scope of Program: 146 awards in FY 1990 (68 in film and media production)
Application/Selection Process:
   Deadline: March 1 (for sponsor's application)
   Preferred Initial Contact: Call for guidelines
   Application Procedure: Sponsor submits application form (artist provides project description for application); artist later submits

supplemental application form, expanded project description, artist's statement (optional), resumé, itemized budget, samples of work
Selection Process: Peer panel of artists, council committee, and board of directors
Notification Process: Letter in 6-8 months after deadline
Formal Report of Grant Required: Yes

911 MEDIA ARTS CENTER

117 Yale Avenue North
Seattle, WA 98109
206-682-6552
CONTACT: ROBIN REIDY, DIRECTOR

EQUIPMENT ACCESS

Video: Production for Hi-8; post-production for VHS, 3/4"
Comments: 911 provides equipment access at low rates to independent producers ($25 membership fee required). Editing grants are also available.

TECHNICAL ASSISTANCE PROGRAMS AND SERVICES

Programs of Special Interest: 911 screens films and videos, maintains a video art library and offers a grantwriting class, media production workshops, and fiscal sponsorship services.

NORTH CAROLINA ARTS COUNCIL

Department of Cultural Resources
Raleigh, NC 27611
919-733-2111
CONTACT: NANCY TROVILLION, ASSISTANT DIRECTOR

PROFILE OF FINANCIAL SUPPORT TO ARTISTS

Total Funding/Value of In-Kind Support: $275,000 (estimate) for FY 1988-89
Competition for Funding: Total applications, 497; total individuals funded/provided with in-kind support, 41
Grant Range: $5,000-$8,000

DIRECT SUPPORT PROGRAMS

➤ **FELLOWSHIPS/PROJECT GRANTS**
CONTACT: VISUAL ARTS DIRECTOR
Purpose: Fellowships recognize exemplary originating artists who have made career commitments to their art; Project Grants support the realization of specific artistic projects by professional artists

Eligibility:
Residency: North Carolina, 1 year
Special Requirements: No students in degree-granting programs; previous grantees ineligible for 3-5 years
Art Forms: Fellowships for music composition, playwriting, visual arts (including photography, crafts, film, video), literature, choreography (offered in odd-numbered years only); Project Grants for visual arts (including photography, crafts, film, video), dance, folk arts
Type of Support: $5,000-$8,000 Fellowships in 1990; up to $5,000 Project Grants
Scope of Program: 26 Fellowships in FY 1987-88; 5 Project Grants in FY 1987-88
Application/Selection Process:
Deadline: February 1
Preferred Initial Contact: Call or write for application
Application Procedure: Submit application form, samples of work, references (optional), resumé, project budget (Project Grants only)
Selection Process: Individuals from outside of organization
Notification Process: Letter within 5 months of deadline
Formal Report of Grant Required: Yes

➤ **LA NAPOULE FOUNDATION RESIDENCY**

CONTACT: VISUAL ARTS DIRECTOR

Purpose: To support long-time residents of North Carolina whose work will significantly advance as a result of an international experience
Eligibility:
Residency: North Carolina
Art Forms: Visual arts, literature (fiction, poetry)
Type of Support: 2- to 4-month residency at the La Napoule Foundation in Southern France, including studio space, housing, meals, travel to and from La Napoule, $1,000 stipend
Scope of Program: 2 residencies (1 visual arts, 1 literature)
Application/Selection Process:
Deadline: February 1
Preferred Initial Contact: Call or write for information
Selection Process: Individuals from outside of organization
Notification Process: June

➤ **DOCUMENTARY PROJECTS**

CONTACT: FOLKLIFE SECTION
Phone: 919-733-7897

Purpose: To encourage the preservation of North Carolina's traditional culture by the professional application of modern documentary technology

Eligibility:
    Special Requirements: Individual or organization must have substantial knowledge of North Carolina's folk art traditions and expertise in professional documentation techniques; preference to projects partly funded by other sources
    Art Forms: Media arts, photography
Type of Support: Up to $10,000; copy of documentation must deposited in archive
Scope of Program: n/a
Application/Selection Process:
    Deadline: March 1
    Preferred Initial Contact: Contact Folklife staff before applying
    Application Procedure: Submit application form, samples of work, resumé, letters of support
    Selection Process: Panel of professional folklife specialists
    Notification Process: Within 4 months of deadline
    Formal Report of Grant Required: Yes

TECHNICAL ASSISTANCE PROGRAMS AND SERVICES

Programs of Special Interest: Artists may submit applications for placement on the North Carolina Arts Council Resident Artists Roster; rostered artists may be considered for residencies in the council's Artists-in-Schools and Visiting Artist programs. North Carolina artists may contact the council for information about 8-week residencies available at the Headlands Center for the Arts in Sausalito, California.

NORTH DAKOTA COUNCIL ON THE ARTS (NDCA)

Black Building
Suite 606
Fargo, ND 58102
701-237-8962
CONTACT: LILA HAUGE, ARTISTS AND EDUCATION SERVICES COORDINATOR

PROFILE OF FINANCIAL SUPPORT TO ARTISTS

Total Funding/Value of In-Kind Support: $25,000 for FY 1991 (includes Professional Development Grants to arts professionals)
Competition for Funding: Total applications, 21; total individuals funded/provided with in-kind support, 9
Grant Range: Up to $5,000

DIRECT SUPPORT PROGRAMS
➤ **ARTIST FELLOWSHIPS**
Purpose: To assist North Dakota artists in furthering their careers

Eligibility:
    Citizenship: U.S.
    Residency: North Dakota
    Age: 18 or older
    Special Requirements: No students pursuing college degrees
    Art Forms: Dance, music, opera/musical theater, theater, visual arts, crafts, photography, media arts, literature
Type of Support: $5,000 in FY 1991
Scope of Program: 3 awards in FY 1991
Application/Selection Process:
    Preferred Initial Contact: Call or write for application/guidelines
    Application Procedure: Submit application form, samples of work, resumé
    Selection Process: Panel of artists and arts professionals
    Notification Process: 6 weeks after deadline
    Formal Report of Grant Required: Yes

➤ **PROFESSIONAL DEVELOPMENT GRANTS**
CONTACT: BRAD STEPHENSON OR LILA HAUGE

Purpose: To provide artists and nonartists with funds for informational/educational opportunities related to the arts and arts development, or for consultants and technical or artistic advice
Eligibility:
    Residency: North Dakota
    Special Requirements: No students
    Art Forms: All disciplines
Type of Support: Up to $300 for professional development project
Scope of Program: $10,000 awarded to individuals and organizations in FY 1991
Application/Selection Process:
    Deadline: None
    Preferred Initial Contact: Call or write for application/guidelines
    Application Procedure: Submit application form, resumé, 2 letters of recommendation
    Selection Process: NDCA Community Programs Committee
    Notification Process: Letter
    Formal Report of Grant Required: Yes

TECHNICAL ASSISTANCE PROGRAMS AND SERVICES

Programs of Special Interest: The NDCA, in conjunction with the South Dakota Arts Council, sponsors the biennial Dakota Arts Congress for artists and arts professionals. The "Opportunities" section of the NDCA's bimonthly newsletter describes other available programs.

NORTHEAST HISTORIC FILM

Route 175
Blue Hill Falls, ME 04615
207-374-2736

EQUIPMENT ACCESS

Film: Post-production for 16mm, 35mm
Video: Post-production for VHS
Comments: Northeast Historic Film's main function is to serve as a regional archive for film and video, but post-production equipment is available at low rates to independent producers. Members receive preference in equipment access.

NORTHWEST FILM AND VIDEO CENTER/OREGON ART INSTITUTE (NWFVC)

1219 S.W. Park Avenue
Portland, OR 97205
503-221-1156
CONTACT: BILL FOSTER, DIRECTOR

PROFILE OF FINANCIAL SUPPORT TO ARTISTS

Total Funding/Value of In-Kind Support: $60,000 annually
Competition for Funding: Total applications, 300 (average); total individuals funded/provided with in-kind support, 12-15
Grant Range: Up to $5,000

DIRECT SUPPORT PROGRAMS

➤ WESTERN STATES REGIONAL MEDIA ARTS FELLOWSHIPS (WSRMAF)
CONTACT: COORDINATOR, WSRMAF

Purpose: To assist independent media artists whose work shows exceptional promise and demonstrates commitment
Eligibility:
  Citizenship: U.S.
  Residency: Alaska, Arizona, California, Colorado, Hawaii, Idaho, Montana, Nevada, New Mexico, Oregon, Utah, Washington State, Wyoming, Pacific territories
  Art Forms: Film, video
Type of Support: Up to $5,000
Scope of Program: 12-15 grants, totalling $60,000, per year

Application/Selection Process:
Deadline: August 15
Preferred Initial Contact: Write for application/guidelines
Application Procedure: Submit application form, supporting materials as requested
Selection Process: Jury
Notification Process: 2 months after deadline
Formal Report of Grant Required: Yes

EQUIPMENT ACCESS
Film: Production and post-production for 16mm, Super 8
Video: Production and post-production (off-line) for VHS, 3/4"
Comments: NWFVC offers equipment access at subsidized rates to independent media artists.

TECHNICAL ASSISTANCE PROGRAMS AND SERVICES
Programs of Special Interest: NWFVC screens a wide variety of films and videos, and holds the regional Northwest Film and Video Festival.

NORTHWEST TERRITORIES DEPARTMENT OF CULTURE AND COMMUNICATIONS

Government of the Northwest Territories
Box 1320
Yellowknife, Northwest Territories
Canada X1A 2L9
403-920-3103
CONTACT: PETER CULLEN, ARTS LIAISON COORDINATOR

PROFILE OF FINANCIAL SUPPORT TO ARTISTS
Total Funding/Value of In-Kind Support: $219,000 for FY 1990
Competition for Funding: Total applications, 41; total individuals funded/provided with in-kind support, 21
Grant Range: $100-$20,900

DIRECT SUPPORT PROGRAMS
➤ **NWT ARTS COUNCIL PROGRAM**
Purpose: To promote the arts in the Northwest Territories by approving funding for artistic work on a project-specific basis
Eligibility:
    Residency: Northwest Territories, 2 years

Art Forms: Visual arts (includes film and video), performing arts, literature
Type of Support: Up to $21,900 for specific project in FY 1990
Scope of Program: 21 awards in 1990
Application/Selection Process:
   Deadline: January 31, April 30 (1 other deadline if funds available)
   Preferred Initial Contact: Call or write for application/guidelines
   Application Procedure: Submit application form, samples of work, 2 letters of support for project
   Selection Process: Members of NWT Arts Council
   Notification Process: Letter within 12 weeks of deadline
   Formal Report of Grant Required: Yes

OHIO ARTS COUNCIL (OAC)

727 East Main Street
Columbus, OH 43205-1796
614-466-2613
TDD: 614-466-4541
CONTACT: SUSAN DICKSON, COORDINATOR, INDIVIDUAL ARTISTS PROGRAM

PROFILE OF FINANCIAL SUPPORT TO ARTISTS
Total Funding/Value of In-Kind Support: $799,172 for FY 1990
Competition for Funding: Total applications, 1,000+; total individuals funded/provided with in-kind support, 148
Grant Range: $228-$25,000

DIRECT SUPPORT PROGRAMS
➤ **INDIVIDUAL ARTIST FELLOWSHIP PROGRAM**
Purpose: To recognize and support originating artists who have created excellent work
Eligibility:
   Residency: Ohio, 1 year
   Age: 18 or older
   Special Requirements: No students; practicing, professional, originating artists only; previous grantees ineligible for 1 year
   Art Forms: Choreography, crafts (contemporary and traditional), creative writing (fiction, nonfiction, playwriting, poetry, criticism of modern and contemporary art activity), design arts, interdisciplinary and performance art, media arts, music composition, photography, visual arts
Type of Support: $5,000-$10,000 award and opportunity to apply to residency programs at the National Studio at P.S. 1 and the Headlands Center for the Arts

Scope of Program: 96 awards in FY 1991

Application/Selection Process:
  Deadline: January 15
  Preferred Initial Contact: Call or write for application/guidelines
  Application Procedure: Submit application form, samples of work
  Selection Process: Peer panel of artists
  Notification Process: Letter within 2 weeks of panel meeting
  Formal Report of Grant Required: Yes

➤ **INDIVIDUAL ARTISTS MAJOR FELLOWSHIP PROGRAM**

Purpose: To support Ohio artists of extraordinary talent and achievement who have contributed substantially to Ohio's artistic vitality

Eligibility:
  Residency: Ohio, 5 years
  Special Requirements: Must have 10- to 15-year record of professional achievement; grantees ineligible for Individual Artists funding for 5 years
  Art Forms: Choreography, crafts (contemporary and traditional), creative writing (fiction, nonfiction, playwriting, poetry, criticism of modern and contemporary art activity), design arts, interdisciplinary and performance art, media arts, music composition, photography, visual arts

Type of Support: 2-year, $50,000 award; recipients must fulfill public service requirement

Scope of Program: 2 or 3 awards per year

Application/Selection Process:
  Deadline: September 1
  Preferred Initial Contact: Call or write for application/guidelines
  Application Procedure: Submit application form, samples of work, resumé
  Selection Process: Peer panel of artists
  Notification Process: Letter within 2 weeks of panel meeting
  Formal Report of Grant Required: Yes

➤ **PROFESSIONAL DEVELOPMENT ASSISTANCE AWARDS (PDAA)**

Purpose: To provide assistance for artists to attend programs or events that will further their professional development

Eligibility:
  Residency: Ohio, 1 year
  Special Requirements: No students; professional, originating artists only; current Fellowship or Major Fellowship recipients ineligible
  Art Forms: Choreography, crafts (contemporary and traditional), creative writing (fiction, nonfiction, playwriting, poetry, criticism of modern and contemporary art activity), design arts, interdisciplinary and performance art, media arts, music composition, photography, visual arts

Type of Support: Up to $1,000 to participate in such activities or programs as workshops, conferences, colonies, seminars, symposia, and rental of studio facilities

Scope of Program: 20 awards, averaging $750, in 1990

Application/Selection Process:

Deadline: 60 days before intended use of funds; awards given on first-come, first-served basis (fiscal year begins July 1)

Preferred Initial Contact: Consult with staff about availability of funds and application process

Application Procedure: Submit samples of work, resumé, financial statement, project budget, information on and letter of acceptance from program or event

Selection Process: Organization staff

Notification Process: Letter within 3 weeks of application

Formal Report of Grant Required: Yes

TECHNICAL ASSISTANCE PROGRAMS AND SERVICES

Programs of Special Interest: The Arts in Education program publishes a directory of artists eligible for residencies in educational, arts, and community settings.

OKLAHOMA VISUAL ARTS COALITION (OVAC)

P.O. Box 18275
Oklahoma City, OK 73154
405-842-6991
CONTACT: JOHN MCNEESE, DIRECTOR

PROFILE OF FINANCIAL SUPPORT TO ARTISTS

Total Funding/Value of In-Kind Support: $8,000 for FY 1991

Competition for Funding: Total applications, 164; total individuals funded/provided with in-kind support, 20

Grant Range: $250-$1,000

DIRECT SUPPORT PROGRAMS

➤ AWARDS OF EXCELLENCE

Purpose: To recognize and reward excellence in the visual arts

Eligibility:

Citizenship: U.S. (permanent residents also eligible)

Residency: Oklahoma, 1 year

Age: 18 or older

Special Requirements: No students; previous recipients ineligible for 1-2 years

Art Forms: Painting, sculpture, ceramics, photography, printmaking, film, video, fiber, drawing, jewelry, performance art, art criticism

Type of Support: $1,000

Scope of Program: 3-5 awards per year

Application/Selection Process:
 Preferred Initial Contact: Call or write for application/guidelines
 Application Procedure: Submit application form, samples of work
 Selection Process: Independent juror
 Notification Process: Letter 1 month after deadline
 Formal Report of Grant Required: No

➤ **SUDDEN OPPORTUNITY FUND**

Purpose: To provide timely assistance to visual artists for career advancement opportunities

Eligibility:
 Citizenship: U.S. (permanent residents also eligible)
 Residency: Oklahoma
 Age: 18 or older
 Art Forms: Painting, sculpture, ceramics, photography, printmaking, film, video, fiber, drawing, jewelry, performance art, art criticism

Type of Support: Up to $250 for career advancement opportunity

Scope of Program: 12-15 grants per year

Application/Selection Process:
 Deadline: Quarterly
 Preferred Initial Contact: Call or write for application/guidelines
 Application Procedure: Submit application form, samples of work
 Selection Process: Panel of artists and arts professionals
 Notification Process: Letter 2 weeks after deadline
 Formal Report of Grant Required: No

ONTARIO ARTS COUNCIL (OAC)

151 Bloor Street West
Suite 500
Toronto, Ontario
Canada M5S 1T6
800-387-0058 (toll-free in Ontario) or 416-961-1660
CONTACT: DAVID CRAIG, FILM, PHOTOGRAPHY AND VIDEO OFFICER

PROFILE OF FINANCIAL SUPPORT TO ARTISTS

Total Funding/Value of In-Kind Support: $4,547,849 for FY 1989-90

Competition for Funding: Total applications, n/a; total individuals funded/provided with in-kind support, 2,207

Grant Range: n/a

DIRECT SUPPORT PROGRAMS

➤ FILM GRANTS

Purpose: To assist individual filmmakers who use the medium as a form of artistic expression

Eligibility:

Citizenship: Canada (landed immigrants also eligible)

Residency: Ontario

Special Requirements: No students; previous applicants ineligible for 1 year; must have directed at least 1 film for "B" Grant, 2 films for "A" Grant; must have acquired substantial creative credits (e.g., writing, cinematography, and editing) for "A" Grant; commissioned, instructional, promotional, and industrial projects ineligible; pilots for commercial or educational television ineligible; filmmaker must have total artistic and creative control of production

Art Forms: Film

Type of Support: Up to $70,000 "A" Grants, up to $20,000 "B" Grants

Scope of Program: $600,000 budget for 1991

Application/Selection Process:

Deadline: April 1, November 1

Preferred Initial Contact: Call or write for application/guidelines

Application Procedure: Submit application form, project description and budget, draft script (dramatic films), outline (documentaries), storyboards (animated films), filmography, resumé, samples of work

Selection Process: Peer panel of artists

Notification Process: Letter

Formal Report of Grant Required: Yes

➤ VIDEO GRANTS

Purpose: To encourage the development of talented professional video artists through assistance with the production costs of their tapes

Eligibility:

Citizenship: Canada (landed immigrants also eligible)

Residency: Ontario

Special Requirements: No students; previous applicants ineligible for 1 year; artist must have total editorial control over production; educational and promotional tapes ineligible; pilots for television series ineligible; "A" Grants applicants must have a number of video productions to their credit; "B" Grants applicants must have directed 1 video production or have creative credits on several projects

Art Forms: Video

Type of Support: Up to $20,000 "A" Grants, up to $5,000 "B" Grants

Scope of Program: 20 grants in FY 1988-89

Application/Selection Process:

Deadline: February 1, August 15

Preferred Initial Contact: Call or write for application/guidelines
Application Procedure: Submit application form, project description and budget, treatment or storyboard (dramatic productions), outline (documentaries), sketches and plans (installations), resumé, samples of work
Selection Process: Peer panel of artists, board of directors
Notification Process: Letter 10-12 weeks after deadline
Formal Report of Grant Required: Yes

➤ **CREATIVE ARTISTS IN SCHOOLS (CAIS) PROJECTS**
CONTACT: SUSAN HABKIRK, ARTS/EDUCATION OFFICER

Purpose: To enable students to explore and develop their individual artistic talents with the guidance of a professional artist in a school setting
Eligibility:
Citizenship: Canada (landed immigrants also eligible)
Residency: Ontario, 1 year
Special Requirements: Professional, originating artists only; project must be developed with school that will pay 25%-35% of artist's fees; projects must fill at least 5 full school days
Art Forms: Visual arts, crafts, literature, theater, music, film, photography, video, dance
Type of Support: Up to $2,625 for 65%-75% of artist's fees (recommended fee $175 per day), travel expenses up to $750 if artist must travel more than 100 km roundtrip, up to $220 for materials
Scope of Program: 204 grants in FY 1988-89
Application/Selection Process:
Deadline: June 1 (for projects after September 1), October 1 (for projects after January 1), January 15 (for projects after April 1)
Preferred Initial Contact: Call or write for application/guidelines
Application Procedure: Submit application form (signed by school), resumé, samples of work, project budget, letter of support from school (optional)
Selection Process: Jury of artists and educators
Notification Process: Letter 8 weeks after deadline
Formal Report of Grant Required: Yes

TECHNICAL ASSISTANCE PROGRAMS AND SERVICES

Programs of Special Interest: The juried Artists and the Workplace program assists professional artists in all fields to work in residence with the trade union movement on projects initiated by the trade union movement to make the arts more accessible to their membership (contact Naomi Lightbourn, Community Arts Development Officer).

OREGON ARTS COMMISSION (OAC)

835 Summer Street, NE
Salem, OR 97301
503-378-3625
CONTACT: VINCENT DUNN, ASSISTANT DIRECTOR

PROFILE OF FINANCIAL SUPPORT TO ARTISTS

Total Funding/Value of In-Kind Support: $54,000 for FY 1990
Competition for Funding: Total applications, 296; total individuals funded/provided with in-kind support, 12
Grant Range: $3,000-$10,000

DIRECT SUPPORT PROGRAMS

➤ **FILM AND VIDEO PRODUCTION GRANTS**

Purpose: To assist outstanding Oregon artists working in the moving image medium, and to advance film and video as significant art forms
Eligibility:
   Residency: Oregon
   Age: 18 or older
   Special Requirements: No students; professional artists only
   Art Forms: Film, video
Type of Support: Up to $10,000
Scope of Program: $10,000 annual budget
Application/Selection Process:
   Deadline: Early September
   Preferred Initial Contact: Call or write for application/guidelines
   Application Procedure: Submit application form, samples of work, resumé, financial statement, project budget
   Selection Process: Peer panel of artists, board of directors
   Notification Process: Letter 3 months after deadline
   Formal Report of Grant Required: Yes

TECHNICAL ASSISTANCE PROGRAMS AND SERVICES

Programs of Special Interest: Video/Filmmaker-in-Schools, funded through the OAC's Arts In Education program, offers residencies in filmmaking, animation, multi-image, film, and video production.

PALENVILLE INTERARTS COLONY

2 Bond Street
New York, NY 10012
212-254-4614

Summer Address (June-Sept):
P.O. Box 59
Palenville, NY 12463
518-678-3332
CONTACT: JOANNA SHERMAN, COLONY DIRECTOR

PROFILE OF FINANCIAL SUPPORT TO ARTISTS
Total Funding/Value of In-Kind Support: $1,600 for FY 1990
(includes stipends only)
Competition for Funding: Total applications, 467; total individuals
funded/provided with in-kind support, 10
Grant Range: n/a

DIRECT SUPPORT PROGRAMS
➤ SUMMER ARTIST RESIDENCIES

Purpose: To encourage new works and new insights by encouraging
interdisciplinary and intercultural communication among recognized and emerging artists, collaborating artists, and groups of
artists of the highest caliber
Eligibility:
    Special Requirements: Minimum 3 years' experience as
    professional artist
    Art Forms: All disciplines
Type of Support: 1- to 8-week residencies include housing, meals,
and studio space as required; residents are asked to pay $175 per
week but stipends and full or partial fee waivers available to artists
in need
Scope of Program: 97 residencies in 1990; 19 artists received full
fee waivers, 10 received $50-$125 weekly stipends
Application/Selection Process:
    Deadline: April 1
    Preferred Initial Contact: Call or write for application/guidelines
    Application Procedure: Submit application form, $10 fee,
    samples of work, references, resumé, supporting documentation
    (if available); accepted artists requesting financial aid submit
    financial statement
    Selection Process: Peer panel of artists, individuals outside
    of organization
    Notification Process: Phone call or letter within 4 weeks of deadline
    Formal Report of Grant Required: No

PENNSYLVANIA COUNCIL ON THE ARTS (PCA)

216 Finance Building
Harrisburg, PA 17120
717-787-6883
CONTACT: DIANE SIDENER YOUNG, MEDIA ARTS PROGRAM DIRECTOR

PROFILE OF FINANCIAL SUPPORT TO ARTISTS
Total Funding/Value of In-Kind Support: n/a
Competition for Funding: n/a
Grant Range: n/a

DIRECT SUPPORT PROGRAMS
➤ **MEDIA ARTS PRODUCTION/NEW WORK PROGRAM**
Purpose: To support organizations and individuals in the production of film, video, and audio/radio works
Eligibility:
  Residency: Pennsylvania
  Special Requirements: Must apply through a nonprofit conduit organization; 1:1 matching funds required (up to 50% of match may be in-kind services); project must take place in Pennsylvania; projects for academic credit ineligible; individuals may receive only 1 fellowship or conduit grant per year
  Art Forms: Film, video, audio/radio
Type of Support: Matching grant
Scope of Program: $100,000 granted in FY 1990-91
Application/Selection Process:
  Deadline: April 1
  Preferred Initial Contact: Consult with Media Artist Program Director before applying
  Application Procedure: Submit application forms, resumé, samples of work, screenplay, project description and budget, financial statement for organization
  Selection Process: Peer panel of artists, board of directors
  Notification Process: Letter

➤ **BROADCAST OF THE ARTS PROGRAM**
CONTACT: BROADCAST OF THE ARTS PROGRAM DIRECTOR
Purpose: To increase both the quantity and quality of arts programming on radio and television in Pennsylvania
Eligibility:
  Residency: Pennsylvania
  Special Requirements: Nonprofit broadcasters, community access cable groups, and arts organizations eligible to apply; individual producers must apply through a nonprofit conduit; must have 1:1 matching funds (50% of match may be in-kind

services); must have letter of intent to broadcast from a Pennsylvania broadcaster

Art Forms: Film, video, audio (eligible content includes news, information, and documentaries about art and artists; broadcasts of live or recorded performances, as well as music, drama, or works of performance art prepared specifically for broadcast are also eligible)

Type of Support: $1,000-$25,000 matching grant

Scope of Program: $200,000 granted in FY 1990-91

Application/Selection Process:
  Deadline: April 1
  Preferred Initial Contact: Consult with Broadcast of the Arts Program Director
  Application Procedure: Submit application forms, resumé, samples of work, screenplay, project description and budget, financial statement for organization, letter of intent to broadcast
  Selection Process: Peer panel of artists, board of directors
  Notification Process: Letter

➤ **MEDIA ARTS FACILITIES ACCESS GRANTS**

Purpose: To encourage computer centers, public and cable television stations, radio stations, media centers, colleges and universities, art schools, museums, municipal and county authorities, and community arts organizations to allow artists access to equipment

Eligibility:
  Residency: Pennsylvania, 2 years
  Special Requirements: Organizations and artists who initiate a proposal with the cooperation of the equipment center are eligible; applicant must supply matching funds
  Art Forms: Media arts

Type of Support: Matching grant for per hour charge for equipment use, artist's stipend, and administrative overhead

Scope of Program: n/a

Application/Selection Process:
  Deadline: April 1
  Preferred Initial Contact: Consult with Media Arts Program Director
  Application Procedure: Submit application forms, artist's biography, list of available equipment, artist's resumé, samples of artist's work, screenplay, project description and budget, financial statement for organization
  Selection Process: Peer panel of artists, board of directors
  Notification Process: Letter

TECHNICAL ASSISTANCE PROGRAMS AND SERVICES

Programs of Special Interest: The Media Arts Program provides exhibition and distribution assistance to organizations. The Arts in Education Program places professional artists in school and community residencies lasting 10-180 days (priority to Pennsylvania artists). Resident artists spend 50% of the residency period working with the site population and the other 50% working on their own creative projects.

PINELLAS COUNTY ARTS COUNCIL (PCAC)

400 Pierce Boulevard
Clearwater, FL 34616
813-462-3327
CONTACT: MAGGIE MARR, SUPPORT SERVICES DIRECTOR

PROFILE OF FINANCIAL SUPPORT TO ARTISTS

Total Funding/Value of In-Kind Support: $7,598 in FY 1990
Competition for Funding: Total applications, 38; total individuals funded/provided with in-kind support, 10
Grant Range: $450-$1,000

DIRECT SUPPORT PROGRAMS

➤ **ARTISTS RESOURCE FUND (ARF)**

Purpose: To provide a source of nongovernmental financial assistance to Pinellas County visual and performing artists for professional development

Eligibility:
 Residency: Pinellas County, 1 year
 Age: 18 or older
 Special Requirements: No students pursuing degrees; previous grantees ineligible for 3 years
 Art Forms: Dance, music, opera/musical theater, theater, visual arts, crafts, photography, media arts

Type of Support: Up to $1,000 for professional development project (e.g., attendance at workshops or seminars, presentation/ documentation of work, materials/supplies for work pivotal to applicant's career)

Scope of Program: 10 awards, totalling $7,598, in FY 1990

Application/Selection Process:
 Deadline: February 1
 Preferred Initial Contact: Call or write for application/guidelines

Application Procedure: Submit application form, samples of work, resumé, project description and budget
Selection Process: Peer panel of artists, board of directors
Notification Process: Letter 6 weeks after deadline
Formal Report of Grant Required: Yes

TECHNICAL ASSISTANCE PROGRAMS AND SERVICES
Programs of Special Interest: PCAC offers workshops, seminars, and personal consultations on topics such as grantwriting and marketing.

THE PIONEER FUND

Box 33
Inverness, CA 94937
415-669-1122
CONTACT: ARMIN ROSENCRANZ. EXECUTIVE DIRECTOR

PROFILE OF FINANCIAL SUPPORT TO ARTISTS
Total Funding/Value of In-Kind Support: $70,000 per year
Competition for Funding: Total applications, 100; total individuals funded/provided with in-kind support, 20
Grant Range: $1,000-$5,000

DIRECT SUPPORT PROGRAMS
➤ THE PIONEER FUND
Purpose: To assist emerging documentary filmmakers and videomakers in advancing their careers
Eligibility:
   Residency: California, Oregon, Washington State (artists must also work in these states)
   Special Requirements: Must be sponsored by a nonprofit organization and have several years practical experience; students and instructional projects ineligible
   Art Forms: Documentary film or video
Type of Support: $1,000-$5,000
Scope of Program: 20 awards per year
Application/Selection Process:
   Deadline: February 1, June 1, October 1
   Preferred Initial Contact: Call for application/guidelines
   Application Procedure: Submit application form, project proposal and budget, resumé, letter of sponsorship
   Selection Process: Panel review

Notification Process: Phone call to recipients, letter to nonrecipients
Formal Report of Grant Required: Yes

PITTSBURGH FILMMAKERS

218 Oakland Avenue
P.O. Box 7467
Pittsburgh, PA 15213
412-681-5449
CONTACT: MARGARET MYERS, EXECUTIVE DIRECTOR

PROFILE OF FINANCIAL SUPPORT TO ARTISTS
Total Funding/Value of In-Kind Support: $118,450 in FY 1989-90
Competition for Funding: Total applications, 218; total individuals funded/provided with in-kind support, 44
Grant Range: $100-$15,000

DIRECT SUPPORT PROGRAMS
➤ MID-ATLANTIC REGION MEDIA ARTS FELLOWSHIPS (MARMAF)
Purpose: To assist independent media artists in the Mid-Atlantic region to complete the pre-production, shooting, editing, distribution, or other definable stages in the making of a film or videotape
   Residency: Pennsylvania, Maryland, New Jersey, West Virginia, Delaware, District of Columbia, 1 year
   Art Forms: Film, video
Type of Support: $500-$7,500 (most grants $2,000-$5,000)
Scope of Program: 30 awards in 1991
Application/Selection Process:
   Deadline: Late February
   Preferred Initial Contact: Call or write for application/guidelines
   Application Procedure: Submit application form, samples of work, resumé, $5 for return shipping
   Selection Process: Peer panel review
   Notification Process: Letter by May 1
   Formal Report of Grant Required: Yes

➤ EMERGING ARTIST GRANTS IN FILM AND VIDEO
Purpose: To assist local filmmakers and videomakers to complete a first work that will make them competitive for other grants
Eligibility:
   Special Requirements: Must be a student at or member of Pittsburgh Filmmakers ($50 membership fee)
   Art Forms: Film, video

Type of Support: Up to $1,000

Scope of Program: $5,500 awarded annually

Application/Selection Process:

   Deadline: Early March

   Preferred Initial Contact: Call or write for application/guidelines

   Application Procedure: Submit application form, samples of work, resumé

   Selection Process: Peer panel review

   Notification Process: Letter 1 month after deadline

   Formal Report of Grant Required: Yes

EQUIPMENT ACCESS

Film: Production and post-production for 16mm, Super 8

Video: Production and post-production for VHS, 3/4"

Comments: Artists may apply for low-cost access to Pittsburgh Filmmakers equipment. Accepted applicants may choose from a $50 Artist Membership, which provides reduced rate rentals ($1-$25 per day), or a $250 Full Access Membership, which provides unlimited access throughout the year.

TECHNICAL ASSISTANCE PROGRAMS AND SERVICES

Programs of Special Interest: Pittsburgh Filmmakers publishes a newsletter, conducts workshops, acts as a fiscal sponsor for independent artists, maintains a resource library for members and students, and exhibits film, video, and photography.

PRINCE EDWARD ISLAND COUNCIL OF THE ARTS

Box 2234
94 Great George Street
Charlottetown, Prince Edward Island
Canada C1A 8B9
902-368-4410
CONTACT: JUDY MACDONALD

PROFILE OF FINANCIAL SUPPORT TO ARTISTS

Total Funding/Value of In-Kind Support: $45,000 (estimate) in 1990

Competition for Funding: Total applications, 49; total individuals funded/provided with in-kind support, 28

Grant Range: Up to $2,000

DIRECT SUPPORT PROGRAMS

➤ **GRANTS PROGRAM—INDIVIDUAL GRANTS/ TRAVEL-STUDY GRANTS**

Purpose: To assist individuals working in any of the arts disciplines

Eligibility:

Citizenship: Canada (landed immigrants also eligible)

Residency: Prince Edward Island, 6 months

Art Forms: Music, dance, theater, writing/publications, film/video, visual arts, crafts, environmental arts

Type of Support: $1,000-$2,000 individual grants; up to $800 travel-study grants

Scope of Program: 28 grants in 1990

Application/Selection Process:

Deadline: April 30, September 15, December 15

Application Procedure: Submit application form, 2 letters of appraisal

Selection Process: Committee review

Notification Process: Letter 4 weeks after deadline

Formal Report of Grant Required: Yes

TECHNICAL ASSISTANCE PROGRAMS AND SERVICES

Programs of Special Interest: The council offers workshops, seminars, a referral service, a resource library, space for artists and arts organizations, and office equipment for in-house use.

PUBLIC ART WORKS

P.O. Box 150435
San Rafael, CA 94915-0435
415-457-9744

CONTACT: JUDY MORAN, EXECUTIVE DIRECTOR

PROFILE OF FINANCIAL SUPPORT TO ARTISTS

Total Funding/Value of In-Kind Support: n/a

Competition for Funding: Total applications, n/a; total individuals funded/provided with in-kind support, 4

Grant Range: $5,500-$6,000

DIRECT SUPPORT PROGRAMS

➤ **ON SITE EXHIBITION**

Purpose: To commission an annual series of temporary installations in public places, usually outdoors

Eligibility:

Art Forms: Disciplines vary according to location and project

Type of Support: $4,000-$4,500 commission and $1,500 honorarium

Scope of Program: 4 commissions per year

Application/Selection Process:
   Preferred Initial Contact: Call or write for information; artists on mailing list receive prospectus
   Application Procedure: Depends on project
   Selection Process: Jury
   Notification Process: Letter or phone call

QUAD CITY ARTS (QCA)

106 East Third Street
Suite 220
Davenport, IA 52801
319-326-5190

PROFILE OF FINANCIAL SUPPORT TO ARTISTS

Total Funding/Value of In-Kind Support: $6,500 in 1991

Competition for Funding: Total applications, 30; total individuals funded/provided with in-kind support, 21

Grant Range: $215-$500

DIRECT SUPPORT PROGRAMS

➤ **ARTS DOLLARS INDIVIDUAL GRANTS**

Purpose: To support specific professional development projects for the creation, completion, presentation, or production of a new work

Eligibility:
   Residency: Illinois (Rock Island, Mercer counties), Iowa (Scott, Clinton, Muscatine counties)
   Special Requirements: Must provide service to residents of the Quad City area
   Art Forms: All disciplines

Type of Support: Up to $500 for specific project

Scope of Program: 21 awards in 1991

Application/Selection Process:
   Call or write for information

TECHNICAL ASSISTANCE PROGRAMS AND SERVICES

Programs of Special Interest: QCA provides artist registry and information services.

RAGDALE FOUNDATION

1260 North Green Bay Road
Lake Forest, IL 60045
708-234-1063
CONTACT: MICHAEL WILKERSON, DIRECTOR

PROFILE OF FINANCIAL SUPPORT TO ARTISTS
Total Funding/Value of In-Kind Support: n/a
Competition for Funding: Total applications, 400; total individuals funded/provided with in-kind support, 150
Grant Range: n/a

DIRECT SUPPORT PROGRAMS
➤ **RESIDENCIES FOR ARTISTS**
Purpose: To provide a peaceful place and uninterrupted time for writers, scholars, and artists who are seriously committed to a specific project
Eligibility:
  Art Forms: Music composition, visual arts, media arts, literature, interdisciplinary
Type of Support: 2-week to 2-month residencies include housing, work space, meals; residents asked to pay $10/day but financial assistance available
Scope of Program: 150 residencies in 1990
Application/Selection Process:
  Deadline: January 15, April 15, September 15
  Preferred Initial Contact: Call or write for application/guidelines
  Application Procedure: Submit application form, samples of work, references, resumé, financial statement (if seeking fee waiver)
  Selection Process: Peer panel of artists
  Notification Process: Letter or phone call 7 weeks after deadline
  Formal Report of Grant Required: Yes

RHODE ISLAND STATE COUNCIL ON THE ARTS (RISCA)

95 Cedar Street
Suite 103
Providence, RI 02903
401-277-3880
CONTACT: EDWARD HOLGATE, DIRECTOR, INDIVIDUAL ARTIST PROGRAMS

PROFILE OF FINANCIAL SUPPORT TO ARTISTS

Total Funding/Value of In-Kind Support: $146,650 for FY 1990

Competition for Funding: Total applications, 311; total individuals funded/provided with in-kind support, 78

Grant Range: $250-$4,350

DIRECT SUPPORT PROGRAMS

➤ **FELLOWSHIPS**

Purpose: To encourage the creative development of originating artists by enabling them to set aside time to pursue their work and achieve specific career goals

Eligibility:
   Residency: Rhode Island, 1 year
   Age: 18 or older
   Special Requirements: Originating artists only; no students; previous recipients ineligible to apply in same category for 3 years; Artist Project awardees ineligible for 1 year
   Art Forms: Choreography, crafts, design, drawing and printmaking, film, video, folk arts, literature, music composition, new genres, painting, photography, 3-dimensional art

Type of Support: $500-$3,000 awards in 1991

Scope of Program: 24 awards in 1991

Application/Selection Process:
   Deadline: April 1
   Preferred Initial Contact: Call or write for application/guidelines
   Application Procedure: Submit application form, samples of work, resumé
   Selection Process: Panels of artists and arts professionals
   Notification Process: Letter in mid-July
   Formal Report of Grant Required: Yes

➤ **ARTIST PROJECTS/TRAVEL GRANTS**

Purpose: Artist Projects awards enable artists to create new works or complete works-in-progress; Travel Grants provide funds to individual artists for impending out-of-state travel opportunities that will significantly impact the artist's work or career

Eligibility:
Residency: Rhode Island, 1 year
Age: 18 or older
Special Requirements: No students; previous recipients ineligible for same grant for 1 year
Art Forms: Choreography, crafts, design, drawing and printmaking, film, video, folk arts, literature, music composition, new genres, painting, photography, 3-dimensional art, performing arts (Travel Grants only)

Type of Support: Artist Projects, $2,000-$5,000 for specific project-related costs (completed work must be publicly presented in Rhode Island); Travel Grants, $100-$1,000 for out-of-state travel for opportunities such as creation, collaboration, or exhibition of work, project-oriented research or study, or attendance at a professional conference or workshop

Scope of Program: 22 Artists Projects awards, 19 Travel Grants in 1990
Application/Selection Process:
Deadline: October 1 (Artist Projects and Travel Grants), April 1 Travel Grants only)
Preferred Initial Contact: Call or write for application/guidelines
Application Procedure: Submit application form, samples of work (Artists Projects), resumé, project or travel budget, documentation of travel opportunity (Travel Grants)
Selection Process: Panel of artists and arts administrators, board of directors
Notification Process: Letter 8-10 weeks after deadline
Formal Report of Grant Required: Yes

TECHNICAL ASSISTANCE PROGRAMS AND SERVICES

Programs of Special Interest: RISCA's Arts in Action workshop series educates artists in practical matters such as marketing, legal issues, and fiscal management. The council maintains the Arts in Education/Artist Roster, which lists artists eligible for school and community residencies.

ROCKEFELLER FOUNDATION

1133 Avenue of the Americas
New York, NY 10036
212-869-8500

PROFILE OF FINANCIAL SUPPORT TO ARTISTS

Total Funding/Value of In-Kind Support: n/a
Competition for Funding: n/a
Grant Range: n/a

DIRECT SUPPORT PROGRAMS

➤ **BELLAGIO STUDY AND CONFERENCE CENTER RESIDENCIES**

CONTACT: SUSAN E. GARFIELD, MANAGER, BELLAGIO CENTER OFFICE

Purpose: To provide a site for artists and scholars who have significant publications, compositions, or shows to their credit to work on projects, particularly projects that will result in publications, exhibition, or performances

Eligibility:
  Special Requirements: Priority given to arts projects that increase artistic experimentation across cultures; previous recipients ineligible for 10 years
  Art Forms: All disciplines

Type of Support: 5-week residency at the Bellagio Center in Milan, Italy, including room and board

Scope of Program: 135 residencies per year

Application/Selection Process:
  Deadline: Quarterly, 1 year before residency
  Preferred Initial Contact: Call or write for brochure
  Application Procedure: Submit application form, project description, resumé, samples of work, reviews of work (if possible)
  Selection Process: Committee
  Notification Process: 2 months after deadline

➤ **INTERNATIONAL FILM/VIDEO FELLOWSHIP PROGRAM**

Purpose: To encourage filmmakers and videomakers whose work can advance international and intercultural understanding in the U.S.

Eligibility:
  Special Requirements: Must be nominated by a designated nominator
  Art Forms: Film, video

Type of Support: $35,000

Scope of Program: 14 grants annually

Application/Selection Process:
  By nomination by designated nominators only; unsolicited applications or nominations not accepted.

ROCKY MOUNTAIN FILM CENTER (RMFC)

Hunter 102
University of Colorado
Campus Box 316
Boulder, CO 80309-0316
303-492-1531

EQUIPMENT ACCESS

Film: Production and post-production for Super 8, 8mm, 16mm
Video: Production for VHS; post-production for VHS, 3/4"
Comments: Film and video equipment available on a 24-hour basis to noncommercial users at very nominal rental rates; reservations must be made weekdays, between 11 a.m. and 2 p.m. only, at the RMFC office or by phone. Access to screening space is free.

TECHNICAL ASSISTANCE PROGRAMS AND SERVICES

Programs of Special Interest: The Filmmakers Bulletin Board office allows filmmakers to contact one another, exchange services, and buy and sell equipment.

SALT LAKE CITY ARTS COUNCIL

54 Finch Lane
Salt Lake City, UT 84102
801-596-5000
CONTACT: KIM DUFFIN

PROFILE OF FINANCIAL SUPPORT TO ARTISTS

Total Funding/Value of In-Kind Support: n/a
Competition for Funding: n/a
Grant Range: n/a

DIRECT SUPPORT PROGRAMS

➤ **DEVELOPMENTAL SUPPORT GRANTS**

Purpose: To support professional development projects such as exhibitions, installations, and collaborative efforts
Eligibility:
   Residency: Preference to Salt Lake City artists
   Special Requirements: Cash match required; project must take place in Salt Lake City
   Art Forms: All disciplines
Type of Support: Matching grant for project

Scope of Program: n/a
Application/Selection Process:
Deadline: June
Preferred Initial Contact: Call or write for application/guidelines
Formal Report of Grant Required: Yes

TECHNICAL ASSISTANCE PROGRAMS AND SERVICES
Programs of Special Interest: Information and technical assistance is available to artists in all areas.

SAN ANTONIO DEPARTMENT OF ARTS AND CULTURAL AFFAIRS (DACA)

P.O. Box 839966
San Antonio, TX 78283-3966
512-222-2787
CONTACT: KATE MARTIN, PROJECT MANAGEMENT SPECIALIST

PROFILE OF FINANCIAL SUPPORT TO ARTISTS
Total Funding/Value of In-Kind Support: $20,000 in FY 1991
Competition for Funding: Total applications, 81; total individuals funded/provided with in-kind support, 12
Grant Range: $1,000-$2,000

DIRECT SUPPORT PROGRAMS
➤ **INDIVIDUAL ARTISTS GRANTS PROGRAMS**
Purpose: To assist both emerging and established artists by supporting work of artistic merit, to encourage innovative projects (e.g., performance art, multi-disciplinary media, new genres), and to support projects by individuals who lack institutional support
Eligibility:
Citizenship: U.S.
Residency: Bexar County
Special Requirements: Originating, professional artists only; no students; previous grantees ineligible for 1 year; project must take place in San Antonio; DACA encourages applications that represent cultural and geographic diversity of San Antonio and that represent women and the disabled; collaborations encouraged
Art Forms: Dance, music, theater, visual arts, crafts, design arts, photography, media arts, literature, multi-disciplinary
Type of Support: Up to $2,000 for project that takes place in San Antonio and leads to a public presentation
Scope of Program: 12 awards in FY 1991

Application/Selection Process:
  Deadline: Spring (usually March)
  Preferred Initial Contact: Call or write for application form
  Application Procedure: Arrange for pre-application interview
  with DACA staff before deadline; submit application form,
  samples of work, resumé, project budget, letter of support for
  public presentation
  Selection Process: Peer panel of artists
  Notification Process: Letter after panel meeting (July)
  Formal Report of Grant Required: Yes

TECHNICAL ASSISTANCE PROGRAMS AND SERVICES
Programs of Special Interest: DACA maintains a library and offers
free workshops for artists on topics such as career development,
legal issues, marketing, and public relations.

SAN FRANCISCO FOUNDATION

685 Market Street
Suite 910
San Francisco, CA 94105
415-543-0223

PROFILE OF FINANCIAL SUPPORT TO ARTISTS
Total Funding/Value of In-Kind Support: n/a
Competition for Funding: n/a
Grant Range: n/a

DIRECT SUPPORT PROGRAMS
➤ **JAMES D. PHELAN ART AWARD**
Purpose: To encourage the work of California-born filmmakers,
videographers, printmakers, and photographers
Eligibility:
  Special Requirements: Applicant must have been born in
  California; previous grantees ineligible
  Art Forms: Eligible disciplines alternate on 2-year cycle between
  film/video and photography/printmaking
Type of Support: $2,500 awards
Scope of Program: 6 awards annually (3 in each eligible discipline)
Application/Selection Process:
  Call for information

Santa Barbara County Arts Commission

112 West Cabrillo Boulevard
Santa Barbara, CA 93101
805-568-3430
CONTACT: PATRICK H. DAVIS, EXECUTIVE DIRECTOR

Profile of Financial Support to Artists
Total Funding/Value of In-Kind Support: $17,000 for FY 1990-91
Competition for Funding: Total applications, 45; total individuals funded/provided with in-kind support, 6
Grant Range: n/a

Direct Support Programs
➤ NEW WORKS GRANTS
Purpose: To encourage artists to present original and challenging work for Santa Barbara County audiences and to enrich the creative process by collaborating with other county artists or arts organizations
Eligibility:
　Residency: Santa Barbara County
　Special Requirements: Artist must be sponsored by a nonprofit organization; originating artists only
　Art Forms: All disciplines
Type of Support: Up to $3,000 for specific project
Scope of Program: n/a
Application/Selection Process:
　Deadline: June 15
　Application Procedure: Sponsor submits application form, financial statement, project description and budget, artist's resumé, samples of work, support materials (e.g., letters of support, reviews)
　Selection Process: Panel of local citizens and arts experts
　Notification Process: 2 months after deadline
　Formal Report of Grant Required: Yes

The School of the Art Institute of Chicago

37 South Wabash Avenue
Chicago, IL 60603
312-899-5100

Profile of Financial Support to Artists
Total Funding/Value of In-Kind Support: n/a
Competition for Funding: Total applications, 74; total individuals funded/provided with in-kind support, 2
Grant Range: $300-$1,500

Direct Support Programs
➤ BARBARA ARONOFSKY LATHAM MEMORIAL GRANTS
CONTACT: OFFICE OF THE DEAN
Phone: 312-899-1236
Purpose: To further the work of emerging talent and to foster the excellence, diversity, vitality, and appreciation of experimental video and electronic visualization art
Eligibility:
Age: 18 or older
Art Forms: Experimental video, electronic visualization art, writing on the history, theory, or criticism of video and electronic visualization art
Type of Support: $300-$1,500 for work-in-progress or new project
Scope of Program: 2 awards in 1989
Application/Selection Process:
Deadline: May 15
Preferred Initial Contact: Call or write for application/guidelines
Application Procedure: Submit application form, samples of work, project description, resumé
Selection Process: Professional jury
Notification Process: 12 weeks after deadline

Technical Assistance Programs and Services
CONTACT: VIDEO DATA BANK
Phone: 312-899-5172
Programs of Special Interest: The Video Data Bank is the largest national distributor of tapes by and about contemporary artists; its collection features experimental and independently produced videos.

SEATTLE ARTS COMMISSION (SAC)
305 Harrison Street
Seattle, WA 98109
206-684-7171
TDD: 206-587-5500
CONTACT: DIANE SHAMASH

Profile of Financial Support to Artists
Total Funding/Value of In-Kind Support: $580,000 (includes commissions)
Competition for Funding: n/a
Grant Range: $1,000-$5,000

DIRECT SUPPORT PROGRAMS
➤ **SEATTLE ARTISTS PROGRAM**
Purpose: To fund the development of new work or works-in-progress in all disciplines
Eligibility:
   Residency: Seattle
   Special Requirements: Originating artists only
   Art Forms: Visual arts, literature (scriptwriting, critical writing/creative nonfiction, fiction/prose, poetry), choreography, music composition, media arts (audio, video, film)
Type of Support: $1,000-$5,000 grant for project
Scope of Program: $80,000 budget
Application/Selection Process:
   Deadline: Fall
   Preferred Initial Contact: Call or write for information

SIERRA ARTS FOUNDATION (SAF)

200 Flint Street
Reno, NV 89501
702-329-1324
CONTACT: VIRGINIA KEENEY, EXECUTIVE DIRECTOR

PROFILE OF FINANCIAL SUPPORT TO ARTISTS
Total Funding/Value of In-Kind Support: $55,000 for FY 1991
Competition for Funding: Total applications, n/a; total individuals funded/provided with in-kind support, 159
Grant Range: $200-$2,000

DIRECT SUPPORT PROGRAMS
➤ **GRANTS PROGRAM**
Purpose: To provide grants-in-aid to individuals, groups, or nonprofit organizations to support projects of educational and community significance as well as imaginative, innovative, or experimental projects
Eligibility:
   Residency: Northern Nevada and neighboring Sierra Nevada region
   Special Requirements: Preference given to applicants who present evidence of matching funds or comparable in-kind support; previous grantees ineligible for 1 year
   Art Forms: All disciplines
Type of Support: Up to $2,000 for project
Scope of Program: 4 grants to individuals in FY 1991

Application/Selection Process:
Deadline: Quarterly
Preferred Initial Contact: Call to check on availability of funds, discuss project with Grants Coordinator/Program Director
Application Procedure: Submit application form, samples of work, project budget, resumé
Selection Process: Organization staff, Grants Committee including board members
Notification Process: Letter 1 month after deadline
Formal Report of Grant Required: Yes

TECHNICAL ASSISTANCE PROGRAMS AND SERVICES
Programs of Special Interest: The Arts-in-Education program places professional artists in month-long residencies in Washoe County elementary schools. SAF maintains an artist registry.

SOUTH CAROLINA ARTS COMMISSION (SCAC)

1800 Gervais Street
Columbia, SC 29201
803-734-8696
CONTACT: MICHAEL FLEISHMAN, CHAIR, ARTIST DEPARTMENT

PROFILE OF FINANCIAL SUPPORT TO ARTISTS
Total Funding/Value of In-Kind Support: $106,588 for FY 1991
Competition for Funding: Total applications, n/a; total individuals funded/provided with in-kind support, 120
Grant Range: n/a

DIRECT SUPPORT PROGRAMS
➤ **GRANTS-IN-AID (SPECIAL PROJECTS)**
Purpose: To help support specific, planned activities such as the production of new work, marketing, and professional development
Eligibility:
Citizenship: U.S.
Residency: South Carolina, 6 months
Special Requirements: No degree-seeking, full-time undergraduate students; professional artists only; matching funds required
Art Forms: All disciplines
Type of Support: Up to 50% of cost of specific project (usually no more than $7,500)
Scope of Program: 13 grants in 1991
Application/Selection Process:
Deadline: January 15
Preferred Initial Contact: Call or write for application/guidelines

Application Procedure: Submit application form, samples of work, resumé, project budget
Selection Process: Board of directors, organization staff, advisory panel
Notification Process: Letter
Formal Report of Grant Required: Yes

TECHNICAL ASSISTANCE PROGRAMS AND SERVICES
Programs of Special Interest: The SCAC's Media Arts Center provides workshops, assistance, film exhibitions, and equipment and studio access for sponsors and media artists in the 9 southeastern states (see the entry on Appalshop, Inc., for information on the Southeast Media Fellowship Program's equipment access grants). Individuals selected for the Approved Artist Roster are eligible for the Arts-in-Education, Visiting Artist, Rural Arts, and Mobile Arts programs.

SOUTH DAKOTA ARTS COUNCIL

108 W. 11th Street
Sioux Falls, SD 57102
605-339-6646
CONTACT: SHIRLEY SNEVE, ASSISTANT DIRECTOR

PROFILE OF FINANCIAL SUPPORT TO ARTISTS
Total Funding/Value of In-Kind Support: $30,000 for FY 1991
Competition for Funding: Total applications, 79; total individuals funded/provided with in-kind support, 10
Grant Range: $1,000-$5,000

DIRECT SUPPORT PROGRAMS
➤ ARTIST FELLOWSHIPS/EMERGING ARTIST GRANTS
Purpose: Artist Fellowships recognize and encourage the creative achievement of South Dakota artists of exceptional talent in any arts discipline; Emerging Artist Grants assist artists in the development of their careers
Eligibility:
   Residency: South Dakota
   Special Requirements: No students; previous grantees ineligible for 2 years (Fellowships) or 3 years (Emerging Artist Grants)
   Art Forms: All disciplines
Type of Support: $5,000 (Fellowships), $1,000 (Emerging Artist Grants)
Scope of Program: 5 Fellowships, 5 Emerging Artist Grants in 1991
Application/Selection Process:
   Deadline: February 1
   Preferred Initial Contact: Call or write for application/guidelines

Application Procedure: Submit application form, resumé, samples of work, support documentation (optional)
Selection Process: Arts disciplines panels, the council
Notification Process: April
Formal Report of Grant Required: Yes

➤ **PROJECT GRANTS**

Purpose: To enable South Dakota artists to reach the public more effectively through special projects (particularly innovative or creative projects and projects that reach disabled, minority, rural, or new constituencies)

Eligibility:
  Residency: South Dakota
  Special Requirements: No students; no applicants for Emerging Artist or Fellowship grants; matching funds required
  Art Forms: All disciplines

Type of Support: Up to 50% of total project costs

Scope of Program: n/a

Application/Selection Process:
  Deadline: February 1
  Preferred Initial Contact: Call or write for application/guidelines
  Application Procedure: Submit application form, resumé, samples of work, support documentation (optional), project description and budget
  Selection Process: Arts disciplines panels, the council
  Notification Process: April
  Formal Report of Grant Required: Yes

TECHNICAL ASSISTANCE PROGRAMS AND SERVICES
Programs of Special Interest: The Artists-in-Schools program endorses artists for 1-week to 1-semester residencies in South Dakota schools.

SOUTHEASTERN CENTER FOR CONTEMPORARY ART (SECCA)

750 Marguerite Drive
Winston-Salem, NC 27106
919-725-1904

PROFILE OF FINANCIAL SUPPORT TO ARTISTS
Total Funding/Value of In-Kind Support: $180,000 (AVA program) for FY 1989-90
Competition for Funding: Total applications, 457; total individuals funded/provided with in-kind support, 10
Grant Range: $15,000

DIRECT SUPPORT PROGRAMS
➤ **AVA (AWARDS IN THE VISUAL ARTS)**

Purpose: To recognize outstanding achievement and potential in the visual arts through a program of national awards, exhibitions, purchases, and publications

Eligibility:
  Citizenship: U.S.
  Residency: U.S.
  Age: 18 or older
  Special Requirements: Must be nominated by designated AVA nominator; previous grantees ineligible
  Art Forms: Visual arts, crafts, photography, media arts, multi-disciplinary

Type of Support: $15,000, touring exhibition of work ($30,000 in purchase awards available each year)

Scope of Program: 10 awards per year

Application/Selection Process:
  Preferred Initial Contact: Nomination by AVA designated nominators only; unsolicited nominations/applications not accepted
  Application Procedure: Nominees submit application form, samples of work, resumé
  Selection Process: Individuals outside of organization
  Formal Report of Grant Required: No

TECHNICAL ASSISTANCE PROGRAMS AND SERVICES

Programs of Special Interest: SECCA maintains an extensive database on southeastern artists.

THE SOUTH FLORIDA CULTURAL CONSORTIUM

c/o Metro-Dade County Cultural Affairs Council
111 N.W. 1st Street
Suite 625
Miami, FL 33128
305-375-4634
CONTACT: BETTY STOETZER, DIRECTOR OF REGIONAL & EDUCATIONAL PROGRAMS

PROFILE OF FINANCIAL SUPPORT TO ARTISTS

Total Funding/Value of In-Kind Support: $90,000 for FY 1991

Competition for Funding: Total applications, 250; total individuals funded/provided with in-kind support, 6

Grant Range: $15,000

DIRECT SUPPORT PROGRAMS
➤ REGIONAL VISUAL ARTISTS FELLOWSHIP

Purpose: To assist South Florida visual and media artists in improving their artistic skills and in furthering their careers

Eligibility:
Residency: South Florida (Dade, Broward, Palm Beach, Martin, and Monroe counties), 1 year
Age: 18 or older
Special Requirements: No students pursuing degrees; professional artists only
Art Forms: Painting, sculpture, drawing, mixed media, printmaking/graphics, media arts (film, video, audio)

Type of Support: $15,000 fellowship; exhibition of grantees' work tours South Florida

Scope of Program: 6 awards in FY 1991

Application/Selection Process:
Deadline: February
Preferred Initial Contact: Call or write for application/guidelines
Application Procedure: Submit application form, samples of work, resumé
Selection Process: Artists and arts professionals outside of organization
Notification Process: Letter within 2 months of deadline
Formal Report of Grant Required: No

SOUTHWEST ALTERNATE MEDIA PROJECT (SWAMP)

1519 West Main
Houston, TX 77006
713-522-8592
CONTACT: TOM SIMS, SPECIAL PROJECTS DIRECTOR

PROFILE OF FINANCIAL SUPPORT TO ARTISTS

Total Funding/Value of In-Kind Support: $50,000 for 1990

Competition for Funding: Total applications, 120; total individuals funded/provided with in-kind support, 12

Grant Range: Up to $5,000

DIRECT SUPPORT PROGRAMS
➤ INDEPENDENT PRODUCTION FUND (IPF)

Purpose: To provide production grants for independent filmmakers and videomakers

Eligibility:
Residency: Texas, Arkansas, Oklahoma, Kansas, Nebraska, Missouri, Puerto Rico, U.S. Virgin Islands, 1 year
Age: 18 or older
Special Requirements: No full-time students or projects associated with degree programs; applicant must have primary control over project
Art Forms: Film, video
Type of Support: Up to $5,000; past IPF grantees not receiving the maximum $5,000 award per project may reapply for additional funds up to a maximum of $2,500 or the difference between the original award and project maximum
Scope of Program: $50,000 available in 1991
Application/Selection Process:
Deadline: May 1
Preferred Initial Contact: Call or write for application/guidelines (mail requests should be addressed to the attention of IPF)
Application Procedure: Submit application form, $3 for return shipping/handling, project description and budget, samples of work, support materials (can include resumé, biography, letters of support, reviews)
Selection Process: Independent peer panel of artists
Notification Process: 12 weeks after deadline
Formal Report of Grant Required: No

TECHNICAL ASSISTANCE PROGRAMS AND SERVICES

Programs of Special Interest: SWAMP coordinates Media Arts Touring and Media Residency activities, and acts as a fiscal sponsor for established film and video artists. The Independent Images Conference promotes independent media production, exhibition, and education in the Southwest and Mid-America region (fees involved).

SQUEAKY WHEEL/BUFFALO MEDIA RESOURCES

372 Connecticut Street
Buffalo, NY 14213
716-884-7172

EQUIPMENT ACCESS

Film: Production and post-production for 16mm, Super 8
Video: Production for Video 8, Hi-8, Beta; post-production for Hi-8 to 3/4"
Comments: Squeaky Wheel offers equipment access at low rates to its members.

TECHNICAL ASSISTANCE PROGRAMS AND SERVICES

Programs of Special Interest: Squeaky Wheel publishes a media directory for upstate New York, exhibits the work of local media artists, conducts technical and grantwriting workshops, and offers consultations on fundraising and distribution.

SUNDANCE INSTITUTE

10202 West Washington Boulevard
Columbia Pictures
Culver City, CA 90232
213-204-2091
CONTACT: CINDY BAGGISH

PROFILE OF FINANCIAL SUPPORT TO ARTISTS

Total Funding/Value of In-Kind Support: n/a
Competition for Funding: Total applications, 1,200; total individuals funded/provided with in-kind support, 15
Grant Range: n/a

DIRECT SUPPORT PROGRAMS

➤ FEATURE FILM PROGRAM

Purpose: To support original, provocative, daring scripts that reflect the independent vision of the writer or writer/director
Eligibility:
    Special Requirements: Sundance is particularly interested in supporting new talent, artists in transition (e.g., choreographers, actors, playwrights), and filmmakers who have already made a feature and are looking for a creative arena for the development of their next project
    Art Forms: Film (directing, screenwriting)
Type of Support: Sundance offers a 5-day Screenwriters Lab (January or June) including one-on-one problem-solving story sessions with professional screenwriters, a June Filmmaking Lab including hands-on directing experience rehearsing, shooting and editing scenes on videotape, a Producer's Conference in July for filmmakers supported in June; airline travel, accommodations, and food for 1 writer/filmmaker per project is provided by the institute, and Sundance will consider paying for accommodations and food for additional partners; if supported projects are produced, Sundance asks writers/directors to contribute 1/2% to 1% of production budget to the institute
Scope of Program: 10-15 projects per year

Application/Selection Process:
Deadline: July 15 (January Screenwriters Lab); November/December (June Filmmakers Lab)
Preferred Initial Contact: Call or write for application/guidelines
Application Procedure: Submit application form for labs, $15 fee, synopsis of project/screenplay; finalists submit full screenplays
Selection Process: Staff, panel of artists
Notification Process: Mid-December (January Lab), mid-April (June Lab)

TECHNICAL ASSISTANCE PROGRAMS AND SERVICES

Programs of Special Interest: The Sundance Film Festival show-cases the talents of emerging filmmakers. To apply, send a request for festival information and a SASE to Sundance Institute. Applications are available in late September and due by November 1.

TENNESSEE ARTS COMMISSION (TAC)

320 Sixth Avenue, N.
Suite 100
Nashville, TN 37243-0780
615-741-1701

PROFILE OF FINANCIAL SUPPORT TO ARTISTS

Total Funding/Value of In-Kind Support: $75,000 for FY 1989

Competition for Funding: Total applications, 150; total individuals funded/provided with in-kind support, 15

Grant Range: Up to $5,000

DIRECT SUPPORT PROGRAMS

➤ INDIVIDUAL ARTISTS FELLOWSHIPS

Purpose: To recognize and support outstanding professional Tennessee artists

Eligibility:
Residency: Tennessee
Special Requirements: No students; professional artists only; previous fellowship winners ineligible
Art Forms: All disciplines (film and video eligible in some years)

Type of Support: $2,500 or more

Scope of Program: 7-8 fellowships; honorable mention awards (under $2,500) sometimes given

Application/Selection Process:
Deadline: January 8
Preferred Initial Contact: Call or write for application/guidelines

Application Procedure: Submit application form, samples of work, resumé, references
Selection Process: Individuals outside of organization
Notification Process: Letter in July
Formal Report of Grant Required: Yes

TECHNICAL ASSISTANCE PROGRAMS AND SERVICES
Programs of Special Interest: Film and video artists may seek 2-week to year-long residencies in schools through the Arts in Education Program.

TEXAS COMMISSION ON THE ARTS (TCA)

920 Colorado Street, 5th Floor
P.O. Box 13406, Capitol Station
Austin, TX 78711
512-463-5535 or 800-252-9415
CONTACT: RITA STARPATTERN

PROFILE OF FINANCIAL SUPPORT TO ARTISTS
Total Funding/Value of In-Kind Support: $73,440 to media artists and organizations
Competition for Funding: Total applications, 33; total individuals and organizations funded/provided with in-kind support, 16
Grant Range: n/a

DIRECT SUPPORT PROGRAMS
➤ ORGANIZATIONAL, PROJECT, AND TOURING
SUPPORT—MEDIA ARTS
Purpose: To support media organizations, media projects, and independents through funding and touring opportunities
Eligibility:
  Residency: Texas
  Special Requirements: Individual artists must apply through a Texas-based nonprofit organization
  Art Forms: Film, video, radio
Type of Support: Grants for organizational, project, and touring support
Scope of Program: 16 grants totalling $73,440
Application/Selection Process:
  Deadline: January 15
  Preferred Initial Contact: Call or write for application/guidelines
  Application Procedure: Submit application form
  Selection Process: Peer panel review
  Notification Process: Letter
  Formal Report of Grant Required: Yes

THEATRE ASSOCIATION OF PENNSYLVANIA

2318 South Queen Street
York, PA 17402
717-741-1269
CONTACT: MARCIA D. SALVATORE, EXECUTIVE DIRECTOR

PROFILE OF FINANCIAL SUPPORT TO ARTISTS
Total Funding/Value of In-Kind Support: n/a
Competition for Funding: n/a
Grant Range: Up to $5,000

➤ **PENNSYLVANIA MEDIA ARTS SCRIPTWRITERS FELLOWSHIP**
Purpose: To recognize and support creative writing for television
and film in dramatic and documentary genres
Eligibility:
  Residency: Pennsylvania, 2 years
  Special Requirements: Minimum 3 years professional experience;
  no students; applicants to Pennsylvania Playwrights Project in-
  eligible; previous grantees ineligible for 3 years; funds may not
  be used for production costs, publishing, or academic projects
  Art Forms: Screenwriting for television and film (dramatic
  and documentary)
Type of Support: Up to $5,000.
Scope of Program: n/a
Application/Selection Process:
  Deadline: June 1
  Preferred Initial Contact: Call or write for application/guidelines
  Application Procedure: Submit application form, project descrip-
  tion and budget, samples of work, sample work description, resumé
  Selection Process: Independent peer panel of artists
  Notification Process: Letter before October 1
  Formal Report of Grant Required: Yes

TUCSON COMMUNITY CABLE CORPORATION (TCCC)

124 East Broadway
Tucson, AZ 85701
602-624-9833
CONTACT: MARK TAYLOR

EQUIPMENT ACCESS
Video: Production for VHS, S-VHS, 3/4"; post-production for VHS,
S-VHS, Video 8, 3/4", Hi-8
Comments: TCCC offers free public access to its equipment and
facilities.

TECHNICAL ASSISTANCE PROGRAMS AND SERVICES

Programs of Special Interest: TCCC annually provides approximately $170,000 in grants to individual artists. The organization is restructuring its grant program; call after July 1, 1991, for more information. TCCC offers free technical assistance services.

UCROSS FOUNDATION

2836 U.S. Highway 14-16 East
Clearmont, WY 82835
307-737-2291
CONTACT: ELIZABETH GUHEEN, PROGRAM DIRECTOR

PROFILE OF FINANCIAL SUPPORT TO ARTISTS

Total Funding/Value of In-Kind Support: n/a
Competition for Funding: Total applications, 250; total individuals funded/provided with in-kind support, 35
Grant Range: n/a

DIRECT SUPPORT PROGRAMS

➤ RESIDENCY PROGRAM

Purpose: To provide individual workspace and living accommodations for selected artists and scholars so that they may concentrate, in an uninterrupted fashion, on their ideas, theories, and works
Eligibility:
  Age: 18 or older
  Special Requirements: Previous residents ineligible for 2 years
  Art Forms: All disciplines
Type of Support: 2-week to 4-month residencies with no charge for room, board, or studio space
Scope of Program: 30-35 residencies per year
Application/Selection Process:
  Deadline: October 1, March 1
  Preferred Initial Contact: Write for application/guidelines, include SASE
  Application Procedure: Submit application form, samples of work, references, resumé
  Selection Process: Peer panel of artists
  Notification Process: Letter 8 weeks after deadline
  Formal Report of Grant Required: No

UNITED ARTS COUNCIL OF GREENSBORO, INC.

Greensboro Cultural Center
200 North Davie Street
P.O. Box 869
Greensboro, NC 27402
919-333-7440
CONTACT: JUDITH K. RAY, COMMUNITY DEVELOPMENT DIRECTOR

PROFILE OF FINANCIAL SUPPORT TO ARTISTS
Total Funding/Value of In-Kind Support: $6,000 for FY 1989
(Emerging Artists Program)
Competition for Funding: Total applications, 21; total individuals
funded/provided with in-kind support, 11
Grant Range: $300-$900

DIRECT SUPPORT PROGRAMS
➤ **EMERGING ARTISTS PROGRAM**
Purpose: To encourage artists in their formative years by helping
them cover the costs of professional development activities such as
presenting their work for exhibits, training, travel, and production
of new work
Eligibility:
  Citizenship: U.S.
  Residency: Guilford County
  Special Requirements: No students
  Art Forms: All disciplines
Type of Support: $250-$1,000 for specific activity
Scope of Program: 11 awards in FY 1989
Application/Selection Process:
  Deadline: March 1
  Preferred Initial Contact: Call or write for application/guidelines
  Application Procedure: Submit application form, samples of
  work, resumé, financial statement, project budget
  Selection Process: Organization staff, board of directors,
  individuals outside of organization
  Notification Process: Letter within 8 weeks of deadline
  Formal Report of Grant Required: Yes

UTAH ARTS COUNCIL (UAC)

617 East South Temple
Salt Lake City, UT 84102
801-533-5895

PROFILE OF FINANCIAL SUPPORT TO ARTISTS

Total Funding/Value of In-Kind Support: $498,770 for FY 1990
Competition for Funding: Total applications, 1,362; total individuals funded/provided with in-kind support, 448 (includes each artist participating in Utah Performing Arts Tour)
Grant Range: Up to $5,000

DIRECT SUPPORT PROGRAMS

➤ **VISUAL ARTS FELLOWSHIPS**

CONTACT: SHERRILL SANDBERG, VISUAL ARTS COORDINATOR
Phone: 801-533-5757

Purpose: To aid practicing artists of exceptional talent and demonstrated ability in their process of aesthetic investigation and creation of original works of art

Eligibility:
   Citizenship: U.S.
   Residency: Utah
   Age: 18 or older
   Special Requirements: No students pursuing degrees; previous recipients ineligible for 3 years
   Art Forms: Visual arts, crafts, video, photography, inter-disciplinary, multi-disciplinary

Type of Support: $5,000

Scope of Program: 2 awards per year

Application/Selection Process:
   Deadline: Mid-April
   Preferred Initial Contact: Call for application/guidelines
   Application Procedure: Submit application form, samples of work, 3 references, resumé
   Selection Process: Individuals outside of organization
   Notification Process: Letter or phone call in October
   Formal Report of Grant Required: Yes

TECHNICAL ASSISTANCE PROGRAMS AND SERVICES

Programs of Special Interest: Artists selected for the council's Artist Bank are eligible for school and community residencies. The council maintains a slide registry (artists pay a $10 registration fee) and administers Utah's 1%-for-Art program.

VERMONT COUNCIL ON THE ARTS (VCA)

136 State Street
Montpelier, VT 05602
802-828-3291
CONTACT: GRANTS OFFICER

PROFILE OF FINANCIAL SUPPORT TO ARTISTS

Total Funding/Value of In-Kind Support: $94,000 for FY 1990 (for Fellowships and New Works Grants)
Competition for Funding: Total applications, 388; total individuals funded/provided with in-kind support, 41
Grant Range: $500-$5,000

DIRECT SUPPORT PROGRAMS

➤ **FELLOWSHIPS**

Purpose: To support the creative development of Vermont artists
Eligibility:
   Residency: Vermont
   Age: 18 or older
   Special Requirements: No students
   Art Forms: All disciplines
Type of Support: $3,500 fellowships; $500 finalist awards
Scope of Program: 17 fellowships, 19 finalist awards in 1990
Application/Selection Process:
   Deadline: March 15
   Application Procedure: Submit application form, resumé, samples of work
   Selection Process: VCA staff, advisory panels, VCA board of trustees
   Notification Process: July
   Formal Report of Grant Required: Yes

➤ **NEW WORKS GRANTS**

Purpose: To fund the creation and presentation of original and innovative work that challenges traditional perceptions of art forms and advances the development and exchange of ideas among artists and between artists and audiences
Eligibility:
   Residency: Vermont (for collaborative projects, at least 50% of participants must be Vermont residents)
   Special Requirements: Artists must apply with a partner non-profit organization; no full-time students; project must include plans for a public presentation in Vermont
   Art Forms: All disciplines
Type of Support: $1,000-$10,000 for specific project

Scope of Program: Total $25,000 granted for 5 projects in 1990
Application/Selection Process:
  Deadline: February 15
  Preferred Initial Contact: Discuss project ideas and application procedure with grants officer
  Selection Process: New Works panel, VCA board of trustees
  Notification Process: May
  Formal Report of Grant Required: Yes

TECHNICAL ASSISTANCE PROGRAMS AND SERVICES
Programs of Special Interest: Artists may apply to participate in the Arts in Education program; information about successful applicants appears in the Artists Register, which is provided to potential sponsors. The council maintains a job bank and lists of other opportunities for artists, as well as the Resource Center, a non-circulating library of information about the arts. The council holds informative workshops, including Grant Seekers Workshops for artists and organizations seeking VCA funding.

VIDEO FOUNDATION TO ASSIST CANADIAN TALENT (VIDEOFACT)

151 John Street
Suite 301
Toronto, Ontario
Canada M5V 2T2
416-596-8696
CONTACT: JULIE THORBURN, PROGRAM DIRECTOR

PROFILE OF FINANCIAL SUPPORT TO ARTISTS
Total Funding/Value of In-Kind Support: $751,536 for FY 1989-90 (includes grants to independent and commercial producers)
Competition for Funding: Total applications, 416; total individuals funded/provided with in-kind support, 107
Grant Range: $3,400-$11,000

DIRECT SUPPORT PROGRAMS
Purpose: To support the number and quality of music videos produced in Canada through providing financial assistance toward the production of music videos
  Citizenship: Canada (landed immigrants also eligible)
  Special Requirements: Producers, managers, artists, record labels, record or video production companies are eligible; video director or production company, or video production facilities must be located

in Canada; 2 of the following must be located in Canada: composer, lyricist, principal performer, performance/production
Art Forms: Music video
Type of Support: Up to 50% of project cost to a maximum of $12,500
Scope of Program: $950,000 available in 1990-91
Application/Selection Process:
    Deadline: 5 per year
    Preferred Initial Contact: Call or write for application/guidelines
    Application Procedure: Submit application form, samples of work, resumé, project budget
    Selection Process: Board of directors
    Notification Process: Phone call or letter 4 weeks after deadline
    Formal Report of Grant Required: Yes

VIRGINIA CENTER FOR THE CREATIVE ARTS (VCCA)

Mt. San Angelo
P.O. Box VCCA
Sweet Briar, VA 24595
804-946-7236
CONTACT: WILLIAM SMART, EXECUTIVE DIRECTOR

PROFILE OF FINANCIAL SUPPORT TO ARTISTS
Total Funding/Value of In-Kind Support: $415,744 in FY 1990
Competition for Funding: Total applications, 3,000; total individuals funded/provided with in-kind support, 280
Grant Range: n/a

DIRECT SUPPORT PROGRAMS
Purpose: To provide a retreat where writers, visual artists, and composers may pursue their work, free from the distractions and responsibilities of day-to-day life
Eligibility:
    Age: Usually 20 or older
    Art Forms: Music composition (chamber, choral, new, orchestral), opera, theater (general and experimental), visual arts, architecture, photography, film, literature, interdisciplinary, multi-disciplinary
Type of Support: 1- to 3-month residencies including room, board, and studio; artists asked to pay $20 per diem fee if possible
Scope of Program: 280 residencies in 1990
Application/Selection Process:
    Deadline: May 25, September 25, January 25
    Preferred Initial Contact: Call or write for application/guidelines

Application Procedure: Submit application form, $15 application fee, samples of work, references, resumé
Selection Process: Peer panel of artists
Notification Process: Letter or phone call 2 months after deadline
Formal Report of Grant Required: No

VIRGINIA COMMISSION FOR THE ARTS

James Monroe Building, 17th Floor
101 North 14th Street
Richmond, VA 23219-3683
804-225-3132 (voice/TDD)
CONTACT: REGIONAL COORDINATORS

PROFILE OF FINANCIAL SUPPORT TO ARTISTS
Total Funding/Value of In-Kind Services: $134,000 for FY 1990
Competition for Funding: Total applications, 1,097; total individuals funded/provided with in-kind support, 29
Grant Range: $1,500-$10,000

DIRECT SUPPORT PROGRAMS
➤ PROJECT GRANTS FOR INDIVIDUAL ARTISTS
Purpose: To encourage significant development in the work of individual artists and in the media in which they work and to support the realization of specific artistic ideas
Eligibility:
  Residency: Virginia
  Art Forms: All disciplines on a rotating basis
Type of Support: Up to $5,000 to support a specific project
Scope of Program: 25 awards, averaging $4,000, in FY 1991
Application/Selection Process:
  Deadline: March 1
  Preferred Initial Contact: Call or write for guidelines/application
  Application Procedure: Submit application form, samples of work, resumé, project budget
  Selection Process: Peer panel of artists, VCA board
  Notification Process: Letter in June
  Formal Report of Grant Required: Yes

TECHNICAL ASSISTANCE PROGRAMS AND SERVICES
Programs of Special Interest: The commission maintains a mailing list of artists categorized by discipline. The commission administers an Artists-in-Education Residency program and provides information about its grant programs through an annual series of application assistance seminars.

VIRGIN ISLANDS COUNCIL ON THE ARTS (VICA)

P.O. Box 6732
41 Norre Gade
St. Thomas, VI 00802
809-774-5984

PROFILE OF FINANCIAL SUPPORT TO ARTISTS

Total Funding/Value of In-Kind Support: $24,490 in FY 1990

Competition for Funding: Total applications, n/a; total individuals funded/provided with in-kind support, 15

Grant Range: $150-$5,000

DIRECT SUPPORT PROGRAMS

➤ **SPECIAL PROJECTS**

Purpose: To financially assist individual artists' projects by providing partial support for research, participation in professional development workshops or seminars, and materials for specific projects

Eligibility:
    Residency: Virgin Islands
    Special Requirements: Must have matching funds
    Art Forms: All disciplines

Type of Support: Up to $5,000 to cover up to 50% of cost of specific project

Scope of Program: 15 grants in FY 1990

Application/Selection Process:
    Application Procedure: Submit application form, project narrative, supplemental materials
    Selection Process: VICA staff and council, panelists
    Notification Process: Letter within 2 weeks of council meeting
    Formal Report of Grant Required: Yes

TECHNICAL ASSISTANCE PROGRAMS AND SERVICES

Programs of Special Interest: VICA staff assist individual artists seeking funding from other sources.

VISUAL COMMUNICATIONS/SOUTHERN CALIFORNIA ASIAN AMERICAN STUDIES CENTRAL, INC.

263 South Los Angeles, #307
Los Angeles, CA 90012
213-680-4462
CONTACT: LINDA MABALOT

PROFILE OF FINANCIAL SUPPORT TO ARTISTS
Total Funding/Value of In-Kind Support: n/a
Competition for Funding: n/a
Grant Range: $500-$1,500 for cash grants

DIRECT SUPPORT PROGRAMS
➤ **FILMMAKERS DEVELOPMENT AND SUPPORT PROGRAM**
Purpose: To support the development of emerging Asian Pacific film and video artists
Eligibility:
   Residency: Southern California
   Special Requirements: Project must be a short film or video focusing on Asian Pacific subjects or themes
   Art Forms: Film, video
Type of Support: Subsidized equipment access and/or grants of $500-$1,500
Scope of Program: 8-10 awards per year
Application/Selection Process:
   Call or write for information

EQUIPMENT ACCESS
CONTACT: AMY KATO
Film: Production for Super 8
Video: Post-production (off-line) for S-VHS
Comments: Visual Communications provides equipment access at discounted rates to members.

TECHNICAL ASSISTANCE PROGRAMS AND SERVICES
Programs of Special Interest: Visual Communications serves as a fiscal sponsor for a limited number of member media artists. Artists must submit a treatment and budget, and projects must focus on Asian Pacific subjects or themes. The organization also selects independent works to be screened at the Los Angeles Asian Pacific American International Film and Video Festival, Los Angeles Freewaves, Pioneering Visions Exhibition Series, and Ethnovisions

Series. These works are programmed to be screened in the community and in the school systems. Consultation services are available for artists seeking funding from Los Angeles city programs and other sources.

VISUAL STUDIES WORKSHOP (VSW)

31 Prince Street
Rochester, NY 14607
716-442-8676

PROFILE OF FINANCIAL SUPPORT TO ARTISTS

Total Funding/Value of In-Kind Support: n/a
Competition for Funding: n/a
Grant Range: Up to $1,000

DIRECT SUPPORT PROGRAMS

➤ **UPSTATE MEDIA REGRANT PROGRAM**

Purpose: To assist emerging media artists and independent producers to advance their work
Eligibility:
  Residency: Upstate New York
  Special Requirements: No students
  Art Forms: Video, audio, time-based computer art
Type of Support: $500
Scope of Program: 9 awards per year
Application/Selection Process:
  Deadline: January
  Preferred Initial Contact: Call for guidelines
  Application Procedure: Submit resumé, samples of work, artist's statement
  Selection Process: Panel of artists and arts professionals
  Notification Process: After panel meeting in February

➤ **NO TV & MOVIES CABLE TELEVISION SERIES**

CONTACT: KAREN CHASE

Purpose: To televise videotapes and films by artists and independent producers from around the country
Eligibility:
  Special Requirements: Applicants must have sole control over every phase of production
  Art Forms: Video, film dubbed to video (maximum length, 28 minutes)

Type of Support: Works broadcast on Greater Rochester Cablevision; artists paid $16.50 per running minute
Scope of Program: n/a
Application/Selection Process:
   Deadline: September
   Preferred Initial Contact: Call or write for guidelines
   Application Procedure: Submit sample of work, artist's statement, resumé, $5 for shipping/handling
   Selection Process: Staff
   Notification Process: Letter or phone call
   Formal Report of Grant Required: No

➤ **ARTIST-IN-RESIDENCE PROGRAM**
Purpose: To allow artists the facilities and time to pursue their work
Eligibility:
   Residency: U.S.
   Special Requirements: No students
   Art Forms: Media arts
Type of Support: 1-month residency including access to facilities, living space, $1,000 honorarium; film and video artists expected to hold screening at the Media Center and, as a visiting artist, attend up to 3 evening classes
Scope of Program: 2 residencies per year
Application/Selection Process:
   Deadline: July
   Preferred Initial Contact: Call for guidelines
   Application Procedure: Submit samples of work, artist's statement, project proposal, list of equipment needs, resumé
   Selection Process: Peer panel of artists, staff
   Notification Process: 3 weeks after deadline
   Formal Report of Grant Required: No

EQUIPMENT ACCESS
CONTACT: MONA JIMENEZ, ACCESS MANAGER
Film: Production and post-production for 16mm, Super 8
Video: Production and post-production for 3/4", Video 8, Hi-8
Comments: Low-cost access is available to independent producers and artists working on noncommercial projects. Further rate reductions are available through the Media Access Program; awards are based on proposals.

TECHNICAL ASSISTANCE PROGRAMS AND SERVICES
Programs of Special Interest: VSW exhibits media installations and work by film and video artists in its screening room and holds week-end workshops on a regular basis.

WASHINGTON PROJECT FOR THE ARTS (WPA)

400 Seventh Street, NW
Washington, DC 20004
202-347-4813
CONTACT: PHILIP BROOKMAN, DIRECTOR OF PROGRAMS

EQUIPMENT ACCESS
Video: Post-production for 3/4", Hi-8
Comments: Access at minimal rates is available for independent producers working on nonprofit projects. A few artists are given free access to facilities and an exhibition opportunity at WPA's discretion.

TECHNICAL ASSISTANCE PROGRAMS AND SERVICES
Programs of Special Interest: WPA conducts workshops in editing and production.

WEST VIRGINIA DIVISION OF CULTURE AND HISTORY

Cultural Center
Capitol Complex
Charleston, WV 25305
304-348-0220
CONTACT: MS. LAKIN RAY COOK, EXECUTIVE DIRECTOR, ARTS & HUMANITIES SECTION

PROFILE OF FINANCIAL SUPPORT TO ARTISTS
Total Funding/Value of In-Kind Support: $20,000 to media artists in 1990
Competition for Funding: Total applications, 5; total individuals funded/provided with in-kind support, 2
Grant Range: Up to $10,000

DIRECT SUPPORT PROGRAMS
➤ **MEDIA ARTS PROGRAM**
Purpose: To assist media arts projects in the areas of artists' fees, production and post-production costs, and presentation costs
Eligibility:
   Residency: West Virginia
   Special Requirements: Must apply with a nonprofit fiscal sponsor; must have matching funds
   Art Forms: Film, video, audio

Type of Support: Up to 50% of project costs, not to exceed $10,000
Scope of Program: $35,000 available in 1991
Application/Selection Process:
   Deadline: April 1
   Preferred Initial Contact: Call or write for information
   Application Procedure: Submit application form, sample of work or extensive treatment
   Selection Process: Peer panel of media artists and administrators, West Virginia Commission on the Arts
   Notification Process: Letter
   Formal Report of Grant Required: Yes

➤ **TRAVEL FUND**

Purpose: To provide artists and arts administrators with financial assistance to attend out-of-state seminars, workshops, conferences, and showcases important to their field of expertise (in-state events of national scope may be funded in some cases)
Eligibility:
   Residency: West Virginia
   Special Requirements: Professional artists and arts administrators only; previous recipients ineligible for 1 year
   Art Forms: All disciplines
Type of Support: 50% of travel costs (maximum $200)
Application/Selection Process:
   Deadline: At least 6 weeks before event (early application encouraged)
   Preferred Initial Contact: Call or write for guidelines/application
   Application Procedure: Submit application form, financial statement
   Notification Process: Within 3 weeks of application

TECHNICAL ASSISTANCE PROGRAMS AND SERVICES

Programs of Special Interest: West Virginia Division of Culture and History provides support for the West Virginia International Film Festival. The Artist/Arts Administrator Opportunities File holds information on workshops, calls for proposals, and job opportunities. The selective West Virginia Artists List and Register contains background information on individual artists. Artists interested in the Arts in the Community program should develop a proposal with a sponsor who will apply for funding; eligible projects include workshops and presentations of media artists' works.

WISCONSIN ARTS BOARD (WAB)

131 West Wilson Street
Suite 301
Madison, WI 53703
608-266-0190
CONTACT: BETH MALNER, PERCENT FOR ART & INDIVIDUAL ARTIST COORDINATOR

PROFILE OF FINANCIAL SUPPORT TO ARTISTS
Total Funding/Value of In-Kind Support: $170,884 for FY 1989
Competition for Funding: Total applications, n/a; total individuals
funded/provided with in-kind support, 89
Grant Range: $350-$5,000

DIRECT SUPPORT PROGRAMS
➤ **INDIVIDUAL ARTIST PROGRAM—MEDIA ARTS**
Purpose: To assist artists in advancing their careers, in pursuing a
specific project, or in developing their skills as a professional
Eligibility:
  Citizenship: U.S.
  Residency: Wisconsin, 6 months
  Special Requirements: No students pursuing degrees; recipients
  of New Work Awards and Development Grants must match
  grants in cash or in-kind support
  Art Forms: Film, video, radio and audio art
Type of Support: Fellowships ($5,000 unrestricted grants), New
Work Awards ($3,500 matching grant for pursuit of a project-
oriented activity), Development Grants ($1,000 matching grant for
professional development activity)
Scope of Program: 2 Fellowships, 2 New Work Awards, 3 Develop-
ment Grants in 1991; media arts awards made in odd-numbered
years only
Application/Selection Process:
  Deadline: September 15
  Preferred Initial Contact: Call or write for application/guidelines
  Application Procedure: Submit application form, samples of
  work and corresponding script treatments, resumé, artist's state-
  ment (optional); artists chosen for New Work Awards and
  Development Grants must submit project description before
  receiving grant
  Selection Process: Peer panel of artists, board of directors
  Notification Process: Letter in January
  Formal Report of Grant Required: Yes

TECHNICAL ASSISTANCE PROGRAMS AND SERVICES

Programs of Special Interest: The WAB sponsors workshops in such areas as grantwriting, audience development, and marketing. Artists selected for inclusion in the Arts-in-Education Artists Directory are eligible for school and community residencies.

WOMEN IN FILM FOUNDATION (WIFF)

6464 Sunset Boulevard
Suite 900
Los Angeles, CA 90028
213-463-6040
CONTACT: MIRIAM REED

PROFILE OF FINANCIAL SUPPORT TO ARTISTS

Total Funding/Value of In-Kind Support: n/a
Competition for Funding: n/a
Grant Range: $2,000-$25,000

DIRECT SUPPORT PROGRAMS

➤ **FILM FINISHING FUND—GENERAL AWARDS/CFI SERVICES AWARDS/LOREEN ARBUS AWARD**

Purpose: To support filmmakers and videomakers who have demonstrated advanced and innovative skills, and whose work relates to WIFF's goals of increasing employment and promoting equal opportunities for women, enhancing the media image of women, and influencing prevailing attitudes and practices regarding and on behalf of women

Eligibility:
    Residency: Los Angeles (for CFI Services Awards only)
    Special Requirements: Independent producers and nonprofit corporations are eligible; substantial number of the creative personnel involved with the project must be women; project must be in progress; project must treat issues of disability (Loreen Arbus Award only)
    Art Forms: Film, video (General Awards and Loreen Arbus Award)

Type of Support: General Awards, up to $5,000 for completion funding; CFI Services Awards, up to $25,000 worth of film post-production services at CFI Labs in Los Angeles; Loreen Arbus Award, up to $5,000 for completion funding
Scope of Program: n/a
Application/Selection Process:
    Deadline: May 10

Preferred Initial Contact: Write for guidelines (include SASE)
Application Procedure: Submit $10 application fee, project description and budget, distribution and exhibition plans, biographies of key personnel, sample of work-in-progress (CFI applicants must submit a rough or fine edit of their work)
Selection Process: Committee
Notification Process: Letter in October

➤ **LIFETIME TELEVISION PRODUCTION COMPLETION GRANTS**

Purpose: To fund the completion of projects whose subject matter relates to women and is of general humanitarian concern
Eligibility:
Special Requirements: Professional film and video artists only; no student projects or college thesis films; dramatic projects ineligible; 50% or more of production personnel must be female; project must relate to women and have strong female viewer appeal; project must be approximately 45 minutes in length or producer must agree to cut work to acceptable telecast length as determined by Lifetime (exceptional 30-minute works also eligible)
Art Forms: Film, video
Type of Support: $25,000-$50,000 completion grant; producer must grant Lifetime Television exclusive exhibition rights for 1 year or 4 telecasts
Scope of Program: n/a
Application/Selection Process:
Deadline: Ongoing
Preferred Initial Contact: Write for guidelines (include SASE)
Application Procedure: Submit project description and budget, professional credentials of key personnel; semi-finalists submit sample of work, completion plans
Selection Process: Committee
Notification Process: Letter

WOMEN MAKE MOVIES (WMM)

225 Lafayette Street
New York, NY 10012
212-925-0606
CONTACT: MICHELLE MATERRE, ASSOCIATE DIRECTOR

PROFILE OF FINANCIAL SUPPORT TO ARTISTS
Total Funding/Value of In-Kind Support: n/a
Competition for Funding: n/a
Grant Range: n/a

DIRECT SUPPORT PROGRAMS
➤ WOMEN MAKE VIDEOS—PRODUCTION ASSISTANCE/INTERNSHIPS

Purpose: To provide production assistance to women video artists and to increase the number of women of color entering the media field

Eligibility:
  Residency: New York State
  Special Requirements: Must be female; internship applicants must be minority women; no students
  Art Forms: Video

Type of Support: Production assistance grants consist of 1-to-1 consultation with WMM staff for pre-production projects, 2 days of video equipment usage for projects in production, or 30 hours usage of post-production facilities for projects near completion; internships include hands-on production experience and a stipend

Scope of Program: 4 production assistance grants, 4 internships available in 1991

Application/Selection Process:
  Deadline: March 15
  Preferred Initial Contact: Write or call for application/ guidelines; free application workshop available
  Application Procedure: Submit application form, project proposal (production assistance grants), sample of work (production assistance grants), personal statement (internships)
  Selection Process: Peer panel of artists
  Notification Process: Recipients by phone, nonrecipients by mail

TECHNICAL ASSISTANCE PROGRAMS AND SERVICES
Programs of Special Interest: WMM acts as a tax-exempt fiscal sponsoring agent for selected media projects that are in accordance with the organization's goals and whose key personnel are WMM members ($30 membership fee). Workshops address areas such as fundraising and film and video production and post-production (fees involved).

WYOMING ARTS COUNCIL

2320 Capitol Avenue
Cheyenne, WY 82002
307-777-7742
CONTACT: RENÉE BOVÉE, COMMUNITY SERVICES COORDINATOR

PROFILE OF FINANCIAL SUPPORT TO ARTISTS
Total Funding/Value of In-Kind Support: $29,000 for FY 1989 (not including AIE residencies)

Competition for Funding: Total applications, 120; total individuals funded/provided with in-kind support, 18

Grant Range: $500-$2,500

DIRECT SUPPORT PROGRAMS

➤ **FELLOWSHIPS/INDIVIDUAL ARTIST GRANTS**

Purpose: Fellowships are designed to assist emerging Wyoming artists at crucial times in their in their careers; Individual Artist Grants support specific projects that promote, preserve, encourage, and stimulate culture in the state

Eligibility:

Residency: Wyoming

Age: 18 or older

Special Requirements: No students; previous Fellowship winners ineligible for 4 years

Art Forms: All disciplines

Type of Support: Fellowships, $2,500; Individual Artist Grants, up to $1,000 matching grant for specific project

Scope of Program: 12 Fellowships; 10 Individual Artist Grants in 1990

Application/Selection Process:

Deadline: September 1 (Visual Arts and Performing Arts Fellowships), August 1 (Literary Fellowships), August 15 (Individual Artist Grants)

Preferred Initial Contact: Call or write for application/guidelines

Application Procedure: Submit application form, samples of work, references, resumé (Individual Artist Grant), project budget and description (Individual Artist Grant), artist's statement (Fellowship)

Selection Process: Peer panel of artists and board of directors

Notification Process: Letter in October/November

Formal Report of Grant Required: Yes

TECHNICAL ASSISTANCE PROGRAMS AND SERVICES

Programs of Special Interest: The council maintains an Artist Registry/Slide Bank to promote the work of Wyoming artists and sponsors Artspeak, an annual gathering of artists that includes workshops. Artists selected for inclusion in the *Arts in Education Program Artist Roster* are eligible for school and community residencies.

ZELLERBACH FAMILY FUND

120 Montgomery
Room 2125
San Francisco, CA 94104
415-421-2629
CONTACT: LINDA HOWE

PROFILE OF FINANCIAL SUPPORT TO ARTISTS
Total Funding/Value of In-Kind Support: n/a
Competition for Funding: n/a
Grant Range: n/a

DIRECT SUPPORT PROGRAMS
➤ COMMUNITY ARTS DISTRIBUTION COMMITTEE
Purpose: To support art-oriented film and video
Eligibility:
Residency: San Francisco Bay Area
Special Requirements: Must be sponsored by a nonprofit organization
Art Forms: Art-oriented film and video
Type of Support: Up to $5,000
Scope of Program: 1 award per year
Application/Selection Process:
Preferred Initial Contact: Call for information
Selection Process: Jury
Notification Process: Letter
Formal Report of Grant Required: Yes

ALPHABETICAL INDEX OF ORGANIZATIONS

INDEX OF ORGANIZATIONS BY GEOGRAPHIC AREA

DISTRICT OF COLUMBIA

Black Film Institute, 37
D.C. Commission on the Arts and
    Humanities, 68
IMAGE Film/Video Center, 95
Mid Atlantic Arts Foundation, 129
Pittsburgh Filmmakers, 171
Washington Project for the Arts, 206

FLORIDA

Appalshop, Inc., 10
Arts Assembly of Jacksonville, Inc., The, 22
Arts Council of Hillsborough County, 26
Florida Division of Cultural Affairs/
    Florida Arts Council, 83
IMAGE Film/Video Center, 95
Pinellas County Arts Council, 169
South Florida Cultural Consortium,
    The, 188

GEORGIA

Appalshop, Inc., 10
DeKalb Council for the Arts, Inc., 69
Georgia Council for the Arts, 86
IMAGE Film/Video Center, 95

HAWAII

Los Angeles Contemporary
    Exhibitions, 113
Northwest Film and Video Center/
    Oregon Art Institute, 157

IDAHO

Helena Presents, 91
Idaho Commission on the Arts, 92
Northwest Film and Video
    Center/Oregon Art Institute, 157

ILLINOIS

Center for New Television, The, 53
Chicago Department of Cultural Affairs, 56
Community Film Workshop, The, 61
Illinois Arts Council, 93
Independent Feature Project, 96
Quad City Arts, 174

INDIANA

Arts Council of Indianapolis, 27
Arts United of Greater Fort Wayne, 32
Athens Center for Film and Video, 34
Center for New Television, The, 53
Indiana Arts Commission, 97
Michiana Arts and Sciences
    Council, Inc., 127

IOWA

Film in the Cities, 82
Intermedia Arts, 98
Iowa Arts Council, 102
Quad City Arts, 174

KANSAS

Intermedia Arts, 98
Kansas Arts Commission, 106
Southwest Alternate Media Project, 189

KENTUCKY

Appalshop, Inc., 10
Athens Center for Film and Video, 34
IMAGE Film/Video Center, 95
Kentucky Arts Council, 107

LOUISIANA

Appalshop, Inc., 10
Contemporary Arts Center, 63
IMAGE Film/Video Center, 95
Louisiana Division of the Arts, 115
New Orleans Video Access Center, 149

MAINE

Boston Film/Video Foundation, 37
Maine Arts Commission, 120
New England Foundation for the Arts, 143
Northeast Historic Film, 157

MARYLAND

Maryland State Arts Council, 124
Mid Atlantic Arts Foundation, 129
Pittsburgh Filmmakers, 171

INDEX OF ORGANIZATIONS BY MEDIUM AND FORMAT

INDEX OF ORGANIZATIONS BY TYPES OF SUPPORT

ABOUT THE AMERICAN COUNCIL FOR THE ARTS

The American Council for the Arts (ACA) is one of the nation's primary sources of legislative news affecting all of the arts and serves as a leading advisor to arts administrators, individual artists, educators, elected officials, arts patrons, and the general public. To accomplish its goal of strong advocacy of the arts, ACA promotes public debate in various national, state, and local forums; communicates as a publisher of books, journals, *Vantage Point* magazine and *ACA UpDate*; provides information services through its extensive arts education, policy, and management library; and has as its key policy issues the needs of individual/originating artists, public and private support for the arts, arts education, multiculturalism, and international cultural relations.

ABOUT VISUAL ARTIST INFORMATION HOTLINE

The Marie Walsh Sharpe Art Foundation in cooperation with the American Council for the Arts (ACA) on October 1, 1990 launched a nation-wide, toll-free information hotline serving American visual artists. The hotline is one of the programs for visual artists initiated by the foundation's Artists Advisory Committee whose members include artists Cynthia Carlson, Chuck Close, Janet Fish, Philip Pearlstein, Harriet Shorr, Rob Storr, and art historian/critic Irving Sandler.

Artists can call 1-800-232-2789 from anywhere in the U.S. and reach the Arts Resource Consortium Library at the American Council for the Arts in New York. Library staff will match the specific needs of callers with a database of information resources for visual artists. The hours of operation for the hotline are Monday through Friday, 2-5 PM Eastern Time.

Primarily a referral service, the hotline gives visual artists details on where to go and whom to contact regarding such issues as funding, insurance, health and law. Included in the database are foundations and government programs funding visual artists, programs of arts councils, arts service organizations and others who provide information, technical assistance or other services to visual artists.

Marie Walsh Sharpe, a Colorado Springs philanthropist, created the foundation before her death in 1985 to benefit visual artists. The foundation established the "Summer Seminars" in 1987, a highly competitive studio institute for high school juniors held at The Colorado College in Colorado Springs, Colorado.

Since 1986 ACA has operated, in partnership with Volunteer Lawyers for the Arts, the Arts Resource Consortium Library, which serves as a national information and referral service for arts managers and individual artists.